BRITISH BUILT AIRCRAFT

VOLUME 5

Northern England, Scotland,
Wales and Northern Ireland

BRITISH BUILT AIRCRAFT

VOLUME 5

Northern England, Scotland,
Wales and Northern Ireland

Ron Smith

TEMPUS

First published 2005

Tempus Publishing Ltd
The Mill, Brimscombe Port
Stroud, Gloucestershire GL5 2QG
www.tempus-publishing.com

© Ron Smith, 2005

The right of Ron Smith to be identified as the Author
of this work has been asserted by him in accordance with the
Copyrights, Designs and Patents Act 1988.

All rights reserved. No part of this book may be reprinted
or reproduced or utilised in any form or by any electronic,
mechanical or other means, now known or hereafter invented,
including photocopying and recording, or in any information
storage or retrieval system, without the permission in writing
from the Publishers.

British Library Cataloguing in Publication Data.
A catalogue record for this book is available from the British Library.

ISBN 0 7524 3487 X

Typesetting and origination by Tempus Publishing.
Printed and bound in Great Britain.

Contents

Introduction		6
Section One:		
The Evolution of the British Aircraft Industry		11
1	Pioneers (1908–1914)	12
2	First World War Mass Production (1914–1918)	15
3	Collapse and Re-birth Between the Wars (1919–1939)	23
4	Second World War Mass Production (1939–1945)	29
5	Post-war (1945–1960)	35
6	Rationalisation – The BAC and the Hawker Siddeley Years (1960–1977)	43
7	Modern Times	47
8	The Genealogy of British Aerospace/BAE SYSTEMS	54
Section Two:		
The Aircraft Manufacturers of Northern England, Scotland, Wales and Northern Ireland		59
Bibliography		240
Cross-reference Index		244
Index		247

Introduction

This volume is the last in a series of five books which provide a complete record of aircraft construction in Britain. Each volume focuses on a different regional area, documenting activity over the whole period from 1908 until the present day, keyed to the places where this enterprise was actually performed. The objective of the whole work is to pay tribute to the heritage of the British aircraft industry, and to create and preserve a record of its lost endeavours. The preceding volumes cover, respectively, aircraft built in Greater London; in South West and Central Southern England; in South East England; and in Central and Eastern England.

As soon as one starts to examine the history of the aircraft industry, it becomes clear that it has developed through a number of distinct phases. These phases can be characterised as: the pioneers (1908 to 1914); First World War mass production (1914 to 1918); collapse and re-birth between the wars (1919 to 1939); Second World War mass production (1939 to 1945); post-war (1945 to 1960); and modern times. A discussion of the evolution of the industry covering these six main periods of activity can be found in Section One. The aim of this review of the evolution of the industry is to place the remainder of the work within the overall context, whilst highlighting developments that are specific to the area covered by this particular volume.

Some twenty-eight years ago, on the formation of British Aerospace (BAe), the American magazine *Aviation Week & Space Technology* wryly commented that the final phase of development of the Society of British Aircraft Constructors (SBAC) had now taken place. Whereas previously the numerous members of the SBAC had reflected the vigour, diversity and inventive spirit of the British industry, it had, following restructuring in 1960, been reduced to the 'Society of Both Aircraft Companies' (namely, the British Aircraft Corporation and Hawker Siddeley Aviation Ltd). The formation of BAe was the final act in the process, with the once great industry reduced to the 'Single British Aerospace Company'.

This light-hearted comment contains an important message. British aircraft industry names, which were once well known to the public, have disappeared from the day-to-day business of manufacturing aeroplanes. Indeed, in many instances, their operating sites have even disappeared from the map. At first sight it seems as if the once vibrant British aircraft industry has contracted virtually to the point of extinction since the Second World War. The entire industry has been reduced to the firms of BAE SYSTEMS, AgustaWestland, Slingsby, and Britten-Norman (surviving, as I write, in its latest manifestation: B-N Group), together with sundry microlight and homebuilt aircraft suppliers.

Many British aircraft manufacturers have disappeared altogether and this has provided the inspiration for this survey of the industry. The regions covered by this volume (Northern England, Scotland, Wales and Northern Ireland) have seen in the last fifty years the demise of such company names as A.V. Roe & Co. Ltd, Blackburn & General Aircraft Ltd, English Electric Aviation Ltd, The Fairey Aviation Co. Ltd, Scottish Aviation Ltd, and Short Bros. & Harland Ltd. Simultaneously, the production of complete aircraft has ceased at many locations across these regions, including, for example, Alloa, Belfast, Blackpool, Dumbarton, Gosforth,

Hornet Moth G-AELO is seen here at Pocklington prior to the 1994 Dawn to Dusk competition flight by Colin Dodds and the author. (Author)

Leeds, Preston, Prestwick, Sherburn-in-Elmet, Speke, Stockport (Heaton Chapel and Errwood Park) and Windermere. Having pondered on these and the many other closures across the country, the idea grew that an effort should be made to record something of Britain's aircraft construction history and heritage.

The first outcome of this desire to document the past achievements of the British aircraft industry was a successful entry in the 1994 Pooley's International Dawn to Dusk Flying Competition by the author, with his colleague Colin Dodds. The entry, under the title *Lost Names in British Aviation*, consisted of the record of a flight made on a single day (between dawn and dusk) in a 1936 de Havilland Hornet Moth, over sites in Britain where aircraft had once been built, by companies that no longer exist. The research carried out in support of that competition entry has been greatly extended to provide the basis for this record of British achievement, innovation, failure and success.

Content

This series of books records British aircraft manufacture in nearly all its manifestations, in the form of a regional survey of the United Kingdom. The scope of the work is deliberately wide, including as many locations as possible where aircraft have been built, whether by their original designers or by contractors. Exclusions are limited to balloons; the majority of gliders and microlight aircraft; and homebuilt aircraft of foreign design, unless substantially modified in the form flown in the United Kingdom. In general, only the prototypes of British-designed homebuilt aircraft are included, rather than every single example of any particular type.

Being centred on the various manufacturing sites, the book allows a wider scope than a mere litany of product histories, allowing additional discussion of people, places and events. As a result, the major players of the industry are recorded alongside the wealth of early activity, light aircraft and one-off designs that provide a rich background to the main scene. Such is the scope of this record that the space allocated to any individual firm is necessarily limited. This mainly has the effect of producing a somewhat condensed view of some of the largest and best-known companies. However, this limitation is, hopefully, compensated for by some of the fascinating but unfamiliar material presented, covering many companies that are likely to be unfamiliar to the reader.

Those interested in the detailed history of the major manufacturers will be able to find many excellent books with which to fill in the detail if they wish. The same cannot be said for companies such as Snellings Light Aircraft Service; John Dawson & Co. (Newcastle-on-Tyne) Ltd; Vulcan Motor & Engineering Co. (1906) Ltd; Noble Hardman Aviation Ltd; and a number of other lesser known companies from Northern England, Scotland, Wales and Northern Ireland that are included here.

Structure

These introductory remarks are followed by a discussion of the evolution of the aircraft industry, highlighting the activities that characterise each of the main periods identified above, and tailored to the specific region covered by this volume. The contraction through successive mergers that has given rise to the present shape of the industry is presented, together with a family tree of British Aerospace (which contains all of the aircraft heritage of the present BAE SYSTEMS).

The main content of the volume follows in Section Two, Volume Five being a survey of aircraft manufacture in Northern England, Scotland, Wales and Northern Ireland. For the purpose of this volume, Northern England is deemed to comprise the geographical areas of Cheshire; Cumbria; Durham and Cleveland; Greater Manchester; Lancashire; Merseyside; Northumberland and Tyneside; and Yorkshire (East, North, South and West). Within Northern England, the presentation structure is alphabetical by county, and then alphabetical by location. Within Scotland, Wales and Northern Ireland, the presentation is alphabetical by location. For most locations, individual manufacturers are then presented alphabetically in sequence.

Where activity at a single site has only involved one firm at any time, or where the evolution of a single major firm has dominated a particular site, the presentation is chronological, rather than alphabetical. Woodford is an example of such a variation.

This series is intended to provide a comprehensive geographic and product history of aircraft construction in the United Kingdom. I have attempted to cover all sites where aircraft manufacture took place, and to select photographs that provide a balanced mix of example products; locations as they are now; and as they were during their heyday; or combinations of these. A number of the photographs are of the sites as taken from the air during the 1994 Dawn to Dusk competition.

At the end of this, the last volume of the series, I have included a cross-reference index that will allow the reader to locate all the sites used by a particular manufacturer, and to determine within which volume of the series those locations may each be found.

Information Sources and Acknowledgements

A number of major reference sources have been used in producing this survey of the British aircraft industry. Chief among these were magazines such as *Flight*, *The Aeroplane*, and *Aeroplane Monthly*, and the following books and publications, which provide particularly useful material across the whole spectrum of the industry: Terence Boughton's excellent *History of the British Light Aeroplane*; A.J. Jackson's *British Civil Aircraft since 1919*; the individual company histories published by Putnam; Ken Ellis' *British Homebuilt Aircraft Since*

1920; R. Dallas Brett's *History of British Aviation 1909-14*; Arthur Ord-Hume's encyclopaedic *British Light Aeroplanes – Their Evolution, Development and Perfection 1920-40*; the equally outstanding *British Aircraft Before the Great War* by Michael H. Goodall and Albert E. Tagg; many editions of *Jane's All the World's Aircraft*; a wide range of test pilot autobiographies; and numerous other sources. A bibliography is provided listing the many reference sources consulted.

In setting out to document the British aircraft industry, I wish to give a flavour of the breadth of the endeavour in terms of the diversity of both products and places used for aircraft manufacture. It is not my intention to provide a definitive record of every aircraft built, nor an encyclopaedia of production quantities. In some cases, I have found the latter aspect clouded with uncertainty; unless clearly definitive data are available, I have used Bruce Robertson's *British Military Aircraft Serials 1878-1987* as a guide when indicating production quantities, at least for aircraft built for UK military service. I have not hesitated to highlight areas where conflicting information may be found in readily available references. It is for others to research and clarify these issues.

Particular thanks are due to my colleague Rob Preece for the loan of his original, unbound, copies of *Flight* covering the period 1911 to 1923, and to Liz and Peter Curtis for access to a complete collection of *Aeroplane Monthly* magazines. Thanks are also due to Chris Ilett for the loan of *Flight* magazines from 1929 and 1930. A further acknowledgement must be made to The Royal Aeronautical Society library; not only are their early copies of *The Aeroplane* bound complete with their advertising pages, but here I also found a copy of R. Borlase Matthews' *Aviation Pocket-Book 1919-20* whose Gazetteer of the industry put me on the track of many unfamiliar companies. I am most grateful for the assistance provided by George Jenks (AVRO Heritage Centre) and Barry Abraham (Airfield Research Group).

Acknowledgement is due to those companies still extant (and not today associated with the aircraft industry) who answered my correspondence. Mention must also be made of the information and photographs suppled for this series by the following: Ken Ellis; Harry Fraser-Mitchell (Handley Page Association); Fred Ballam (Westland); Chris Hodson (Folland Aircraft Ltd); Olivia Johnston (Bombardier Aerospace, Belfast); Sir Arthur Marshall and Sarah Beavis (Marshall Aerospace plc); Dougal McIntyre (son of the co-founder of Scottish Aviation Ltd, for photographs of that company's machines); Mick Ames (International Auster Club Heritage Group); John Collier (additional Auster material); Weir Group plc; Ray Williams (material related to Sir W.G. Armstrong Whitworth Aircraft Ltd); Paul Lawson and colleagues (BAE SYSTEMS Brough Heritage Group); Michael Rutter (Slingsby Aviation Ltd); and Del Hoyland (Martin-Baker Aircraft Co. Ltd). I am also immensely grateful to G. Stuart Leslie who, as steward of the late J.M. Bruce's collection, alongside his own archive, has made many rare early photographs available for use in this volume.

I must further acknowledge the access provided to photographic material by my present employer, BAE SYSTEMS, including the Heritage Groups at Brough, Farnborough and Warton, and public relations staff at Prestwick. In making this acknowledgement, I should also stress that all opinions expressed herein are entirely my own. I also acknowledge the permission received from BAE SYSTEMS plc, which enables me to reproduce a number of advertisements from BAE SYSTEMS legacy companies in this volume. Every effort has been made to provide the correct attribution for the illustrations used. Please inform the publisher should any errors or omissions have been made and these will be rectified at the earliest opportunity.

Finally, as indicated earlier, the research for this book was triggered by the successful entry in the 1994 Pooley's International Dawn to Dusk competition. This could not have been made without the support, encouragement, experience and competence of my colleague Colin Dodds, who flew the aircraft, and the generosity of David Wells, who made his aircraft, G-AELO, available for the competition flight.

Not Yet Found (and Imperfect Knowledge Disclaimer)

In a work of this scope, it is inevitable that mistakes and omissions will be made; for these I apologise, throwing myself upon the mercies of a hopefully sympathetic readership. Any additions and corrections made known to me will be most welcome and will be incorporated in any further edition that the publisher sees fit to print.

Whilst the original intention was to list companies that built complete aircraft, lack of information about the actual products of some companies means that (particularly in the First World War) the content has certainly strayed into the component supply industry. Although this may stretch the scope of the menu beyond the taste of some, it does at least add richness to the feast.

Some firms, which sound like aircraft factories, may have only built parts (for example, Northern Aircraft & Engineering Ltd); others, which entered the industry to build parts, ended up building complete machines (for example, C. Portass & Son Ltd, and Alexander Stephen Ltd (as part of the 'Scottish Group' of shipbuilders)); finally there are those which might have done almost anything (for example, The Liverpool Aviation Co. Ltd and Haithwaite Aviation Co. Ltd). Once again, I must trust that any blurring of definitions as to what to include or exclude will be forgiven.

The scope of the content has also been broadened in the modern era, as I have chosen to include the contributions of a number of companies that specialise in aircraft restoration and replica construction. The scope, quality and complexity of the work undertaken by these firms exceeds, in many cases, the difficulty of the original manufacturing task. Furthermore, I wish to draw specific attention to the contribution of these organisations to the preservation of Britain's aviation heritage. The primary example in this volume is, perhaps, the Northern Aeroplane Workshops.

Mention must also be made of aircraft and companies that are definitely known to have existed, but for which I have been quite unable to establish a location. At the time of writing, these are:

The **Buckle** parasol monoplane. Illegally flown, unregistered, in 1929, the Buckle monoplane was constructed by Mr S.L. Buckle for the princely sum of £17. Sopwith Snipe wings, ailerons, rudder, elevator and tailplane were used. A simple rectangular section fuselage was built, and power was supplied by a 45hp six-cylinder Anzani radial. The propeller was obtained from a shed at Brooklands and cut down until the Anzani provided a satisfactory rpm. (Source: *Aeroplane Monthly*, April 1979)

The **Newport Aircraft Co.** A question was asked in Parliament in November 1918 in relation to unpaid wages and bonuses at this company.

In addition, the following companies whose addresses are unknown: **Cambrian Aircraft Constructors Ltd**, and **Northwold Aircraft Co. Ltd**.

The Evolution of the British Aircraft Industry

This section presents a summary of the overall development of the aircraft industry in Britain, highlighting specifically (in this volume) activities in Northern England, Scotland, Wales and Northern Ireland. This area is notable for the number of major manufacturers present and their contributions to aircraft manufacturing from the earliest days of the pioneer, through to the present day. Specific activities include:

- A crop of pioneers exploiting the lakes and beaches across the region.
- Sir W.G. Armstrong, Whitworth & Co. Ltd at Newcastle.
- A.V. Roe & Co. Ltd (and its successors) at a number of factories in the Greater Manchester area.
- The aircraft manufacturing activity of The English Electric Co. Ltd (and its successors) at Preston, Warton and Samlesbury.
- The Blackburn Aeroplane & Motor Co. Ltd (and its successors) at Leeds, Brough and Dumbarton.
- Scottish Aviation Ltd at Prestwick.
- Short Bros. & Harland (and its successors) in Northern Ireland.
- The Glasgow shipbuilders' contribution to First World War production.
- Shadow factories and Second World War production: Vickers-Armstrongs Ltd (and later the de Havilland Aircraft Co. Ltd and its successors) at Chester/Broughton in Wales; Vickers-Armstrongs Ltd (and later Hawker Aircraft Ltd) at Blackpool; Rootes Securities Ltd at Speke; and A.V. Roe & Co. Ltd at Yeadon.
- Contract production of more than 800 Proctor aircraft by F. Hills & Sons Ltd at Barton.
- Light aircraft manufacture by Slingsby Aviation Ltd, and the Europa Aircraft Co., both at Kirkbymoorside.

The enduring legacy of these companies is reflected in continued production of aircraft and components under BAE SYSTEMS and/or Airbus at Brough, Broughton, Chadderton, Prestwick, Samlesbury, Warton and Woodford; and continued production by Bombardier Aerospace Inc. in Belfast.

1
Pioneers
(1908–1914)

Flying in Europe began in France in 1906, with the flights of Santos Dumont in October and November of that year. By 1908, practical machines were being flown in France by such pioneers as Farman, Voisin and Blériot. The Wright brothers astounded their audiences with the performance and controllability of their craft when it was publicly displayed at Le Mans in the autumn of 1908. The time was now right for Britain's pioneers to take to the air.

A.V. Roe had been experimenting for some time at Brooklands, but his short flights of 8 June 1908 failed to achieve official recognition. S.F. Cody flew at Farnborough in October 1908. J.T.C. Moore-Brabazon flew at Eastchurch at the end of April 1909, and by July 1909 A.V. Roe's triplane was performing well at Lea Marshes. In February 1909, the Short brothers took a licence to manufacture Wright biplanes for the Aero Club, setting up a factory at Leysdown on the Isle of Sheppey. Britain now possessed an aircraft industry.

The pioneering period prior to the First World War was marked by adventure, experiment and innovation – the techniques of building and of flying aeroplanes were not yet understood. There was no right or wrong solution to any aspect of design, and consequently almost every possible configuration was attempted and many blind alleys were explored. Potentially good designs were let down by poor detail design, inadequate control arrangements, or heavy, inefficient and unreliable engines.

From 1911, Robert Blackburn flew a successful series of monoplanes at Filey, Brooklands and Hendon. His factory was set up in Leeds, with Brough coming into use during the First World War. (J.S. Smith)

The Northern Aircraft Co. Ltd, Seaplane School, at Windermere.

Learning often came slowly: A.V. Roe advertised throughout the First World War that he was the pioneer of the tractor biplane, although, with his initial interest in the triplane configuration, it was 1911 before his Avro D flew. F. Warren Merriam, instructor at the Bristol School, remarked on how long it took to understand that a seat belt could save lives. In a number of cases, lives were lost because pilots simply fell off their machines. Quite trivial landing accidents could also cause death and injury as a result of the pilot being thrown from an aircraft that was otherwise little damaged. It also took a considerable time before the importance of pointing into wind for take-off and landing was understood. In the technical arena, incorrect assumptions were commonplace, for example, in the inadequate stressing of monoplanes against down loads. Even *Flight* is found in May 1913 expressing great surprise that the Eastbourne Aviation Co. monoplane should have adopted ailerons for lateral control when wing warping has 'become almost standard practice'.

The pioneer aircraft included in this series are, in the main, those that are known to have flown successfully. In some cases, where the fact of flight is not entirely certain, aircraft have been included which at least have the appearance that they might have flown successfully (e.g. Sanders Type 2, Beccles). Known freaks have been excluded (e.g. The Aerial Wheel Monoplane, which was built in Birmingham and entered in the 1912 Military Trials at Larkhill).

The main flying locations prior to the First World War were Brooklands, Eastchurch, Hendon and Shoreham. There was, however, also substantial activity in the areas covered by this volume, examples including:

Northern England

- Manufacturing activity by A.V. Roe & Co. Ltd at Brownsfield Mills and Miles Platting, Manchester.
- Robert Blackburn at Filey Sands and Leeds.
- The Lakes Flying Co. (later The Northern Aircraft Co. Ltd) at Windermere.
- Planes Ltd and the Mersey Aeroplane Co. at Freshfield Sands.

Scotland

- W.H. Ewen at Lanark, and later at Alloa.
- The Scottish Aviation Co. Caledonia and Dart monoplanes at Barrhead.
- The Barnwell brothers monoplane at Stirling.
- J.W. Dunne experimenting at Glen Tilt and Blair Atholl.

Wales

- William Ellis Williams in Anglesey.
- The Watkins monoplane at Cardiff.
- The James brothers at Narbeth.

Northern Ireland

- J.B. Ferguson at various sites in the Belfast area.
- Lillian Bland at Carnamoney.

By the outbreak of the First World War, the Short Brothers, A.V. Roe, C.R. Fairey, Robert Blackburn, Frederick Handley Page, The British & Colonial Aeroplane Co. Ltd (later to become The Bristol Aeroplane Co. Ltd), Vickers Ltd, T.O.M. Sopwith, Harry Hawker, and Geoffrey de Havilland were already active in the industry. Despite the diversity of the pioneering efforts, and the many bizarre and unsuccessful designs, the seeds of today's configurations, and of today's industry, were sown during this period of adventure. Great fruit was to be harvested once these seeds found the fertile ground of warfare.

2
First World War Mass Production (1914–1918)

The First World War saw an exponential growth in aircraft production, which is reflected in this survey of aircraft production in Northern England, Scotland, Wales and Northern Ireland. The importance of the aeroplane during the First World War, and the reasons for the rapid growth in production demand are therefore discussed in some detail below.

The Aircraft as a Machine of War

At the outbreak of the First World War, the utility of the aeroplane had only just begun to be appreciated by the Services. It was then slow, fragile and unarmed; moreover, very few were available. Thus the Royal Flying Corps (RFC) had a total of only sixty-three first line aeroplanes, with a further thirty-nine landplanes and fifty-two seaplanes available to the Royal Naval Air Service (RNAS).

The war developed into static trench warfare, with major actions or 'pushes' preceded by artillery barrages. An early use was found in reconnaissance and artillery observation, and this role became the cornerstone of military aviation. General von Below is quoted by Maurice Baring, in *Flying Corps Headquarters 1914-1918*, as stating in a memorandum: 'The main object of fighting in the air is to enable our photographic registration and photographic reconnaissance to be carried out, and at the same time to prevent that of the enemy.' The use of fighters to prevent reconnaissance operations was therefore a natural development, followed by the application of the aeroplane to bombing operations, anti-submarine patrols and operations against airships.

Changing operational roles and the rapid development of aircraft and armament meant that existing in-service types were quickly rendered obsolete. New designs were essential, and had to be rushed into large-scale production. Aircraft were flown intensively, and losses were high through both enemy action and accidents. A large-scale training activity was required to maintain a supply of pilots to the operational squadrons, giving rise to its own losses of both men and machines.

All of this required a rapid expansion of production of all types, a process hampered by the fact that many of the potential workforce were enlisting in the Services. This problem could only be solved by bringing into the production effort industrial enterprises that had no prior experience of aircraft manufacture. The furniture and motor trades were both critical in this respect, as is evident in this region. Similarly, the work force needed to be augmented, and many women entered the production lines of the munitions factories (including the aircraft industry) for the first time.

The types that were most widely contracted out included the designs of the Royal Aircraft Factory (such as the BE2, BE12, RE8, FE2 and SE5A), training aircraft (notably the Avro 504 and DH6), Felixstowe-designed flying boats, patrol seaplanes (Short 184), and

Production of the Royal Aircraft Factory BE2 was widely contracted during the First World War, these examples being manufactured by Wm. Beardmore & Co. Ltd at Dalmuir. (JMB/GSL collection)

The flying boat played an important role during the First World War with standing anti-submarine patrols being mounted from Felixstowe. (JMB/GSL collection)

combat aircraft (Sopwith Pup, Camel, 1½ Strutter and Snipe; Bristol F.2B Fighter; AIRCO DH4, DH9, DH9A). Toward the end of the First World War significant orders were placed for the contract manufacture of long-range bomber types, such as the Handley Page O/400 and Vickers Vimy. Many of these orders were cancelled following the Armistice.

Loss Rates

The expansion of production during the First World War was, in truth, an enormous enterprise. Because of its significance, it is worth reflecting on some of the facts and figures associated with this accelerated production programme. As background, one needs to appreciate the intensity of air operations, and of the high rate of loss and *matériel* consumption involved, as indicated by the following contemporary data:

> *The average life of an aeroplane at the battlefront is not more than two months. To keep 5,000 aircraft in active commission for one year it is necessary to furnish 30,000. Each machine in the period of its activity will use at least two motors, so that 60,000 motors will be required.*

M. Flaudin, head of the Allied Air Board (quoted in the American magazine *Flying*, September 1917).

These figures seem extraordinary, but closely match the levels actually achieved by the end of the conflict.

Aircraft losses in late 1918 were running at some 200 per month. In fact, aircraft destroyed by the enemy, and in training accidents, together with those that had to be scrapped as being obsolete, represented some 60 per cent of the total constructed during the war. Sadly, training exacted a heavy toll. A question in Parliament during the 1918 Air Estimates debate revealed that during 1917 more men were lost at the training schools than were lost flying on all fronts. Winston Churchill also spoke in Parliament on 4 April 1917 on the subject of the heavy losses being suffered by the RFC during training.

Data published in 1919 (in *Flight* and elsewhere) indicate that the total casualties over the whole period of the war were 6,166 killed, 7,245 wounded and 3,128 missing. A total of 330 British airmen lost their lives in April 1917, the so-called 'Bloody April'. At this time, the expected operational life of an RFC pilot was no more than seventeen-and-a-half flying hours. Peter King in *Knights of the Air* indicates that losses in every month of 1918 were equal to the entire strength of the RFC at the start of the First World War.

The demands imposed by these short service lives and high attrition were considerable; how were the resultant production needs to be met?

Expansion of the Production Programme

Production at existing aircraft companies was rapidly expanded, and contracts were placed with established industrial concerns, particularly in the motor car and furniture trades, to boost supply. Many new companies were also founded specifically to meet this growing demand, and to provide a sub-contract infrastructure. The resultant explosion of industrial activity was truly amazing, and has been inadequately recorded.

In May 1917, less than three years after the outbreak of the First World War, the position was summarised by the 'British Comptroller of Aeronautic Supplies' in a statement to the Board of Governors of the Aero Club of America. He stated that 'there are 958 firms in England engaged on work for the British Directorate of Aeronautic Supplies, 301 of which are direct contractors and 657 are sub-contractors'. The report further states that 'the total number of hands employed by the fifty firms of most prominence is 66,700. [...] The present British budget for aeronautics in the present year totals $575,000,000' (reported in *Flying* magazine, June 1917). These are impressive figures by any standard.

The *Aviation Pocket-Book of 1919-20* listed 148 aeroplane manufacturers and many other suppliers, and commented on the adequacy of its Gazetteer thus: 'It does not pretend to include the names of all who are accustomed to making aeroplane parts, for many firms were

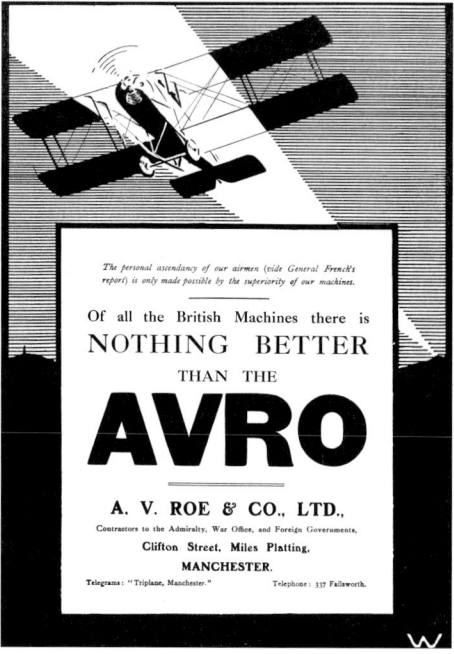

Above: *Sir W.G. Armstrong, Whitworth & Co. Ltd made an important contribution to First World War production with their own FK3 and FK8 designs in addition to contract production of the BE2 and Bristol Fighter. (JMB/GSL collection)*

Left: *A.V. Roe & Co. Ltd used the slogan 'Nothing Better' from 1913 onwards.*

doing so for the period of the war only – in fact there is hardly a motor car or motor car accessory or wood-working firm that was not fully occupied with aviation work at the time of the Armistice. [...] Possibly, however, some names are not included that ought to be, since it is not an easy task, when compiling a directory of this nature, to ensure its being absolutely complete.' The author must echo these sentiments in respect of the present work.

Manufacture was split between aircraft manufacturers, with their own design teams, capable of producing original designs; contractors, who built established designs to order; and component suppliers. With the dispersion of production to many enterprises, it was found necessary to create a number of regional Acceptance Parks, to which contractors delivered their aircraft for inspection and acceptance. Contractors in some cases delivered wings, tail and fuselage separately by road or rail to the acceptance aerodromes, prior to assembly and flight-test.

Within the area covered by this volume, the most significant aircraft manufacturing concerns (each of whom built at least 400 aircraft, with a combined total of more than 9,000 aircraft) were:

- A.V. Roe & Co. Ltd at Manchester – particularly Miles Platting and Newton Heath.
- Vulcan Motor & Engineering Co. (1906) Ltd at Southport.
- Sir W.G. Armstrong, Whitworth & Co. Ltd at Newcastle.
- Angus Sanderson Ltd at Newcastle.
- The Blackburn Aeroplane & Motor Co. Ltd at Leeds and Brough.
- Wm. Beardmore & Co. Ltd at Dalmuir.
- The 'Scottish Group' of engineering and shipbuilding companies, including G. & J. Weir Ltd.
- Harland & Wolff Ltd in Belfast.

Smaller concerns included: Dick, Kerr & Co. Ltd at Preston; John Dawson & Co. Ltd at Newcastle; Pegler Bros & Co. (Doncaster) Ltd; Phoenix Dynamo Manufacturing Co. Ltd at Bradford; March, Jones & Cribb at Leeds; The British Caudron Co. Ltd at Alloa; and Arrol-Johnston Ltd at Dumfries.

Production Quantities

The achievements of the rapidly expanding industry were remarkable. This is illustrated rather graphically by the following statement made by Winston Churchill, Minister of Munitions, speaking in Parliament on 25 April 1918, when presenting the Estimates of the Ministry of Munitions:

We are now making in a single week more aeroplanes than were made in the whole of 1914, in a single month more than were made in the whole of 1915, and in a single quarter more than were made in the whole of 1916.

The total British production during the First World War is widely reported as 55,093 airframes (other figures are also quoted, see below), with an additional 3,051 purchased abroad. Very significant production was also undertaken in France and the USA, with American production running at around 12,000 aircraft per year by the end of the war. Data published after the First World War (as a Parliamentary Paper on 24 April 1919) gave the following figures for British production.

First World War Aircraft Production

Period	Duration (months)	Aircraft built	Aircraft per month
August 1914 to May 1915	10	530	53
June 1915 to February 1917	21	7,137	340
March 1917 to December 1917	10	13,521	1,352
January 1918 to October 1918	10	26,685	2,669

(Note: This gives a total of 47,873, some 7,200 less than is given by more recent sources.)

The expansion in production is also reflected in the numbers of aircraft on charge with the RFC and RNAS, as follows: August 1914, 272; January 1917, 5,496; January 1918, 11,091; October 1918 (RAF), 22,171. These figures, from the same source as the production numbers, show that in four years the aircraft establishment of the flying services had been increased more than eighty fold, with the production rate increasing more than fifty fold. To provide a comparison with United Kingdom production, one should acknowledge that this enormous acceleration in the field of aviation was evident among all combatants.

As an inevitable consequence of the fighting, a large number of wrecked, damaged and unserviceable aircraft congregated at the operational and training bases. A significant reconstruction activity used cannibalised parts to produce new aircraft to return to operations. Serial blocks were allocated to as many as 500 such aircraft at a time (rebuilt from depots in France, for example). To illustrate the scale of this effort, some examples of units within the repair organization, and activities down to Squadron level, are provided in the table below (which is by no means comprehensive):

Organisation	Location (if known)	Example output
No.1 (Southern) Aircraft Repair Depot	Farnborough	700 aircraft covering at least eighteen types
No.2 (Northern) Aircraft Repair Depot	Coal Aston	Reservations for some 500 aircraft including FK.8, RE8, FE2B, BE2E, etc.
No.3 (Western) Aircraft Repair Depot	Yate	At least 200 aircraft including Camel, RE8, SE5A, Avro 504, Bristol F.2B, BE2E
No.5 (Eastern) Aircraft Repair Depot	Henlow	Fifty allocations including F.2B, Avro 504, Camel, DH4, DH9A
6 Wing Aircraft Repair Station	Dover	Nine Pup, three Camel, DH5, BE2C, DH4, Avro 504, 1½ Strutter
19 Repair Station	Northolt	DH2 from spares A5211
18 Repair Station	Montrose	Twelve BE2C and a Bristol Scout from spares
3 Training Depot Station	Lopcombe Corner	Three Camel
43 Training Depot Station	Chattis Hill	Seven Camel, two as two-seaters
23 Training Wing Aircraft Repair Station	South Carlton	Avro 504 and two-seat Camel
26 Wing Aircraft Repair Station	Thetford	Small numbers of BE2E, Pup, Avro 504, Farman S.11, DH6, RE8, etc.
7 Wing Aircraft Repair Station	Norwich	Small numbers of Pup, Avro 504, DH6, Shorthorn, DH4, BE2D/E, RE8, FK.3
RAF Ascot	Ascot	Twenty-five DH9A built up from spares
Central Flying School	Upavon	Four Sopwith Camel
63 Training Squadron	Joyce Green	Sopwith Pup B9440

There were a number of Aircraft Depots in France (for example, at St Omer and Candas), together with mobile Aircraft Parks to assist in maintaining supplies and spare parts.

Production Difficulties

Significant production difficulties were encountered (and were to be re-encountered in the Second World War) due to the difficulty of building up production among a large number of dispersed and sometimes inexperienced sub-contractors. The requirement to accelerate production was hampered by the steady depletion of the workforce as more and more were

This DH9A was a product of No.1 (Southern) Aircraft Repair Depot at Farnborough. (T.C. Treadwell and A.C. Wood)

called up for service in France. Near continuous industrial unrest resulted due to the heavy demands on the individual, and the Defence of the Realm Act was much used to maintain stability in the munitions industries.

Engine suppliers had great difficulty maintaining pace with airframe manufacture. Early in 1915 a serious shortage of 90hp RAF engines occurred leaving Sir W.G. Armstrong, Whitworth & Co. Ltd with no less than 100 engineless BE2 machines hanging three or four deep from the ceiling. Similarly, in January 1918, no less than 400 SE5A were waiting for engines. The lower than expected performance of the Siddeley Puma proved to be a problem for the DH4. Martinsyde F.3 production was reduced because of the need for Rolls-Royce Falcon engines to power the Bristol Fighter. The lack of availability of Falcon engines also resulted in the Bristol Fighter being flown (with variable success) with 300hp Hispano-Suiza, Siddeley Puma and Sunbeam Arab engines. Production of the FE2D was also constrained by the shortage of supply of its Rolls-Royce Eagle engine. The 200hp Hispano-Suiza engine fitted to the Sopwith Dolphin suffered from frequent connecting-rod failures. The supply of engines was further hampered by the need to create a new industry to supply magnetos, the manufacture of which, until the outbreak of the First World War, had been the almost exclusive province of German industry.

At the end of the First World War, engine orders were running at around 65,000 per year, more than 8,500 of these orders being for the disastrous ABC Dragonfly. F. Warren Merriam commented, 'There is no doubt that at this late stage in the war, our aero engines were becoming less and less reliable.' Shortages affected nearly every type. Standardisation was absent; in early 1918, Mr Pemberton Billing pointed out that forty-four different types of engine were in use. Ironically, the attempt to standardise on the Dragonfly was also an ignominious failure. In 1918, with vast numbers of engines on order from thirteen contractors, the Dragonfly was achieving a typical engine life of only two-and-a-half hours before failure.

Scarcity of Resources

The needs of aircraft production resulted in a tremendous drain on resources, and even had an impact on the agricultural landscape, through the demand for flax to supply the need for aircraft linen. In July 1917, Dr Addison, Minister of Munitions gave a specific indication of the strategic requirements of the aircraft industry, as follows:

> *The fact that no fewer than 1,000 factories are engaged on some process or other connected with the construction and equipment of the flying machine proves the magnitude of the work we have in hand. The needs of the aeroplane programme are enormous, almost passing belief. For our present programme of construction, more spruce is required than the present annual output of the United States, more mahogany than Honduras can supply – and Honduras is accustomed to supply the requirements of the World. Besides this, all the linen of the type required made in Ireland, the home of the linen industry, and the whole of the alloyed steel that England can produce can be used. As for flax, the Government has actually to provide the seed from which to grow the plant essential for its purposes.*

Flax seed was supplied free to growers, who were further encouraged with significant subsidies, and guaranteed prices. The scheme was administered by the Flax Production Branch of the Board of Agriculture. Further financial assistance to growers was offered in July 1918 as a result of the Flax Companies (Financial Assistance) Bill. So successful were these measures that by the time of the Armistice, production of aircraft fabric was running at 7 million yards (nearly 4,000 miles) per month. By April 1919, the Ministry of Munitions had in stock and available for disposal no less than 31,970,725 yards of linen. In mid-1919, the total surplus (by now 40,000,000 yards, or nearly 23,000 miles of fabric, in sixteen varieties and widths of 25–72ins) was sold to one individual, Mr J.L. Martin, for about £4,000,000.

The Government requested in late 1917 that farmers carry out a census of ash trees, where potential supply problems were causing some concern. In supporting this request it was stated that 'The Government requirements for the next twelve months [i.e. 1918] are expected to exceed 200,000 trees'. In all, about one third of the volume of timber standing at the outbreak of war was felled, much being used in aircraft manufacture.

Overall, perhaps the most striking feature of the First World War mass production effort was that the entire enterprise, involving more than a thousand companies, was created within ten years of the construction of Britain's first aeroplane.

Foundation of the SBAC

On 23 March 1916, forty of the main constructing firms came together to form an interest group through which to voice their common concerns. This was the Society of British Aircraft Constructors (SBAC), an organisation that continues to be a spokesman for the industry today.

Not a single one of the SBAC founders survives today, as a wholly British aircraft manufacturer, although Shorts (as a subsidiary of Bombardier) and Italian-owned AgustaWestland are honourable near-survivors

3
Collapse and Re-birth Between the Wars (1919–1939)

The early inter-war period was marked by the near-complete collapse of the military aircraft market, and the return of the majority of contractors to their original products and markets. The larger companies were restructured to avoid Excess Profit Duty, and they all faced competition from their own products, now being marketed by The Aircraft Disposal Company. Military sales were very limited in number.

By the 1930s, the growing light aircraft movement resulted in expansion of civil production, and many new concerns were established, only to be cut off at the start of the Second World War. The de Havilland Aircraft Co. Ltd found a sustained civil market with a succession of designs following on from the groundbreaking DH60 Moth. Airspeed Ltd, Phillips & Powis/Miles Aircraft Ltd, Taylorcraft Aeroplanes (England) Ltd and Percival Aircraft Ltd all succeeded and were able to make a valuable contribution to Britain's efforts during the Second World War. Military rearmament began in 1935, and provided a lifeline for the main manufacturers.

Post-war Collapse

What brought about the initial collapse? Quite simply, the need for aircraft evaporated virtually overnight. Once the war stopped, the country had neither the resources, nor the need, to sustain the aircraft production juggernaut. Many orders were cancelled, and the enormous stock of war surplus aircraft was sold on favourable terms to The Aircraft Disposal Company at Croydon. In consequence, any firm attempting a new aircraft venture during the immediate post-war period inevitably found itself competing with its own, or its competitors', second-hand products.

When this difficulty was combined with the effects of Excess Profits Duty, it is not surprising that wholesale reorganisation took place. Most of the sub-contractors either went into liquidation, or returned to their former trades. In this region, The English Electric Co. and Wm. Beardmore & Co. Ltd ceased aircraft manufacture, whilst the Clydeside shipbuilders and Harland & Wolff returned to their accustomed trade. The surviving companies also reorganised, slimmed down, or went into liquidation; many flirted with the motor trade and other forms of diversification. A number of those that entered voluntary liquidation emerged in new, fitter, guises to carry on in the aircraft business. The survivors drew the protective cloak of the SBAC tightly around themselves.

The scale of the contraction after the Armistice was incredible. On 11 November 1918, 25,000 aircraft were on order. The Air Ministry sought to shut down production of all obsolete types immediately, and only accept delivery of those contracts from which they positively could not extricate themselves. Those obsolete types that could not be cancelled would be delivered directly to store. By cancellation of these orders, the number of aircraft that the Ministry was obliged to accept was reduced to 13,432. Scrapping for the recovery of useful parts proved not to be very economic, and it was recommended that greater savings would be made if the engine were to be removed, and the rest of the machine burned.

By the end of 1920, the Aircraft Manufacturing Co. Ltd (AIRCO); The British & Colonial Aeroplane Co. Ltd; Nieuport & General Aircraft Co. Ltd; Martinsyde Ltd; The Central Aircraft Co.; The Grahame-White Aviation Co. Ltd; and Sopwith Aviation & Engineering Co. Ltd had variously closed, entered receivership, or reorganised. By June 1922 only ninety-seven British civil aircraft had Certificates of Airworthiness, down from 240 in 1920. By the mid-1920s, the industry had reduced to sixteen major manufacturers – Sir W.G. Armstrong, Whitworth Aircraft Ltd; A.V. Roe & Co. Ltd; The Blackburn Aeroplane & Motor Co. Ltd; Boulton & Paul Ltd; The Bristol Aeroplane Co. Ltd; The de Havilland Aircraft Co. Ltd; Fairey Aviation Ltd; The Gloucestershire Aircraft Co. Ltd; Handley Page Ltd; H.G. Hawker Engineering Co. Ltd; George Parnall & Co. Ltd; S.E. Saunders Ltd; Short Brothers (Rochester & Bedford) Ltd; The Supermarine Aviation Works Ltd; Vickers Ltd; and Westland Aircraft Works (Branch of Petters Ltd).

Military Production in the 1920s and 1930s

From this point onwards, military aircraft manufacture was virtually reduced to the modification and development of the existing in-service types, and the development of a smattering of prototypes. The prototype activity was spread across the industry and just about sustained the industrial base. The lack of active operations meant that only small production volumes of largely obsolescent aircraft were required to fulfil the needs of the RAF. Shorts, for example, built less than forty aircraft during the whole of the 1920s.

Within this region A.V. Roe & Co. Ltd built upon the record of its outstanding Avro 504 trainer, leading to a long and successful series of single-engine biplanes for military and civil use. These included the Avro 504N, Avian, Tutor, Prefect and Cadet, which were followed by large-scale production of the twin-engine Avro Anson. The Blackburn Aeroplane & Motor Co. Ltd produced a variety of aircraft throughout this period, many for naval use. Notable types included the Dart, Ripon, Baffin, Shark, Skua and Roc, as well as the civilian Bluebird and numerous prototype designs. In 1928, Sir W.G. Armstrong, Whitworth & Co. Ltd joined with the Siddeley-Deasy Motor Car Co. Ltd of Coventry, leading to the formation of the Armstrong Whitworth Development Co. Ltd. The aircraft interests of this company were then transferred to Coventry as Sir W.G. Armstrong Whitworth Aircraft Ltd. Fairey Aviation Ltd occupied the former National Aircraft Factory No.2 of the First World War, which had subsequently been used by Willys Overland Crossley Ltd, to build the Fairey Hendon and then the Battle.

One measure of the desperation of the industry was that key military requirements, likely to lead to significant production contracts, would lead to a rash of official and private venture prototypes being produced. An example is provided by the influential requirement F.7/30 for a new fighter aircraft, issued in 1931. The aircraft that competed for a contract against this requirement were as follows:

- Blackburn F.7/30 (K2892).
- Bristol Type 123 biplane (private venture, unmarked).
- Bristol Type 133 monoplane (private venture, R-10).
- Gloster SS.37 (private venture, G.37) – eventually ordered into production as the Gladiator.
- Hawker (private venture, I-PV3).
- Supermarine F.7/30 (K2890).
- Westland F.7/30 (K2891).

Bristol Fighter E2058/G-EBCU was built by Sir W.G. Armstrong, Whitworth Aircraft Ltd, and was subsequently delivered to the Queen of the Belgians by the Aircraft Disposal Co. Ltd in May 1922. (JMB/GSL collection)

Four of the seven types flown were constructed on a private venture basis, and none of the three officially funded designs was selected for production.

Specification F.7/30, in addition to producing the RAF's last biplane fighter, was also instrumental in the genesis of the Supermarine Spitfire. R.J. Mitchell's proposal for an improved solution to this requirement led to funding for the development of a new design (the Type 300) against a modified specification (F.37/34). This specification was superseded by F.10/35, which the Type 300 was modified to meet (although the aircraft was still referred to by the firm as the F.37/34). F.10/35 sought a fighter aircraft with eight guns and a speed advantage over 'the contemporary bomber' of at least 40mph at 15,000ft. A speed of 310mph was required at the same altitude, with an enclosed cockpit providing a good pilot field of view, particularly in the upper hemisphere. Thus was the Spitfire, as the Air Ministry subsequently named the type, born.

The military market remained stagnant until, during the late 1930s, tension rose within Europe leading to progressive rearmament from 1935. From this point onward, the military manufacturers saw increasing orders and the start of sub-contract/dispersed production to increase capacity.

Civil Production and the Light Aeroplane Movement

Immediately after the First World War, there were limited attempts to generate an air transport market, with A.V. Roe & Co. Ltd (Avro Transport Service), Blackburn (North Sea Aerial Navigation Co. Ltd), Handley Page (Handley Page Transport Ltd) and AIRCO (Aircraft Transport & Travel Ltd) all starting airline services, mainly using converted military aircraft. These efforts were unsuccessful and, although small numbers of commercial aircraft were sold to independent airlines, there was no real demand for air travel. Even after the formation of Imperial Airways, airliner production in Britain was restricted to modest production runs from Armstrong Whitworth, de Havilland, Handley Page, and Shorts.

The appearance of the de Havilland Dragon (1932), and Dragon Rapide (1934), saw production quantities increase. It is fair to say, however, that, with the exception of de Havilland,

A typical between-the-wars prototype, the Avro 566 Avenger was built in Manchester and assembled and test flown at Hamble, Hampshire. (BAE SYSTEMS plc)

Specification F.7/30 resulted in a number of extraordinary confections, this being the Blackburn offering. This competition was, however, influential to the eventual development of the Spitfire. (BAE SYSTEMS plc)

and Empire flying boat production at Shorts, military aircraft production dominated the affairs of most of the larger companies.

Whilst the Lympne Light Aeroplane Competitions of 1924 and 1926 generated much publicity for the potential of privately owned aircraft, the competing aircraft themselves were not a great success. The appearance of the de Havilland Moth, and the availability of subsidies for flying schools, radically changed this picture. New companies emerged and prospered,

Like a number of other manufacturers, Blackburn flirted with the air transport industry after the First World War. Their airline, the North Sea Aerial Navigation Co., was equipped with converted Blackburn Kangaroos. (JMB/GSL collection)

Phillips & Powis (Aircraft) Ltd, later Miles Aircraft Ltd, was one of a number of successful firms producing light aircraft in the 1930s. Miles were noted for their touring and racing aircraft, typified by Miles M.2L Hawk Speed Six G-ADGP. (Author)

including the famous names of Airspeed (at York and then Portsmouth), de Havilland (initially at Stag Lane, and then Hatfield), General Aircraft (Croydon and then Hanworth), Percival Aircraft (Gravesend and then Luton), and Miles (then as Phillips & Powis (Aircraft) Ltd, at Woodley). Much of this activity was concentrated in, and near, London, as flying gathered popularity as a fashionable activity. Private aircraft production in this region included the Avro Avian, Avro Cadet and the Avro-built Cierva C.30A Autogiro; the

Blackburn Bluebird; the Comper Swift produced at Hooton Park; and the Hillson Praga, which was built at Barton, Manchester.

A new phenomenon also arose in the form of the craze for the Flying Flea sparked by the design of the tandem wing *Pou de Ciel* by Henri Mignet. Although ultimately (and in some cases tragically) unsuccessful, the Flea served to legitimise the eccentric British habit of constructing home-built aircraft. This had originated in the pioneering period with the enthusiasm of the likes of Mr Jezzi at Eastchurch, being continued after the First World War by such characters as F.H. Lowe at Heaton, and the Blake brothers at Winchester. This tradition has been carried on to this day in Britain by individuals such as John Isaacs, John Taylor, Ivan Shaw and many others, now under the very professional administration of the Popular Flying Association at Turweston.

4
Second World War Mass Production (1939–1945)

Rearmament and the Shadow Factory Scheme

The expansion of the aircraft production programme against the threat of war built up gradually from 1935 and is inseparably linked to the Second World War aircraft production effort. Whilst to many eyes the move to rearm Britain's forces came perilously late, moves began some five years before the Second World War broke out. The first step was the adoption of an expansion plan in July 1934, known as Scheme A, to increase the size of the Royal Air Force. Under this scheme the Metropolitan Air Force was intended to grow to 1,252 operational aircraft by the spring of 1939.

Hitler had become Chancellor in January 1933, but his repudiation of the Treaty of Versailles, reoccupation of the Rhineland, the Austrian Anschluss, the annexation of Czechoslovakia and the Nazi–Soviet Pact were still years ahead. It is clear, therefore, that some early positive decisions were made and as a result the armaments industry began to grow. The real difficulty lay in the lack of investment in modern designs and technology, combined with the drastic reduction in production capacity caused by the lean years of the 1920s and early 1930s.

The pace of rearmament in the aircraft industry quickened with Scheme C, which was instituted in May 1935 and which brought about further significant increases in both the size of the RAF and the production of new aircraft types. From October 1936 the need for increased production led to the formation of the 'shadow factory' scheme. New factories were constructed using public funds, owned by the Government, but run by private industry to boost the production of (initially) aero engine components, where the shortfall in production capacity was even more marked than in the airframe industry. The contractual complexities of the shadow factory scheme introduced uncertainty in some instances over the precise responsibility for site management and aircraft production/assembly at particular sites. This is an area that would benefit from further research.

In addition to Bristol (whose engines were to be produced), the five companies initially involved in the shadow factory scheme were Austin Motor Co. Ltd, The Daimler Co. Ltd, Rootes Securities Ltd (Humber), The Rover Company Ltd and the Standard Motor Co. Ltd. In February 1937 the scheme was extended to allow Austin and Rootes to construct airframes as well as engines. Despite this early recognition that engine availability was critical to the acceleration of airframe production, there were periods, as in the First World War, when engineless airframes were in plentiful supply.

The early expansion schemes favoured light day bombers such as the Fairey Battle and Vickers Wellesley. Unfortunately, the concept of the light day bomber proved to be a blind alley, with the Battle, in particular, suffering from high operational losses whilst trying to stem the Blitzkrieg across the Low Countries during 1940. (Fairey Battle losses between 10 and 14 May 1940 were no less than sixty aircraft, out of the 108 deployed, during attacks against troop concentrations and the Albert Canal bridges). Other types that entered production in this period included the Hampden, Whitley and Blenheim. These types were to make an

HS158 *is one of the many Fairey Swordfish aircraft to have been built by Blackburn at Sherburn-in-Elmet.* (BAE SYSTEMS plc)

important contribution in the early years of the Second World War, but lacked the performance and payload to remain in front-line service throughout the coming conflict. From 1936 onward, types such as the Wellington, Hurricane and Spitfire began to be ordered in quantity through parent and shadow factories. Later on, the focus switched to heavy bomber production (particularly the Halifax and Lancaster), anticipating the need for a bomber offensive against Germany.

Wartime saw an increase in activity in Northern England, Scotland, Wales and Northern Ireland due in part to the establishment of substantial additional production capacity to supplement that of the major aircraft firms. Examples include:

- Vickers Wellington production at Brooklands/Weybridge was supplemented by actories at Broughton (Chester) and Blackpool.
- A.V. Roe & Co. Ltd began operations at Yeadon, building the Anson and Manchester.
- Blackburn Aircraft Ltd reinstated production at Sherburn-in-Elmet and began production at Dumbarton.
- The Fairey Aviation Co. Ltd added production capacity at Heaton Chapel and Errwood Park.
- Contract production of more than 800 Percival Proctor aircraft by F. Hills & Sons Ltd at Barton.
- The English Electric Co. Ltd (at Preston/Samlesbury) re-entered aircraft production to manufacture the Hampden and Halifax.
- Metropolitan-Vickers built the Avro Manchester and Lancaster at Trafford Park.
- Rootes Securities Ltd at Speke provided additional capacity for the production of the Bristol Blenheim and Handley Page Halifax (with additional Blenheim production at Blythe Bridge, Staffordshire).
- Short & Harland Ltd in Belfast began manufacturing the Bristol Bombay and Handley Page Hereford before moving on to the Stirling and Sunderland.
- Short Sunderland production at Windermere and Dumbarton.

Elsewhere, Sir W.G. Armstrong Whitworth Aircraft Ltd created additional production capacity at Baginton and Bitteswell. Hawker capacity was increased with operations at Langley supplementing those at Kingston and Brooklands. Vickers-Armstrongs Ltd

(Supermarine) managed a large shadow factory at Castle Bromwich and another factory at South Marston, in addition to dispersed production across Southern England. (The initial management of the Castle Bromwich Aeroplane Factory was with the Nuffield Organisation, Vickers-Armstrongs Ltd being subsequently asked to take over its management). Gloster Aircraft Co. Ltd was used to provide additional Hurricane production capacity and to take responsibility for the Henley and Typhoon. Austin Motors Ltd of Birmingham built the Fairey Battle day bomber, Hawker Hurricane fighter, and the Short Stirling and Avro Lancaster heavy bombers. Rootes Securities managed a shadow factory at Blythe Bridge, building the Blenheim and Beaufighter. Tiger Moth production was transferred to Morris Motors at Cowley to allow the de Havilland Aircraft Co. Ltd to concentrate its resources on the Mosquito. Brush Coachworks at Loughborough undertook DH89 Dominie production, and Standard Motors at Coventry/Ansty built the Mosquito. The London Aircraft Production Group (at Aldenham and Leavesden) added to the output of Halifax bombers produced by Handley Page Ltd and the other contractors. The heavy bomb damage sustained at Rochester resulted in production of the Short Stirling at Swindon and South Marston.

Production Difficulties

Large-scale orders and expanded capacity were one thing: production proved to be quite another problem. Production difficulties were encountered with the accelerating demands placed on both airframe and engine manufacturers, particularly as the British industry was only just accommodating retractable undercarriages, variable pitch propellers, and all-metal stressed skin monoplanes. In contemporary reports one finds reference to:

- Poorly organised initial production by Supermarine at Woolston, with mismatched wing and fuselage production rates.
- Similar problems at Filton with the Blenheim, with thirty-two fuselages produced before any wings appeared.
- The initial inability of the Morris-run Castle Bromwich shadow factory to get the Spitfire into production.
- Miles Master development and production dictated by availability of particular engine types.
- Master, Oxford and Tiger Moth airframes dispersed into storage to await their engines.
- Fairey's problems of excessive dispersal of its factories, including delays to the Albacore due to problems with its Taurus engine. The delays to Albacore production led to a further delay of about a year in establishing Firefly production. A delay of two years to the Barracuda was attributed to priority being given to other types in production by Fairey at Heaton Chapel and Errwood Park. Sir Stafford Cripps intervened to introduce new personnel and reorganise project management at Fairey Aviation.
- Bristol's engineless Beaufighters towed by road from the factory at Filton to Whitchurch to await completion.
- Production levels in 1937/38 running at around one-third of those planned for the Battle and Blenheim, and virtually zero for the Spitfire.
- Dozens of Typhoons at Brockworth without engines being ferried to maintenance units using 'slave' engines. The engines were then removed, sent back to the Gloster factory, and refitted to the next aircraft for its delivery.

The setting up of the shadow factory scheme was, itself, a drain on the resources of the parent firms, due to their need to produce additional drawings and tooling, and to provide oversight of the expansion factories. One should not, however, forget the scale of the task, and the depleted production resource initially available for the effort.

Production Quantities and Standardisation

Despite all these difficulties, expansion in the immediate pre-war period was more successful than has been widely acknowledged. In 1935, 893 military aircraft were produced. This figure was more than doubled in 1936, and by 1939 reached 7,940, a nearly nine-fold increase in only five years. In 1941, the figure was more than 20,000, and by 1944 it exceeded 26,000.

The main production effort during the Second World War was split between the following organisations:

- The main design firms of A.V. Roe & Co. Ltd, Sir W.G. Armstrong Whitworth Aircraft Ltd, Blackburn Aircraft Ltd, Bristol Aeroplane Co. Ltd, the de Havilland Aircraft Co. Ltd, the Fairey Aviation Co. Ltd, Gloster Aircraft Co. Ltd, Handley Page Ltd, Hawker Aircraft Ltd, Short Brothers (Rochester & Bedford) Ltd, Vickers-Armstrongs Ltd and Westland Aircraft Ltd.
- Shadow and dispersed factories controlled either by aircraft industry parent firms, or by the motor industry (Rootes Securities Ltd, The Austin Motor Co. Ltd, Morris Motors Ltd, Standard Motor Co. Ltd, etc.), mainly in the Midlands and the north-west of England. This activity included contract production by The English Electric Co. Ltd at Preston and Samlesbury (Hampden, Halifax and Vampire), London Aircraft Production Group at Leavesden (Halifax) and Short & Harland Ltd in Belfast (Bombay, Hereford, Sunderland and Stirling).

New production capacity was required to meet the needs of the Second World War. The English Electric Co. Ltd returned to aircraft production, this photograph showing engine installation on Halifax EP234 at Samlesbury in September 1944. (BAE SYSTEMS plc)

The distinctive Barracuda dive bomber was a major wartime product of Fairey Aviation at Stockport, although the type was also the subject of contract production by other manufacturers. (BAE SYSTEMS plc)

- Smaller companies such as Airspeed (1934) Ltd, Cunliffe-Owen Aircraft Ltd, Folland Aircraft Ltd, Heston Aircraft Ltd, Phillips & Powis (Aircraft) Ltd/Miles Aircraft Ltd, Percival Aircraft Ltd, and Taylorcraft Aeroplanes (England) Ltd. Scottish Aviation Ltd at Prestwick played a valuable role in the reception and preparation of US-built aircraft ferried across the Atlantic, and also were responsible for a Spitfire and Hurricane repair organisation.
- Firms within the Civilian Repair Organisation such as Air Service Training, Marshall of Cambridge, Morrisons, Brooklands Aviation Ltd, and many others; manufacturer's repair organisations such as the Handley Page repair organisation at Clifton/Rawcliffe; Westlands at Doncaster; SEBRO at Cambridge; railway companies (e.g. LMS at Derby and Barassie); and RAF Maintenance Units such as Henlow and Kemble. Many aircraft that were nominally repaired and returned to service were substantially new airframes by the time that 'repair' had been completed.

The risk of bomb damage to main factory sites led every firm to set up dispersed operations. As in the First World War, large numbers of firms were involved, and as early as mid-1939, some 1,200 companies were involved in sub-contract aircraft production. Peak production in the Second World War reached 2,715 aircraft per month (March 1944), with, in addition, more than 500 aircraft per month returned to service after repair.

Unlike the First World War, there was a general policy of limiting the number of types in production. The increased efficiency and production volume that resulted offset the loss of some potentially outstanding designs (such as the Martin-Baker MB5), the production of which was blocked. As production gathered momentum, a number of companies were diverted from building their own types, in favour of the standardised designs. Examples in this area included production by Blackburn Aircraft Ltd of the Swordfish, Barracuda and Sunderland; Blenheim production by A.V. Roe & Co. Ltd; and the manufacture by Fairey Aviation Ltd of the Beaufighter and Halifax.

The main Second World War production types are summarised in the following table:

Main Second World War Production Types

Fighter	Bomber	Trainer/Liaison	Other
Defiant	Hampden	Tiger Moth	Swordfish
Hurricane	Battle	Oxford	Sunderland
Spitfire	Blenheim	Master	Firefly
Typhoon	Wellington	Magister	Seafire
Tempest	Stirling	Anson	Walrus
Beaufighter	Halifax	Auster	Lysander
	Lancaster	Proctor	Beaufort
	Mosquito	Dominie	Barracuda

By about 1941, most of the production capacity for front-line machines had been grouped on the Stirling, Halifax and Lancaster bombers, together with the Beaufighter, the Mosquito, the Spitfire, and the Barracuda. The reduced number of types produced reflects the technical maturity of the industry; it was no longer possible for the enemy to produce a new design that would completely change the balance of air power overnight. The Messerschmitt Me 262 might have had such an effect, had it been available earlier and in larger numbers, but in general it was found that progressive improvement of existing designs could keep pace with new enemy designs. Thus, the Spitfire was able to maintain its operational utility, through progressive engine, carburation and airframe developments, in the face of the Focke Wulf Fw190 and its developments.

Figures released at the end of the War by the Ministry of Aircraft Production stated that wartime production totalled some 125,000 complete aircraft, largest numbers being (in sequence) Spitfire, Hurricane, Wellington, Anson, Lancaster, Mosquito, Halifax, Beaufighter, Blenheim and Oxford (all 5,000 aircraft or more). (Note that the total figure is undoubtedly larger than is given above, as the published list does not include non-operational types such as the Tiger Moth, more than 8,800 of which were built).

It is also worth noting, in the light of the post-war domination of the industry by the USA, that although starting later, the US industrial machine outstripped United Kingdom production by a comfortable margin. The US built some 360,000 aircraft in the Second World War, nearly 96,000 of them in 1944 alone.

5
Post-war
(1945–1960)

When peace came, the various Government-owned shadow factories were no longer required for aircraft production, and were closed, or converted for car and engine manufacture. The aircraft industry set about meeting the challenges that it faced. These were the relatively unfamiliar demands of the commercial market, and the race to exploit the new technologies of war as tensions mounted between the West and the Soviet Bloc. The industry's efforts were made more difficult by the weakness of Britain's war shattered economy. Although the conditions facing the industry were not as drastic as those after the First World War, some companies still found themselves diversifying into new products. Many of the contract manufacturers simply returned to their original trade.

Commercial Aircraft Developments

A key decision, which has shaped the post-war commercial aircraft industry, was that wartime transport aircraft production was allocated to the United States of America. As a result, the excellent C-47 Dakota or DC-3 was immediately available for opening up the post-war air routes, with longer range services provided by the DC-4 (C-54 Skymaster), the later DC-6 and the Lockheed Constellation. Not only were these excellent aircraft in their own right, but they also proved capable of development into a line of successful derivative aircraft.

What then of Britain? New aircraft types were needed – Britain's pre-war airliners had, after all, not exactly led the world in their performance or technology. Despite the strain on the economy, an attempt was made, through the Brabazon Committee, to identify and develop a fleet of new aircraft covering a wide range of commercial applications. Unfortunately, these designs could not be created overnight, and, in the short-term, stop-gap designs and converted bombers were all that was available to compete for airline markets. Worse was to follow, as when the new types appeared, they were (with a couple of notable exceptions) not well suited to the prevailing market conditions. One common fault seems to have been the specification of too few passenger seats. Perhaps this reflected the view that few people could afford to fly, and those that could, would expect a suitably civilised environment!

To modern eyes, and admittedly with the benefit of hindsight, the first post-war commercial offerings from British industry seem brave but, in many cases, doomed from the outset. Among these were:

- The hurriedly converted bombers – the Lancastrian, Halton, and Stirling V.
- Britain's only true transport of the war, the Avro York – itself a development of the Lancaster bomber.
- The Sunderland flying boat conversions and developments – the Hythe, Sandringham and Solent.
- Non-starters – Armstrong Whitworth Apollo, Bristol Brabazon, Cunliffe-Owen Concordia, Portsmouth Aerocar, Percival Merganser and Saunders-Roe Princess.

The production of pre-fabricated housing was a feature of the immediate post-war aircraft industry. The kitchen of this prefab is being fitted out as it passes down the production line at Hawarden. (BAE SYSTEMS plc)

The Bristol Freighter sold successfully for civil and military transport. This RCAF example is delivering engines for overhaul by Scottish Aviation Ltd at Renfrew in May 1960. (Colin Lourie)

- The honourable exceptions – the new designs which reached production. These were the Airspeed Ambassador, Avro Tudor, Bristol Freighter, Bristol Britannia, de Havilland Comet, de Havilland Dove, Handley Page Hermes, Handley Page (Reading) Marathon, Percival Prince, Vickers Viking and Vickers Viscount.

Sadly, the vast majority could not compete with the operational economics of the American designs, nor the economies of scale afforded by the US industrial machine. Of British commercial aircraft in the immediate post-war period, only the de Havilland Dove and the Vickers Viscount were unqualified successes. It is indeed tragic that the Comet, which could have achieved a generation of British leadership in the skies, proved to be unexpectedly flawed. Although redesign of the Comet eventually produced a robust and successful aircraft, the moment had been lost as far as British domination of the commercial air transport market was concerned.

Military Aircraft Programmes

On the military side, the defeat of Germany and Japan brought peace, but no reduction in tension, because of the development of the 'Cold War' with the Soviet Union. The end of the war had seen the development of long-range surface-to-surface rockets, jet and rocket-propelled aircraft, and the atomic bomb. German technical progress with the development of the thin swept wing had also opened the door to much higher speeds, and the prospect of supersonic flight. Britain, and indeed the whole developed world, therefore plunged into a race to develop and exploit these technologies in the military field. Jet aircraft production continued at pace after the end of the Second World War, with production of most types being undertaken at several sites simultaneously. Examples include:

- Vampire production by de Havilland at Hatfield, Christchurch and Broughton (Hawarden); by Fairey Aviation at Stockport; and by English Electric at Preston and Samlesbury.
- Hunter production by Hawker at Dunsfold and Blackpool; and by Armstrong Whitworth at Bitteswell.
- Canberra production by English Electric at Preston and Samlesbury; A.V. Roe & Co. Ltd at Woodford; Handley Page Ltd at Radlett; and Short Bros. & Harland at Belfast.
- Production by Sir W.G. Armstrong Whitworth Aircraft Ltd of the Gloster Meteor, Hawker Sea Hawk and Gloster Javelin.

Although Britain's brilliant lead in jet engine technology saw operational fruit with the Meteor and Vampire, it was rapidly surpassed by the pace of development in both the USA and the USSR. In these nations, the significance of German swept-wing developments was better understood and acted upon, resulting in the superlative North American F-86 Sabre and the

The Handley Page Hermes found only modest sales success; this is the prototype Hermes 4, twenty-five of the type serving with BOAC from 1950 to 1952. (BAE SYSTEMS plc)

Mikoyan & Guryevich MiG 15/17. Despite 'super-priority' programmes, Britain was unable to bring its own Swift or Hunter quickly into service and had to suffer the indignity of the interim operation of the F-86 Sabre in order to preserve a credible operational capability. Naval aviation relied upon the propeller-driven Sea Hornet, Sea Fury and Wyvern, with jets being introduced in the form of the Attacker, Sea Venom, Sea Hawk and DH110 Sea Vixen. As the 1950s came to an end, Britain began the development of V/STOL combat aircraft with initial trials of the Hawker P.1127, which was to lead, via the Kestrel, to the production of the Harrier close support aircraft.

In the field of bombers, the superb Canberra was flown in 1949 and continues in RAF service in 2005, more than fifty years later. The Canberra was followed by the challenging V-Bomber programme, which demonstrated that Britain could indeed produce world-class designs. How extraordinary, however, that after all its deprivations in the Second World War, the country could actually afford to carry all three V-Bombers – the Valiant, Victor and Vulcan – into production in the face of the Cold War threat.

Transport and training aircraft programmes also delivered some long serving types including the Vickers Valetta and Varsity, Handley Page Hastings, Blackburn Beverley, de Havilland Devon and Chipmunk, and the Percival/Hunting Percival Prentice, Pembroke and Provost.

Westland transitioned to the manufacture of helicopters based upon the licence-built construction of Sikorsky designs, initially in the form of the WS-51 Dragonfly, and the WS-55 Whirlwind. A wider rotorcraft industry developed with a range of home-grown designs from Bristol (Sycamore and Belvedere), Fairey (Ultra-Light, Gyrodyne and Rotodyne) and Saunders-Roe (Skeeter and P.531).

In Scotland, Scottish Aviation began aircraft manufacture with a single-engine, high-wing utility aircraft designed for operation from short, rough airfields, the Pioneer, following this with a twin-engine machine for the same role, the Twin Pioneer.

Re-structuring of the Industry

As the 1950s came to a close, it was clear that an industry where every company built every type of aircraft could not be sustained. During this decade, all the manufacturers competed to develop and produce virtually every major class of aircraft, as indicated by the examples given in the table below:

Class of Aircraft	Manufacturers	Example Types
Bomber	A.V. Roe & Co. Ltd	Shackleton, Vulcan, Canberra (contract production)
	The English Electric Co. Ltd	Canberra
	Handley Page Ltd	Victor, Canberra (contract production)
	Vickers-Armstrongs Ltd	Valiant
	Short Brothers & Harland Ltd	Canberra (contract production)
Fighter	The de Havilland Aircraft Co. Ltd	Venom
	The English Electric Co. Ltd	Lightning
	Folland Aircraft Ltd	Gnat (export)
	The Gloster Aircraft Co. Ltd	Meteor, Javelin
	Hawker Aircraft Ltd	Hunter
	Vickers-Armstrongs Ltd	Swift, Scimitar
	Sir W.G. Armstrong Whitworth Aircraft Ltd	Hunter, Meteor and Javelin (contract production)
Military transport	Sir W.G. Armstrong Whitworth Aircraft Ltd	A.W.660 Argosy

Post-war (1945–1960) 39

The Hawker P.1067 Hunter prototype WB188, shows its graceful lines. (BAE SYSTEMS plc)

It now seems incredible that Britain should simultaneously produce three completely different types of strategic bomber – the V-bomber force. The incomparable Vulcan will long be remembered by all who saw it, both for its manoeuvrability and the thunderous, body-shaking noise of its take-off. (BAE SYSTEMS plc)

	Blackburn & General Aircraft Ltd	Beverley
	The Bristol Aeroplane Co. Ltd	Freighter, Britannia
	Handley Page Ltd	Hastings
	Vickers-Armstrongs Ltd	Valetta, Varsity
	Short Brothers & Harland Ltd (contract)	Britannia
Utility and communication	A.V. Roe & Co Ltd	Anson
	The de Havilland Aircraft Co. Ltd	Devon, Dove, Heron
	Hunting Percival Aircraft Ltd	Pembroke
	Scottish Aviation Ltd	Pioneer, Twin Pioneer

Scottish Aviation's most famous product was the Twin Pioneer. Eighty-seven were built, but the type could not compete with a copious supply of second-hand C47/DC3 aircraft. (Author)

Naval aircraft	Sir W.G. Armstrong Whitworth Aircraft Ltd	Sea Hawk (contract production)
	Blackburn & General Aircraft Ltd	NA.39 Buccaneer
	The de Havilland Aircraft Co. Ltd	Sea Vixen
	The Fairey Aviation Co. Ltd	Gannet
	Hawker Aircraft Ltd	Sea Hawk
	Westland Aircraft Ltd	Wyvern
Civil transport	Sir W.G. Armstrong Whitworth Aircraft Ltd	A.W.650 Argosy
	A.V. Roe & Co. Ltd	HS748 (first flew in 1960)
	The Bristol Aeroplane Co. Ltd	Britannia
	The de Havilland Aircraft Co. Ltd	Comet
	Handley Page Ltd	Herald
	Vickers-Armstrongs Ltd	Viscount, Vanguard
Helicopter	The Bristol Aeroplane Co. Ltd	Sycamore, Belvedere
	The Fairey Aviation Co. Ltd	Gyrodyne, Rotodyne (experimental types)
	Saunders-Roe Ltd	Skeeter
	Westland Aircraft Ltd	Sikorsky products and developments thereof

With anything up to seven manufacturers competing for business to supply a single class of aircraft, the industry was looking at an unsustainable future. The Government recognised that this situation was unacceptable, and applied great pressure on the industry to produce rationalisation.

Duncan Sandys' 1957 Defence White Paper of 4 April 1957 *Outline of Future Policy* has become somewhat notorious for its suggestion that missile technology was now maturing at such a rate that it would replace manned aircraft in many roles. It stated that in view of 'the good progress made towards the replacement of the manned aircraft of RAF Fighter

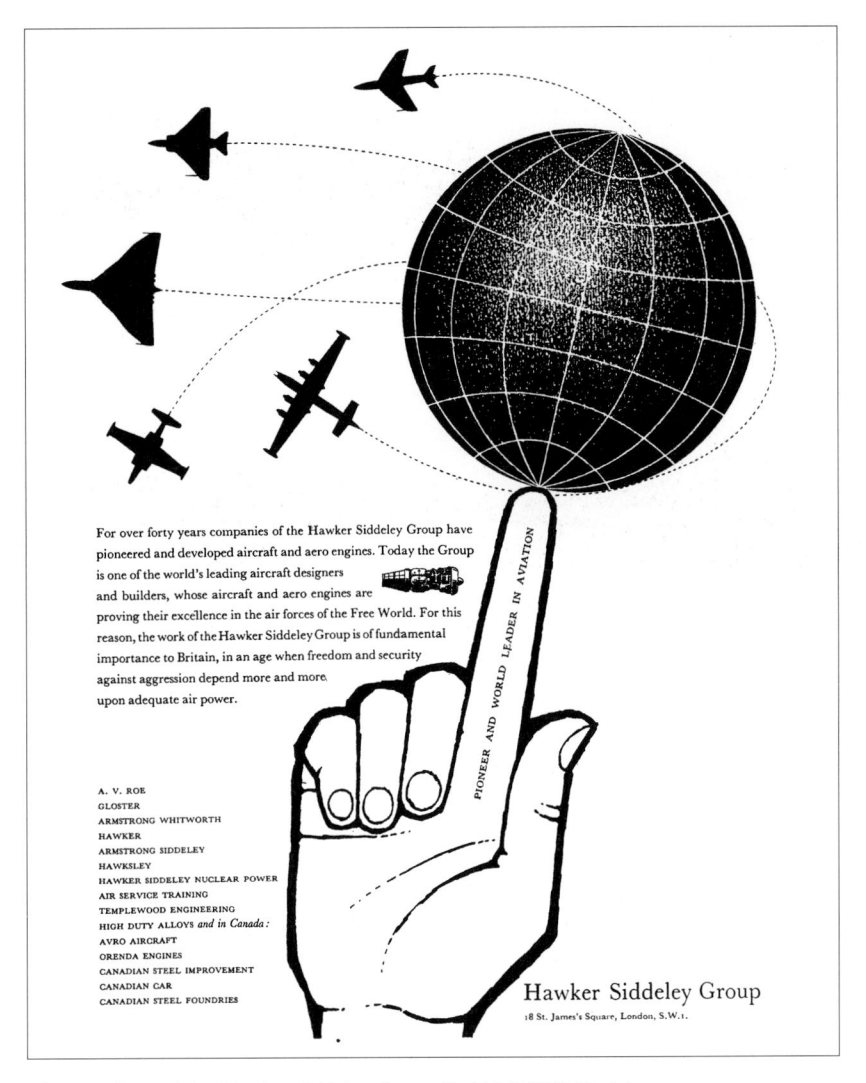

The members of the Hawker Siddeley Group (© BAE SYSTEMS plc)

Command with a ground to air missile system, the RAF is unlikely to have a requirement for fighter aircraft of types more advanced than the supersonic P.1, and work on such projects will stop'. Development of a supersonic manned bomber was not to be started, emphasis being switched to atomic weapons and guided missiles.

Clearly great changes in the aircraft industry were becoming inevitable. The first step was the announcement of the formation of the British Aircraft Corporation Ltd in January 1960, the Government having indicated that it would only support the TSR.2 programme if it were to be produced by a single company. This resulted in the aviation interests of Vickers, Bristol and English Electric joining forces, with Hunting Aircraft following shortly afterwards. In parallel, the companies in the Hawker Siddeley Group – Armstrong Whitworth, A.V. Roe & Co. Ltd, Blackburn, Gloster and Hawker found themselves being progressively joined by new bedfellows. These consisted of Folland (in 1959); de Havilland and its Airspeed Division (in 1960); and Blackburn (also in 1960). In July 1963, this group was further reorganised to create Hawker Siddeley Aviation Limited.

Thus was created what *Aviation Week & Space Technology* has called the 'Society of Both Aircraft Companies'. This was something of an exaggeration, as Short Bros. & Harland Ltd continued in Belfast, as did Scottish Aviation Ltd at Prestwick; Handley Page Ltd at Radlett; and Auster Aircraft Ltd at Rearsby. The helicopter industry was the subject of a similar Government-dictated rationalisation, in which Westland acquired the helicopter interests of its competitors: Saunders-Roe Ltd (in 1959); Bristol (in 1960); and Fairey Aviation (also in 1960).

FIFTY OUT OF FIFTY

Since 1912 the member companies of British Aircraft Corporation
have been providing aircraft and weapons for Britain's air defence. It was
with these weapons and aircraft that the men of the
Royal Flying Corps—later the Royal Air Force—made such vital contributions
in two world wars and have maintained security ever since.
British Aircraft Corporation salutes the Royal Air Force and looks
forward to providing its weapons and wings of the future.

BRITISH AIRCRAFT CORPORATION

The fiftieth anniversary of the British Aircraft Corporation (© BAE SYSTEMS plc)

6
Rationalisation: The BAC and Hawker Siddeley Years (1960–1977)

Market Trends – Commercial and General Aviation

BAC and Hawker Siddeley inherited a civil market that was struggling to break out from American domination. It is unfortunate that during the initial post-war period, a unique British ability to market the wrong products had resulted in the commercial market for piston-engined aircraft being dominated by the USA. It was doubly unfortunate, then, that despite the success of the Viscount, the Comet disasters opened the door to the Boeing 707 and DC-8.

If possible, worse was to follow. Myopic specifications from Britain's nationalised airlines (BEA and BOAC) and political indifference to the commercial aircraft industry undermined the potential of the Vanguard and VC10, BAC One-Eleven and Trident. The technically brilliant Concorde was economically, politically and environmentally flawed, particularly after the oil price shock of the 1970s, and the on-off-on development of the HS146 (later the BAe 146 and Avro RJ family) appeared to be driven by pure politics.

In a significant move for the future, the Hatfield Division of Hawker Siddeley entered into an agreement to develop wings for the new European consortium Airbus Industrie. This followed an inter-governmental agreement to support the Airbus project definition, which was signed in September 1967. From May 1969, the United Kingdom government withdrew from further project funding, but Hawker Siddeley took the decision to continue in the project on a purely commercial basis.

In the field of general aviation, the 1960s scene seemed more positive; Beagle (British Executive and General Aviation Limited) was set up in October 1960, drawing upon the creative abilities of Auster at Rearsby, and F.G. Miles at Shoreham. New designs emerged in the shape of the Beagle Pup, the twin-engine Beagle 206, and the Bulldog military trainer. De Havilland had seen the value of the executive jet market and designed their DH125, initially known as the Jet Dragon, which was taken up and marketed by Hawker Siddeley as the HS125 with great success worldwide.

At Bembridge, Isle of Wight, John Britten and Desmond Norman had, through their operation of agricultural aircraft in some of the more basic areas of the world, identified the need for a simple robust utility aircraft capable of operation from short airstrips in all climates. The design that resulted, the Islander, fulfilled the designers' concept in every respect. On a larger scale, Shorts were also successful in bringing the utilitarian Skyvan into production for both civilian and military users.

In the helicopter arena, Westland Helicopters Limited built a solid base from its manufacture of Sikorsky products under licence. The Whirlwind and Wessex attracted large-scale orders, and the Saunders-Roe P.531 was developed successfully into the Scout and Wasp. Westland boomed in the 1970s as the Anglo-French helicopter deal came to fruition, with WHL building its own Lynx, and the Aerospatiale-designed Puma and Gazelle. Simultaneously, the company secured large national and export orders for the Sea King helicopter, which it built under licence from Sikorsky in the USA.

Although developed into a robust and long-lived design, the structural failures of the initial Comet 1 meant that Britain's opportunity to gain a world lead in air transport was lost. This is the elegant Comet 3, seen at Hatfield. (BAE SYSTEMS plc)

Commercial Casualties

Handley Page Ltd, having achieved only modest sales with the HPR.7 Dart Herald, conceived a twin turboprop feeder liner, the Jetstream. The Jetstream was greeted with enormous enthusiasm in the marketplace, with significant sales achieved before its first flight. This sales success was in large measure dependent upon the aircraft delivering its declared performance, within its FAA certification limited maximum weight of 12,500lb. In the event, this could not be achieved.

Handley Page Ltd had invested in tools and facilities for large-scale production, and were now faced with a difficult and expensive development programme, whilst bearing the costs

The TSR2 programme proved to be a major catalyst for the enforced rationalisation of the aircraft industry. This photograph shows the TSR.2 on arrival at Warton from Boscombe Down in February 1965. (BAE SYSTEMS plc)

Above: *Two early prototypes of Hawker Siddeley's long-lived Dakota replacement, the HS748 (initially known as the Avro748).* (BAE SYSTEMS plc)

Right: *The Buccaneer saw long service with the Royal Navy and then with the RAF. This S. Mk 2 is one of two modified by Marshall Aerospace in 1974 for flight trials of the Tornado avionics fit.* (Marshall Aerospace plc)

Short Belfast XR371 is preserved at the RAF Museum at Cosford. (Author)

of their unfulfilled production expectations. The company proved unable to withstand the financial pressures and entered voluntary liquidation in August 1969, ceasing to trade in June 1970. The subsequent development of the aircraft by British Aerospace shows that this was, regrettably, another case of that British trait, most familiar in the field of sport, of defeat snatched from the jaws of victory.

Similar difficulties were encountered at Beagle. Here, despite the sale of nearly 400 Beagle Pup aircraft, the Government withdrew financial support to the company in December 1969. Beagle eventually produced 152 Pup aircraft and eighty-five Beagle 206. Even the hugely popular Islander suffered from the problems brought about by sales success. Although the aircraft survived and remains in limited production, the company suffered a series of financial crises, including a number of periods in receivership.

Military Developments and Collaborative Ventures

In the military field, an almost mortal blow was struck when BAC, having been drawn together to produce the TSR.2, saw it cancelled by Dennis Healey in April 1965. BAC military efforts were then concentrated at the ex-English Electric sites of Preston, Samlesbury and Warton on the completion of Lightning production, supplemented by export Canberra refurbishment and the development of the pressurised Jet Provost T. Mk 5, and the BAC167 Strikemaster. BAC then moved on to the collaborative development of the Jaguar.

In the late 1960s, the RAF identified the requirement to reduce its number of front-line types, whilst achieving the following aims:

- The progressive replacement, from the late 1970s, of the Canberra and the V-bomber fleet.
- To establish the capability to carry out the low-level penetration roles that were to have been the province of the TSR.2.
- In the longer term, to phase out the Lightning and Phantom from their air defence roles.
- Also in the longer term, to replace the Buccaneer in its low-level strike, reconnaissance and maritime strike roles.

With all these objectives in mind, a further collaborative project emerged, known as the Multi-Role Combat Aircraft, or MRCA – later named Tornado. BAC joined with MBB and Aeritalia to form Panavia to produce the Tornado, which first flew in 1974.

Hawker Siddeley faced its own political traumas, with the cancellation of the supersonic V/STOL P.1154 project, the Royal Navy variant being cancelled by Peter Thorneycroft in February 1964. The RAF P.1154 version followed under the Healey axe of 1965, which also saw the cancellation of the HS.681 V/STOL transport. Despite these difficulties, Hawker Siddeley prospered on the strength of the products that it had inherited from its parent companies. Of particular note were the Harrier from Hawker, the HS.748 from A.V. Roe & Co. Ltd, and the HS125 from de Havilland. Other work included the Buccaneer (ex-Blackburn), the Nimrod maritime patrol aircraft, Hunter refurbishment, and production of the Trident. In Belfast, Shorts built the Belfast strategic transport, but must have been deeply disappointed that only ten were ordered, these only serving with the RAF from 1966 until the end of 1976.

During this period Hawker Siddeley designed what may prove to be Britain's last purely home-grown military aircraft, the HS.1182 Hawk trainer, which first flew in 1974, and continues to be one of the world's most successful trainer aircraft. In 1977, the next major stage in the development of the British Aircraft industry took place: the creation of British Aerospace – the 'Single British Aircraft Company'.

7
Modern Times

The Nationalisation and Privatisation of British Aerospace

British Aerospace (BAe) was formed as a nationalised corporation in April 1977, as a result of the Aircraft and Shipbuilding Industries Act 1977. In January 1981, BAe converted from a nationalised corporation to a public limited company (plc) in preparation for privatisation. The United Kingdom Government sold 51.57 per cent of its shares in February 1981, and all but a single £1 'golden share' in May 1985. When BAe was founded, it employed some 50,000 people on eighteen sites – Bitteswell, Brough, Broughton (Chester), Chadderton, Christchurch, Dunsfold, Filton, Hamble, Hatfield, Holme-on-Spalding Moor, Hurn, Kingston, Preston, Prestwick, Samlesbury, Warton, Weybridge and Woodford.

Throughout its existence, BAe (now BAE SYSTEMS) has developed an ever more international flavour. The BAC collaboration on Jaguar was followed by the tri-national Tornado programme. Tornado production for Saudi Arabia has now ended, and BAE SYSTEMS has started production of Eurofighter, in partnership with Spain, Italy and Germany. Transatlantic military co-operations include the T-45 Goshawk for the US Navy, and the AV-8B Harrier II and II Plus with McDonnell Douglas (now Boeing). Further ahead is the JSF programme, with BAE SYSTEMS teamed with Lockheed Martin to produce the supersonic CTOL/ASTOVL F-35 multi-role strike fighter for the USAF, US Navy, US Marine Corps and the RAF. Development work is underway on an extensively modified Nimrod, the MRA.4, (with new wings and engines) to preserve Britain's maritime patrol capability.

Something of a defining moment for the industry came on 24 December 1998 when new-build Sea Harrier FA.2 NB18 was 'bought off' by the Royal Navy customer. The completion of this aircraft was said by BAe to mark the last delivery of an all-British fighter aircraft to the UK armed services. One national programme, the Hawk, continues to go from strength to strength. Private venture developments of the Hawk 100 and Hawk 200 have allowed the type to remain effective, and it continues to be selected as the preferred training and light attack aircraft of many armed forces around the world. The latest order for the type was announced on 3 September 2003, the Indian Government procuring sixty-six Hawk aircraft for the Indian Air Force Advanced Jet Trainer programme.

By the time of the merger of British Aerospace with Marconi Electronic Systems to form BAE SYSTEMS on 30 November 1999, the number of sites manufacturing aircraft components was down to eight – Brough, Broughton (Chester), Chadderton, Filton, Prestwick, Samlesbury, Warton and Woodford – less than half the number of sites taken over in 1977.

BAe/BAE SYSTEMS Commercial Programmes

In the civil field, the establishment of the Airbus consortium has at last introduced a note of success into Britain's involvement in commercial aviation. Much against many observers' expectations, Airbus has proved to be a worthy rival to Boeing, achieving initial market

An impressive array of military aircraft from the British Aerospace stable. (BAE SYSTEMS plc)

The future of BAE SYSTEMS' military aircraft production is focused on Eurofighter Typhoon and Nimrod MRA.4, together with the JSF and FOAS projects. (Author)

penetration with the A300 and A310. These types have been followed up by the smaller, and hugely successful, A320 family, and the A330 and A340 long-haul transports. Airbus has now launched its super-wide body project, the A380, and is also the nominated project management organisation for a joint European military transport project, the Future Large Aircraft A400M. On 14 December 2004, Airbus announced the go-ahead for the marketing of the A350, a 235-285-seat developed version of the A330 to compete head-on with the Boeing 7E7.

Elsewhere, the civil market has not proved a happy experience for British Aerospace/BAE SYSTEMS. Corporate jet activity was continued with production of the BAe125 (previously HS125, previously DH125). The aircraft has been extensively developed throughout its production life, the final BAe production versions being the Hawker 800 and Hawker 1000. BAe sold its corporate jet business to the Raytheon Corporation in June 1993.

BAe's regional turboprop products were the Jetstream and the Advanced Turbo-Prop, or ATP, a stretched and re-engined development of the Avro/HS.748. The ATP was manufactured at Woodford until October 1992, when production was transferred to Prestwick, and the aircraft re-launched under the designation Jetstream 61. At Prestwick, meanwhile, a growth version of the Jetstream, the Jetstream 41, was launched. Market conditions proved initially unfavourable due to production over-capacity in this sector. BAe responded by forming an alliance with Aerospatiale and Alenia known as Aero International (Regional), AI(R), with a view to rationalising product lines. An early casualty was the ATP/Jetstream 61, which, together with the original Jetstream 31, was not taken up by the AI(R) consortium. BAe continued with the Jetstream 41, but announced in May 1997 that the production line would close by the end of 1997. The AI(R) consortium was, itself, disbanded in 1998.

In the regional jet market, BAe produced the BAe 146, taken over from Hawker Siddeley. Although produced in significant numbers, initially at Hatfield, and then at Woodford, the type was not a financial success for BAe. Production costs were high and many aircraft were leased on terms that ultimately proved unprofitable to BAe. The aircraft was re-launched as a family of types known as the Avro RJ (Regional Jet) series. Unfortunately, the terrorist attack on the New York World Trade Center on 11 September 2001 sounded the death knell for the RJ/RJX programme. On 27 November 2001, BAE SYSTEMS announced that it would be withdrawing from the construction of commercial aircraft at Woodford and would close the RJ and RJX programmes, with a consequential loss of 1,669 jobs. This decision, following the earlier suspension of the Jetstream 41 and 61 programmes at Prestwick, marked the end of BAE SYSTEMS construction of complete aircraft for the civil market.

The Wider Industry

Outside of BAe/BAE SYSTEMS, Shorts produced the SD330 and SD360 developments of their 'ugly-duckling' Skyvan, and went on to supply the RAF with an extensively developed

The Nimrod MRA.4 programme achieved a major milestone with the first flight of PA01 ZJ516 from Woodford in August 2004. (BAE SYSTEMS plc)

The first Airbus A380 F-WWOW emerges at Toulouse in January 2005 proir to its first flight on 27 April 2005. (French Frogs Airslides)

Opposite above: Commercial aircraft success for BAE SYSTEMS has come through its stake in the Airbus programme, some 5,000 Airbus aircraft having been sold by summer 2004. (Author)

version of the Embraer Tucano for basic training. The last SD360 was built in 1991, and the last Tucano in 1992. Purchased by Bombardier in 1989, the company has become increasingly centred upon aerospace component manufacture and assembly and it is unlikely that it will ever build another complete aircraft.

The boom that Westland experienced in the late 1970s could not last. Partly as a result of its ill-starred WG30 civil helicopter venture, Westland found itself in financial difficulties in 1986. A huge political row erupted over whether WHL should accept a possible European rescue package, or one offered by Sikorsky. After much acrimony, including the resignation of Michael Heseltine from the cabinet, the Sikorsky option was taken.

Westland, like BAe, has taken an increasingly international route to secure its future. This has centred on the EH101 Merlin helicopter developed with Italy. WHL was purchased by GKN in 1994 and, in 1998, GKN announced its intention to combine its helicopter operations with those of the Italian company Agusta SpA. This merger has resulted in the formation of a new company, AgustaWestland, which has a mix of civil and military products, and involvement in both the EH101 and NH90 programmes. In the UK, the company has the EH101 and the WAH-64 Apache in production. The Lynx also remains in production, having gained new export success in the form of the Super Lynx 300.

The helicopter marketplace worldwide still features over-capacity, and AgustaWestland will continue to need good penetration in export markets to secure its long-term future. With EH101 export sales to Denmark, Portugal and Japan, and the selection of the type as the

US101 as the next helicopter for the US presidential fleet, helicopter production at Yeovil looks set to continue for some time to come. The selection of the US101 was announced on 28 January 2005; a total of twenty-three aircraft will be delivered between 2009 and late 2014. On 26 May 2004, GKN announced its agreement in principle to sell its 50 per cent shareholding in AgustaWestland to Finmeccanica, thereby passing control of the British helicopter industry into Italian hands.

In the general aviation sector, the almost immortal Islander continues in limited production. Private aircraft have, for the most part, remained a bleak area for the British industry. In this context, the chequered histories of the ARV Super 2, Optica and SAH1/FLS Sprint demonstrate the difficulties presented by this sector. Success has, however, been achieved by three products – the Slingsby T67 Firefly, the CFM Shadow, and the Europa.

- Slingsby redesigned the Fournier RF6 (T67A), adopting an all-composite structure and installing increased power to produce a highly successful fully aerobatic trainer, which has found favour at entry level with a number of air forces around the world.
- The CFM (Cook Flying Machines) Shadow was designed by David Cook of Leiston, Suffolk: more than 400 of these aircraft have been built in a number of variants, including the high performance Streak Shadow which flies at up to 105 knots on its 64hp. The Shadow and Streak Shadow have been sold in more than thirty-six countries, and have completed many notable flights, including from England to Australia. As with so many British aircraft manufacturers there have been trading difficulties along the way. CFM Metal Fax Ltd went into liquidation in November 1996 and was taken over by CFM Aircraft Ltd in 1997. CFM Aircraft Ltd was, itself, in receivership in autumn

Below: *The DH125 continued in production under the stewardship of both Hawker Siddeley and British Aerospace, until the design was sold to Raytheon in 1993. It remains in production as this book is written in 2004.* (Author)

Above: *The Sherpa military derivative of the Short SD330. The Sherpa was supplied to the US Air Force as the C-23A and the US Army National Guard as the C-23B.* (Bombardier Aerospace Belfast)

Right: *AgustaWestland became fully owned by the Italian firm Finmeccanica in 2004. Production in Yeovil includes the EH101 Merlin and uprated versions of the Lynx family.* (Author)

The Singsby T67 achieved a notable success with its selection by the USAF. These Slingsby T67M260-T3A were photographed at Hondo, Texas. (Slingsby Aviation Ltd)

2002, before being taken over by CFM Airborne Inc. of Texas who announced in November 2002 the setting up of a UK facility, CFM Airborne (UK) Ltd.
- Ivan Shaw's all-composite Europa, designed for the homebuilt and kit construction market first flew in September 1992. The aircraft was built by The Europa Aircraft Co., which, after a management buy-out became Europa Management (International) Ltd on 1 August 2001. On 24 November 2003, Europa Management (International) Ltd announced that the total number of kits sold had passed the significant total of 1,000 in thirty-four countries. Following financial difficulties, the company was re-launched as Europa Aircraft (2004) Ltd 'to continue to develop and sell the Europa range of aircraft'.

Future Prospects

Where does the future of the British industry lie? Shrinking defence markets have forced rationalisation in the United States of America. To some extent, this was also the engine for the creation of Hawker Siddeley and BAC, and subsequently the formation of British Aerospace and BAE SYSTEMS. Today the industry is faced with the routine achievement of in-service lives in excess of thirty-five years, combined with intervals between major projects of fifteen years or more. With the exceptions of the C-17, EH-101 Merlin, Tucano and Eurofighter, the majority of the aircraft operated by the British armed services – Apache, Canberra, Chinook, Gazelle, Harrier, Hawk, Hercules, HS125, Jaguar, Jetstream, Lynx, Nimrod, Puma, Tornado, TriStar, and VC10 – all now have a heritage stretching back more than thirty years. The presently projected out-of-service date for the Harrier is 2015, forty-nine years after the first flight of the first Harrier development aircraft and fifty-five years after the first flight of the P.1127. These are the pressures that have driven an increasing trend toward collaborative projects, and when combined with the large scale of investment required to launch new projects, it is inevitable that aerospace is rapidly moving towards being a global business.

Lockheed, Martin Marietta, General Dynamics (Fort Worth Division), IBM, Loral, and Vought have already coalesced into a single corporation. Northrop and Grumman have merged to become Northrop Grumman, and Boeing has absorbed the earlier combine of McDonnell and Douglas. Faced with these giant businesses, European re-structuring has become inevitable. British Aerospace took a 35 per cent share in Saab of Sweden and spent a period in ultimately unsuccessful restructuring discussions with DaimlerChrysler Aerospace of Germany (DASA).

On 19 January 1999, BAe and GEC announced that they had reached agreement on the merger of BAe with the GEC defence interests (Marconi Electronic Systems). This merger, effective from the end of November 1999, created BAE SYSTEMS, then Europe's largest defence company, ranking at third largest in the world with a workforce of nearly 100,000 employees. In response to the creation of BAE SYSTEMS, DaimlerChrysler announced in June 1999 that they were acquiring the Spanish company CASA, thereby strengthening their position for future restructuring discussions. An agreement with Aerospatiale Matra followed, leading to the formation of EADS (European Aeronautic Defence and Space Company) on 10 July 2000. EADS is the world's third largest defence organisation, behind Boeing and Lockheed Martin, displacing BAE SYSTEMS from this position.

With transatlantic projects such as JSF looking to secure global export markets, overtures from the major players in the USA may not be long delayed. A future global aerospace business may yet be created by one of the major US defence conglomerates acting in partnership with BAE SYSTEMS and/or EADS. Over recent years, the press has at various times linked BAE SYSTEMS with overtures from Lockheed Martin, Boeing and General Dynamics. In ten years' time, it is hard to believe that the current structure of the industry will not have seen further upheaval – we will have to wait and see. By that time, indeed, it may seem almost quaint to refer to the British Aircraft Industry.

8
The Genealogy of British Aerospace/BAE SYSTEMS

The preceding narrative has charted the evolution of the British aircraft industry. Much of the manufacturing capacity of the industry is now in the hands of only two companies: BAE SYSTEMS, previously British Aerospace plc, manufacturing military fixed-wing aircraft and commercial aircraft components, and AgustaWestland (previously GKN Westland Helicopters Ltd) manufacturing military helicopters in the UK.

The narrative has shown how political and commercial imperatives led to progressive re-structuring of the industry. The impact of these changes is best appreciated when presented in the form of a family tree. BAE SYSTEMS came into being with the merger between British Aerospace and the defence interests of GEC, Marconi Electronic Systems (MES). As MES did not include any UK aircraft manufacturers in its heritage, the following family tree represents only the British Aerospace heritage that passed into BAE SYSTEMS. Three diagrams are presented:

1. British Aerospace: The Big Picture
2. BAe: Hawker Siddeley Companies
3. BAe: British Aircraft Corporation and Scottish Aviation

Whilst, in many respects, these diagrams speak for themselves; a few observations are worth making:

- British Aerospace was formed in 1977 by the merging of three companies: Hawker Siddeley Aviation Ltd, the British Aircraft Corporation (BAC) and Scottish Aviation Ltd. Short Bros. & Harland were the only major fixed-wing aircraft manufacturer that remained independent of this group.
- Because Scottish Aviation Ltd had acquired the rump of the Beagle Aircraft Ltd and Handley Page Ltd activities, they effectively brought with them into the BAe family tree the heritage of these firms. This encompasses (via Handley Page Ltd) Martinsyde Ltd and Phillips & Powis/Miles Aircraft Ltd, and (via Beagle) Auster Aircaft Ltd and Taylorcraft Aeroplanes (England) Ltd.
- Hawker Siddeley Aviation Ltd (HSAL) added Blackburn and General Aircraft Ltd, The de Havilland Aircraft Co. Ltd and Folland Aircraft Ltd to the group of Hawker Siddeley companies which had already been merged in 1935, although continuing to trade under their original identities (A.V. Roe & Co. Ltd, Hawker Aircraft Ltd, Gloster Aircraft Company Ltd, and Sir W.G. Armstrong Whitworth Aircraft Ltd).
- The less familiar antecedents of HSAL include H.H. Martyn & Co. (via Gloster), Wm Denny & Bros Ltd, General Aircraft Ltd and CWA Ltd (via Blackburn), and Airspeed Ltd, May, Harden & May and Wycombe Aircraft Constructors (via AIRCO/de Havilland).

The VC10 remains in RAF service more than forty years after the type was first flown. Service lives in excess of thirty years are becoming the norm, even for front-line types. (Author)

- Only four companies were grouped into BAC, these being English Electric Aviation Ltd, Bristol Aircraft Ltd (previously the Bristol Aeroplane Co. Ltd), Vickers-Armstrongs (Aircraft) Ltd and Hunting Aircraft Ltd (previously Percival Aircraft Ltd). The Vickers-Armstrongs heritage includes The Supermarine Aviation Works Ltd and Pemberton-Billing Ltd. The aircraft interests of The English Electric Co. Ltd were originally formed by merging the aircraft activities of Coventry Ordnance Works, Phoenix Dynamo Co. Ltd and Dick, Kerr & Co. in December 1918.
- Between 1919 and 1921 many company names were changed, and a number of new companies were founded following the closure of closely linked predecessors. This reflects the impact of taxation imposed after the First World War on companies that were considered to have made excess profits.

BAe: The Big Picture

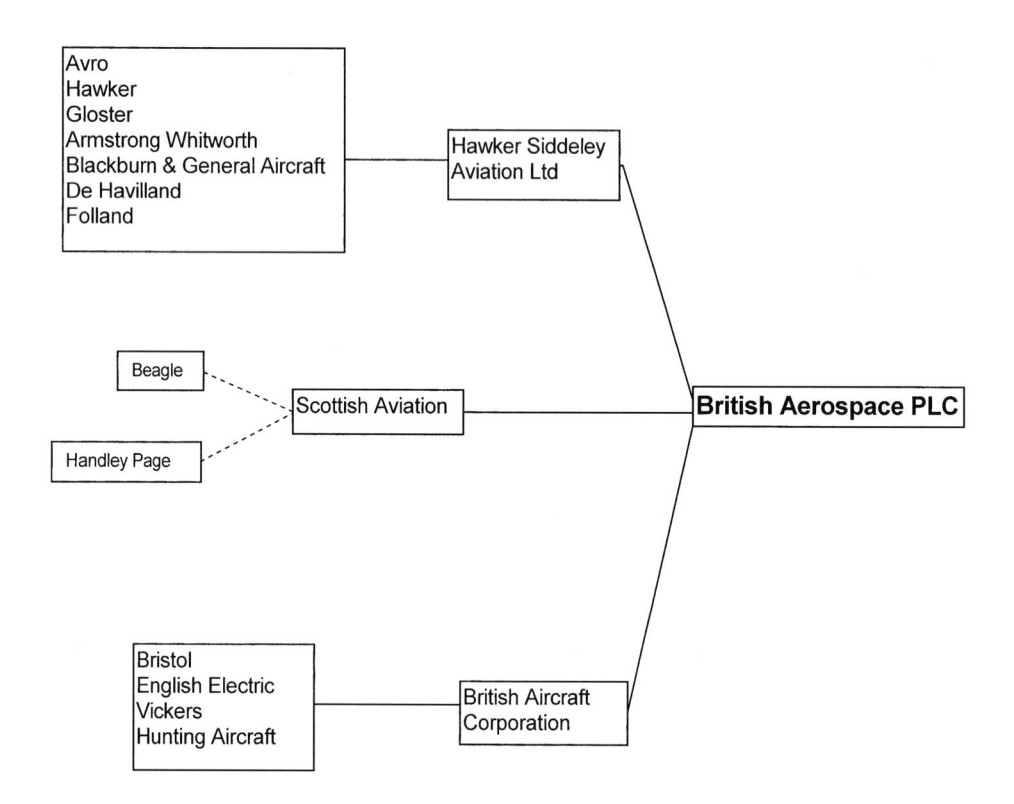

- Avro
- Hawker
- Gloster
- Armstrong Whitworth
- Blackburn & General Aircraft
- De Havilland
- Folland

→ Hawker Siddeley Aviation Ltd

- Beagle
- Handley Page

→ Scottish Aviation

- Bristol
- English Electric
- Vickers
- Hunting Aircraft

→ British Aircraft Corporation

→ **British Aerospace PLC**

British Aerospace - Hawker Siddeley Companies

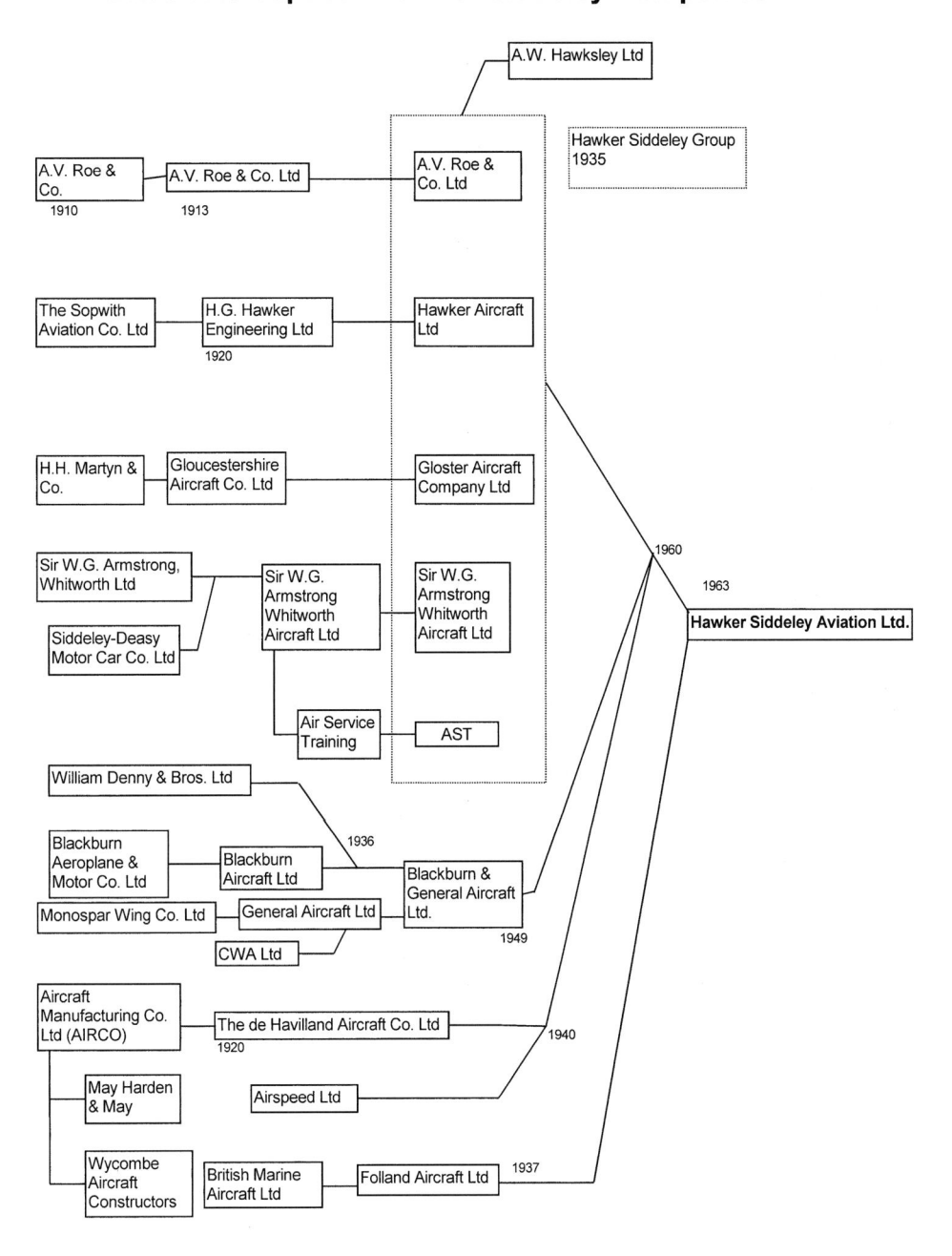

Hawker Siddeley Group 1935

- A.W. Hawksley Ltd

- A.V. Roe & Co. (1910) → A.V. Roe & Co. Ltd (1913) → A.V. Roe & Co. Ltd

- The Sopwith Aviation Co. Ltd → H.G. Hawker Engineering Ltd (1920) → Hawker Aircraft Ltd

- H.H. Martyn & Co. → Gloucestershire Aircraft Co. Ltd → Gloster Aircraft Company Ltd

- Sir W.G. Armstrong, Whitworth Ltd / Siddeley-Deasy Motor Car Co. Ltd → Sir W.G. Armstrong Whitworth Aircraft Ltd → Sir W.G. Armstrong Whitworth Aircraft Ltd

- Air Service Training → AST

1960 / 1963 → **Hawker Siddeley Aviation Ltd.**

- William Denny & Bros. Ltd

1936

- Blackburn Aeroplane & Motor Co. Ltd → Blackburn Aircraft Ltd
- Monospar Wing Co. Ltd → General Aircraft Ltd
- CWA Ltd

→ Blackburn & General Aircraft Ltd. (1949)

- Aircraft Manufacturing Co. Ltd (AIRCO) → The de Havilland Aircraft Co. Ltd (1920)
- May Harden & May
- Wycombe Aircraft Constructors
- Airspeed Ltd

1940

- British Marine Aircraft Ltd → Folland Aircraft Ltd (1937)

BAe: British Aircraft Corporation & Scottish Aviation

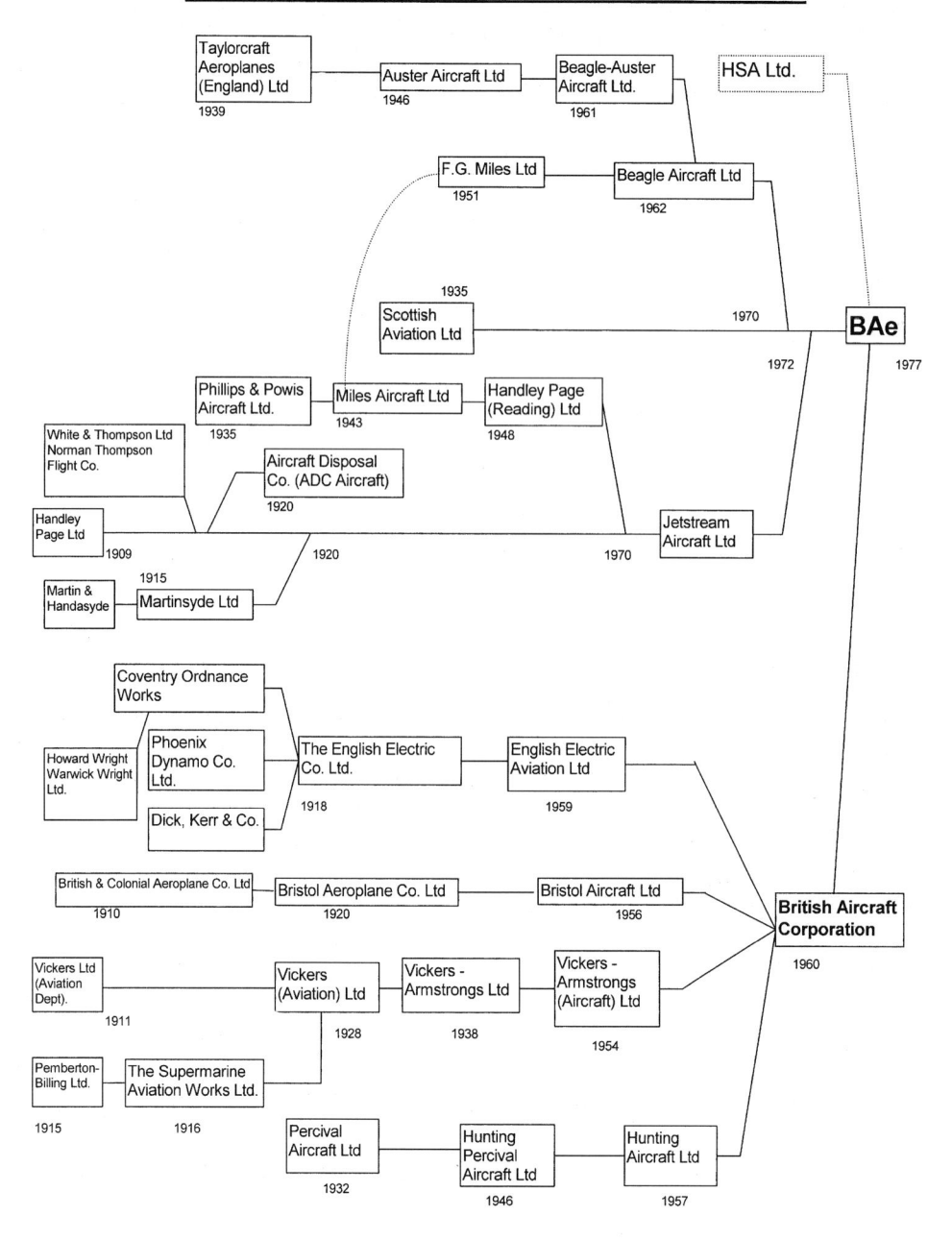

- Taylorcraft Aeroplanes (England) Ltd — 1939 → Auster Aircraft Ltd — 1946 → Beagle-Auster Aircraft Ltd — 1961
- HSA Ltd.
- F.G. Miles Ltd — 1951 → Beagle Aircraft Ltd — 1962
- Scottish Aviation Ltd — 1935 → BAe (1970)
- BAe — 1977
- Phillips & Powis Aircraft Ltd. — 1935 → Miles Aircraft Ltd — 1943 → Handley Page (Reading) Ltd — 1948
- White & Thompson Ltd / Norman Thompson Flight Co.
- Aircraft Disposal Co. (ADC Aircraft) — 1920
- Handley Page Ltd — 1909
- Jetstream Aircraft Ltd — 1970
- Martin & Handasyde → Martinsyde Ltd — 1915
- Coventry Ordnance Works
- Howard Wright / Warwick Wright Ltd.
- Phoenix Dynamo Co. Ltd.
- Dick, Kerr & Co.
- The English Electric Co. Ltd. — 1918 → English Electric Aviation Ltd — 1959
- British & Colonial Aeroplane Co. Ltd — 1910 → Bristol Aeroplane Co. Ltd — 1920 → Bristol Aircraft Ltd — 1956
- British Aircraft Corporation — 1960
- Vickers Ltd (Aviation Dept). — 1911 → Vickers (Aviation) Ltd — 1928 → Vickers - Armstrongs Ltd — 1938 → Vickers - Armstrongs (Aircraft) Ltd — 1954
- Pemberton-Billing Ltd. — 1915 → The Supermarine Aviation Works Ltd. — 1916
- Percival Aircraft Ltd — 1932 → Hunting Percival Aircraft Ltd — 1946 → Hunting Aircraft Ltd — 1957
- BAe — 1972

The Aircraft Manufacturers of Northern England, Scotland, Wales & Northern Ireland

Northern England

For the purpose of this volume, Northern England is deemed to comprise the geographical areas of Cheshire; Cumbria; Durham and Cleveland; Greater Manchester; Lancashire; Merseyside; Northumberland and Tyneside; and Yorkshire (East, North, South and West). Within Northern England, the presentation structure is alphabetical by county, and then alphabetical by location.

Cheshire

Byley (Cranage)

Vickers-Armstrongs Ltd used dispersed facilities at Byley (Cranage) for Wellington production.

Chester

The Broughton/Hawarden factory (used by **Vickers-Armstrongs Ltd**, **The de Havilland Aircraft Co. Ltd**, **Hawker Siddeley Aviation Ltd**, **British Aerospace plc**, **Raytheon Corporation**, **British Aerospace Airbus Ltd/BAE SYSTEMS Airbus Ltd**) is in Flintshire, and its entry can therefore be found in the Wales section of this volume.

Crewe

Rolls-Royce Ltd: A Rolls-Royce Merlin engine factory was set up at Crewe in 1938 as a shadow factory to support the pre-war expansion of the aircraft industry. The first Crewe-built engine was delivered on 20 May 1939.

Hooton Park

The **Comper Aircraft Co. Ltd** was founded by Nick Comper on 14 March 1929, with the first CLA7 Swift G-AARX flying in January 1930. The attractive Swift was noted for its racing and long-distance flights, particularly those of Charles A. Butler whose flights included a record-breaking trip from England to Australia starting at the end of October 1931.

Comper advertising in 1930 spells out the characteristics of the type and its high level of equipment:

> The Comper Swift single-seater monoplane in cost and performance is in a class by itself. It is designed as a touring and sporting aircraft combining both speed and comfort with the highest degree of safety to the owner pilot. The cockpit is roomy and visibility is exceptionally good. Careful design and thorough testing have resulted in an absolutely reliable aircraft which requires no effort to fly, and in which maintenance routine has been reduced to its simplest

Vauxhall's car factory has spread across the airfield at Hooton Park, home of the Comper Swift. (Author)

terms. The SWIFT (when folded) can be housed in an ordinary garage measuring 19ft by 9ft. Price (with 50hp Salmson engine) £475 ex works includes full set of Instruments, Cockpit and Engine Covers, Picket Screws, all Tools, Leather Suitcase in special locker, Map Case and Log Book.

Sales price with the 40hp ABC Scorpion engine used by the prototype was £400, increasing to £525 for the high performance Pobjoy powered version. The Swift was also flown with the 50hp Salmson AD-9 radial and the 75hp Pobjoy R. Racing examples were fitted with the 120hp Gipsy III (G-ABWH, G-ACBY), or 130hp Gipsy Major I (G-ABWW).

The type was also advertised as 'The world's cheapest single seater – a monoplane of exceptional performance and high aerobatic certification'. A further example was:

Comper Swift – points to remember:
- High performance
- Slow landing speeds
- Easy to fly
- Perfect visibility
- No rigging to maintain
- Low consumption

Cruising speed 120mph, climb 1,400ft/min. Take off in still air 60 yards or 5H seconds.

To quote Harald Penrose, 'Top speed was an amazing 125mph, and it climbed like a fighter at 1,400ft/min. Forward view was as bad as a DH9...' (not quite consistent with the advertising quoted above). *Flight* described the performance of the Swift as 'perfectly astounding'. In racing trim, the diminutive Swift lived up to its name, turning in speeds of nearly 150mph. In 1932, the King's Cup entry included eight Swifts, and seven were entered in 1933. A total of forty-one Comper Swift were built. The company transferred to Heston in the spring of 1933, for which see further details in Volume One of this series.

An autogyro derivative of the Swift, the Cierva C.25 G-ABTO, was first flown at Hooton Park on 21 April 1932 (20 March is also quoted), and was later operated at Heston and Hanworth after the company's move to Heston.

In 1930, two Ford Trimotors, 4-AT-E G-ABEF and 5-AT-C G-ABFF, were assembled at Hooton Park for the **Ford Motor Co. Ltd**. The aircraft were unloaded at Ellesmere Port on 16 October 1930, being erected and tested within a few days at Hooton Park. This led to Ford placing the following advertisement: 'Ford Motor Co. Ltd, Aircraft Department, 88 Regent Street, London W1. With their worldwide background of reliability, Ford planes now reach England. Under the auspices of the Ford Motor Co. Ltd, reliability trials will be conducted this autumn in Great Britain and in four other countries. Do not miss this opportunity – whatever your interest in air transport may be – of personally inspecting these planes, world-renowned for strength, lightness, speed and safety.'

Martin Hearn Ltd: Martin Hearn was an Avro 504 joy-riding pilot, and an intrepid wing walker. Martin Hearn Ltd operated the last of the civil Avro 504N conversions, G-AFRM, until it was destroyed in July 1940.

During the Second World War, Martin Hearn Ltd carried out Anson and Mosquito repairs and sub-contract production of Mosquito assemblies at Hooton Park. 258 Mosquito aircraft were returned to service following repair by Martin Hearn Ltd. The company was also responsible for the No.7 Aircraft Assembly Unit, which carried out the erection and test of a number of American-built aircraft, including Douglas Boston and North American Harvard, together with eighty Canadian-built examples of the Handley Page Hampden. Other types handled by No.7 AAU included the North American Mustang and the first Sikorsky R-4 Hoverfly to be flown in the UK.

In March 1946, Slingsby Sailplanes Ltd announced the establishment of an associate company agreement with Martin Hearn Ltd of Hooton Park, Cheshire, for the construction of five types of glider, these being the Cadet, Tutor, Kite Mk II, Kite Mk III and the Tandem Tutor. The reason given for this arrangement was that Martin Hearn Ltd had manufacturing capacity available, and could provide low production costs. Martin Hearn built twenty-five Tutor and twenty-five Cadet gliders for Slingsby during 1946/47. Subsequent production included nineteen T21B Sedbergh for the Air Training Corps.

A popular racing and sporting aircraft, the diminutive Comper Swift was also used for notable long-distance flights. (J.S. Smith)

Three examples of the Crosby BA4B were built, this immaculate example being seen at the PFA Rally at Cranfield. (Author)

Pobjoy Airmotors Ltd was formed on 14 August 1930 with capital of £8,400 to produce Pobjoy engines, initially for the Comper Swift. In June 1935, the company name was changed to **Pobjoy Airmotors and Aircraft Ltd**.

In February 1936 Hooton Park was promoting its facilities thus: 'Merseyside Air Park, Hooton, Cheshire for Aircraft Factories, Service Depots, Airline Terminal. Buildings to total floor area greater than 125,000 sq. ft. Adjoining 200 acre landing field. Excellent road and rail communications. The Air Park controlled by practical airmen.'

In 1998, Hooton Park was part of the Vauxhall car plant at Ellesmere Port – 'the home of the Astra'. Although some Belfast hangars survived on the western side of the site, active development was underway, with a near continuous stream of lorries moving around the site. About half the airfield was still visible from the air in mid-1994, but it seems likely that much of this will shortly disappear from sight. The hangars themselves have been threatened by Vauxhall's development plans, but are likely to be preserved following vociferous local protest.

Knutsford

Three **Crosby** BA-4B aircraft G-AYFU, 'YFV, and 'YFW were built by **Crosby Aviation Ltd**, Archery House, Leycester Road, Knutsford in 1972-1974. These aircraft were test flown at Ringway, the first flying on 25 March 1973. The BA-4B is a modified version of the Andreasson BA-4 single-seat sporting biplane. Two additional aircraft G-BEBS and G-BEBT were constructed by Hornet Aviation (Dave Fenton) at Sherburn-in-Elmet.

Stretton/Warrington

The Fairey Aviation Co. Ltd managed repair facilities at Burtonwood, Warrington (ex-shirt factory), Reddish, Parrs Wood and Stretton. Fairey Barracuda aircraft were repared/rebuilt in Warrington and then taken to Stretton for assembly. The airfield is now bisected by the M56 motorway, but the two 'A1' hangars used by Fairey for Barracuda assembly are used as a storage and distribution depot by Guinness.

Cumbria

Barrow in Furness

A.V. Roe & Co. Ltd: Barrow was the scene of early seaplane flying, including flights of the Avro Type D seaplane flown during 1911 and 1912 by S.V. Sippe and Commander Schwann at Cavendish Dock. Although trials commenced at the beginning of August 1911, the aircraft did not succeed in becoming airborne until 18 November, following extensive experiments with different float configurations. Unfortunately, the first landing was not as successful as the take off. It was not until April 1912 that successful take off and landing manoeuvres were being made reliably. Despite the capsize of the aircraft after landing, the flight made on 18 November 1911 is regarded as the first successful British flight from water.

Cavendish Dock was also the site used by **Messrs Vickers, Sons & Maxim Ltd** for the construction of the abortive rigid airship HMA No.1 'Mayfly', which was destroyed (having never flown) on 24 September 1911.

Carlisle

Lynden Aurora: The Lynden Aurora is a single-seat shoulder-wing homebuilt light aircraft, the first example G-CBZS being flown for the first time at Carlisle Airport on 11 October 2003. The Aurora is of all-wood construction and in general configuration resembles the Tipsy Nipper, albeit with slightly larger dimensions. The strut-braced wing is swept forward by four degrees to improve visibility from the cockpit. The Aurora is powered by a 56hp HKS700S flat-twin engine of 700cc capacity, driving a two-bladed 60in-diameter ARPLAST propeller. Empty weight is 500lb and maximum take-off weight is 750lb. By 2 January 2004, the aircraft had flown for a total of seven hours twenty minutes and was showing very promising performance figures for its relatively modest power. These included a cruise speed of 70 knots, stall speed of 37 knots and climb rate of 500ft/min.

Wren Aircraft Co. This company built a single-seat, low-wing monoplane, the Goldcrest G-AICX (a registration subsequently re-issued to the author's Luscombe 8A). The Goldcrest was powered by a 28hp Scott Squirrel and was flown in 1947 at Kirklington. In appearance, the aircraft had something of the lines of the later Taylor monoplane.

Windermere

Flying from Lake Windermere has its origins with the activities of **The Lakes Flying Co.** and its successors, which are described below, followed by a review of other manufacturers' activities on the lake.

One of the most recent new types of British design, the Lynden Aurora was flown for the first time in October 2003. (Joe Lynden)

An evocative photograph of the Lakes Water Hen on Lake Windermere. (JMB/GSL collection)

W. Rowland Ding in the cockpit of the Lakes Sea Bird. This aircraft started life as the Avro-built Duigan biplane. (JMB/GSL collection)

In 1911, Edward Wakefield put up a couple of hangars 'to the dismay of local scenery lovers'. This refers to a letter written by Canon Rawnsley to *The Times* in January 1912, complaining that the hangars at Bowness were spoiling its beauty. Mr Wakefield replied that he was erecting one shed near Cockshott Point, 'painted a quiet green' to match the surrounding foliage. At the end of March 1912, a gale destroyed the hangar (judgement from on high, some thought), which had to be replaced. The collapse of the hangar also destroyed the Lakes Water Bird. In June 1912, there were two aeroplane sheds and slipways at Hill of Oaks, Lake Windermere. The Bowness hangar had an arched roof, with the words '**The**

Lakes Flying Co.' written around the inside of the roofline on the face of the hangar overlooking the lake.

The Lakes Flying Co. was taken over by **The Northern Aircraft Co. Ltd**, of Bowness-on-Windermere, on 11 November 1914. In the same month, the new owners advertised the school's facilities as follows: 'Tractor and pusher biplanes and monoplanes. Flying area the largest in Great Britain. Eight mile straight flights without obstruction, circuits 1¼ mile diameter over water.' The instructor and general manager was Mr Rowland Ding, who learned to fly at Hendon with the Beatty School, and subsequently flew for Handley Page Ltd. There were three sheds in use, one as the works, and the firm claimed that their 'Waterplane School of Flying has the largest aerodrome as it is twelve miles long'. The company's telegraphic address was 'Aircraft, Windermere'.

The company used evocative descriptions in their advertising. A particularly fine example was: 'The Seaplane School – The go-ahead school. The Northern Aircraft Café, adjoined to the School Hangars is now open. Breakfasts, Luncheons and Teas at moderate prices. Work has commenced on the Dormy House in the School Grounds. Twenty bedrooms, spacious Dining and Billiard Rooms, fitted with central heating throughout. The Northern Aircraft Co. Ltd, Bowness-on-Windermere.'

The Lakes Water Bird, which first flew from Lake Windermere on 25 November 1911, was the first truly successful British seaplane. It was adapted from a 'Curtiss-type' biplane built by A.V. Roe & Co. Ltd at Brownsfield Mills, Manchester. After testing as a landplane at Brooklands, where it was first flown on 19 July 1911, the aircraft was taken to Windermere, fitted with a central float made locally in Bowness by **Messrs Borwick & Sons**, and tested as noted above. A highly successful design, the aircraft made sixty flights in its first thirty-eight days of operation. The Water Bird was destroyed on 30 March 1912 as a result of the hangar collapse referred to above.

The Water Bird was followed by the Water Hen and Sea Bird, which were also outstanding flyers. In May 1912, the Lakes Flying Co. Water Hen was flying very successfully at Windermere. Unlike the Water Bird, the Water Hen was designed and built by The Lakes Flying Co. (albeit as a modified version of the Water Bird). The Water Hen flew on 30 April 1912 and during seven months of that year made around 250 flights. One novel feature was the use of a large central pontoon float with a bungee suspension to absorb shocks. The central pontoon float was later replaced with a conventional twin-float arrangement. This very successful aircraft was used early in the First World War for RNAS training at Windermere, continuing in this role until the school was taken over by the Government in 1916.

The Sea Bird was a conventionally configured two-seat biplane with a 50hp Gnome engine, which was used for joy-riding over Lake Windermere. This machine used a fuselage modified from that of an Avro machine originally built for J.R. Duigan, which had been purchased by the Lakes Flying Co. and moved to Windermere on 4 June 1912. The first flight of this aircraft in its seaplane configuration took place at Windermere on 28 August 1912, and the type continued in use until 3 June 1915. Once again, a single broad central float was used, although later the aircraft was modified to the more familiar twin-float configuration of modern seaplanes.

The final Lakes Flying Co. type was a large, but relatively unsuccessful, pusher monoplane. This machine was designed by Gnosspelius and built by Borwick & Sons. After initial flights with a single central float in September 1914, the machine was subject to a number of incidents before emerging for trials on twin floats on 1 May 1915. By this time, it was known as the Northern Aircraft Co. monoplane, reflecting the change in ownership of the company. It remained largely unsuccessful and had been withdrawn from use by the end of May.

By November 1914, at the time that the company was taken over by **The Northern Aircraft Co. Ltd**, the facilities had expanded to some five additional sheds apart from the original 'Lakes' hangar. One of the instructors was J. Lankester Parker – Chief Test Pilot to

66　British Built Aircraft – Northern England, Scotland, Wales and Northern Ireland

THE SEAPLANE SCHOOL

Your Country Needs You

HOW BETTER CAN YOU SERVE YOUR COUNTRY THAN BY FLYING FOR IT

WE MAKE THAT —— POSSIBLE ——

THE NORTHERN AIRCRAFT CO., Ltd., Bowness-on-Windermere

'Phone— 114 Windermere.　　Wire— "Aircraft, Windermere."

The Seaplane School.

WITHIN a short period, the School equipment will include the following seaplanes:

BIPLANES.
100 h.p. Anzani tractor.
75 h.p. Anzani tractor.
65 h.p. Green propeller.
50 h.p. Gnome propeller.

MONOPLANES.
100 h.p. Anzani tractor.
80 h.p. Gnome propeller.
50 h.p. Gnome tractor.

Others are being arranged for so that the **Seaplane School** shall remain

The Best Equipped School in England.

Instructors: Mr. W. Rowland Ding, assisted by Messrs. J. Lankester Parker and W. Laidler. Secure your certificate here, and commence your career with a reputation.

Send for booklet to:—
THE SECRETARY,
NORTHERN AIRCRAFT CO., LTD.,
BOWNESS-ON-WINDERMERE.

Phone: 114 Windermere.　　Wire: "Aircraft, Windermere."

THE SEAPLANE SCHOOL

It is the quality of our tuition which we wish to emphasise.

You leave this school competent to fly high-powered machines, on sea or land.

You need not spend large sums on extra practice; we make that unnecessary.

Send for booklet to:—
THE SECRETARY,
NORTHERN AIRCRAFT CO., LTD.,
BOWNESS-ON-WINDERMERE.

Phone: 114 Windermere.　　Wire: "Aircraft, Windermere."

NAC's 100 H.P. MONO.

This page: *A selection of adverts for Northern Aircraft Co. Ltd.*

THE SEAPLANE SCHOOL

100 H.P. DUAL CONTROL MONOPLANE

Tuition safely, quickly and efficiently on high-powered machines of modern design.

For particulars apply to
THE SECRETARY,
NORTHERN AIRCRAFT Co., Ltd.,
BOWNESS-ON-WINDERMERE.

The Blackburn Improved Type I (or Land/Sea monoplane) taxiing at speed on Lake Windermere. (BAE SYSTEMS plc)

Short Brothers for many years. He also undertook freelance flight-testing with the Prodger-Isaac Aviation Co. organisation. Lankester Parker learned to fly with the Vickers School at Brooklands in 1914, and taught seventy-five pilots to fly at the Lakes School. Another instructor was Cecil Pashley of Shoreham, who moved here in March 1915, travelling on to the Grahame-White School at Hendon in autumn 1915.

Under the control of The Northern Aircraft Co. Ltd, one further design was produced, this being a twin-float pusher biplane, the PB.1. This machine was subsequently re-engined (a Gnome replacing the Green engine of the PB.1) and in this form was known as the PB.2. The design was characterised by having a triangular fin and rudder which hung below the tailplane, allowing the rudder to operate directly in the slipstream of the pusher propeller.

By September 1915, the fleet consisted of four biplanes and three monoplanes, with an additional, 100hp Anzani powered, Blackburn twin-float monoplane being added in November 1915. This latter was the two-seat Blackburn 'Improved Type I monoplane', originally built with an 80hp Gnome rotary. Sold to W.R. Ding at Windemere, it first flew on floats on 26 Octover 1915 and is also known as the 'Blackburn Land Sea Monoplane'. The school was taken over by the Government in mid-1916. In October 1917, The Northern Aircraft Co. Ltd was in voluntary liquidation, selling one complete Sopwith seaplane, one Blériot, one pusher, and one Blackburn monoplane together with one Avro and one Curtiss-type biplane dismantled. Also included in the 18 October auction were buildings and the motor launch *Sarah*. The pusher referred to was presumably the PB.2.

There is some doubt as to the identity of the Blackburn machine mentioned in this advertisement. The aforementioned Land Sea Monoplane capsized at Bowness on 1 April 1916 and was written off. In *British Aircraft Before the Great War* it is suggested that the second Blackburn Type I monoplane (a single-seater flown on 14 December 1913) was acquired by the Northern Aircraft Co. Ltd. This machine was converted to twin floats, but was not satisfactory and was not flown. This does not accord with A.J. Jackson's account in *Blackburn Aircraft since 1909*, but might explain the inclusion of a Blackburn monoplane in the assets of the company in 1917.

A.V. Roe & Co. Ltd: The Avro 501 was first tested as a seaplane at Windermere in January 1913, before being modified to landplane configuration and being delivered to the Admiralty at Eastchurch. The Avro 501 was still flying in 1914.

A.V. Roe & Co. Ltd also operated a joy-riding base at Bowness in 1919. The hangar and slipway used by Avro were those of the Lakes Flying Company. To advertise their operation, the hangar was painted with the words 'A.V. Roe & Co. Ltd Seaplane Base, Works Manchester, Southampton, Passenger Flights'. Two Avro 504L floatplanes were used, H2581 and H2582, which later became G-EADJ and G-EADK.

Gnosspelius: Experiments were carried out at Windermere between 1910 and 1914 on a series of experimental hydroplanes designed by Mr O.T. Gnosspelius and built in the local Borwick & Sons boatyard. The No.2 monoplane flew successfully between 1912 and 1914, being reported by *Flight* to be flying successfully in February 1912 (its first flight was made on 13 February 1912). This aircraft was a monoplane with a fuselage of triangular section and used a single central pontoon float.

Mr Gnosspelius designed a two-seat tractor biplane fitted with twin floats, which was flown on 20 September 1913. It is reported in *British Aircraft Before the Great War* that this machine operated only for a short period, being last flown on 11 November 1913. Despite (or perhaps because of) its thoroughly workman-like appearance, this machine was apparently too heavy to fly successfully under the power of its 100hp Green engine. Major Gnosspelius was subsequently appointed to the position of engineer for the Lakes Flying Co.

Lake Windermere was used for the unsuccessful tests of the **Perry Beadle** flying boat in 1914.

Short Brothers (Rochester & Bedford) Ltd had a Sunderland repair and manufacturing facility at Calgarth during the Second World War. This was in operation from September 1942 until May 1944 and, in addition to aircraft repair, thirty-five Sunderland III were built here (DP176-DP200, EJ149-158). Like the earlier activities of The Lakes Flying Co., construction of the Shorts' facility was less than welcome, being described as 'an abomination', and being the subject of a protesting deputation to Lord Beaverbrook. The facilities at Whitecross Bay were completely dismantled when Shorts left, an undertaking to this effect having been given (by Lord Beaverbrook) to The Friends of the Lake District, when the factory was established. The concrete foundations, operating pads and slipways were subsequently incorporated into the fabric of the Whitecross Bay caravan park.

A number of sheds still stand at Bowness and are in use by boatyards and marinas. Some of the sheds even have 'quiet green' doors!

Durham & Cleveland

Spennymore

Mr Ernest Brooks, the proprietor of Brooklands Garage, Ferryhill, Co. Durham set up **Brooklands Rotorcraft Ltd** to manufacture his Mosquito autogyro. The Brooklands Mosquito G-ATSW was first flown in July 1966. Production details are somewhat confused, but it appears that some twelve aircraft were produced between 1966 and 1970, a number as Gyroflight Hornet, see below.

The **Gyroflight** Hornet was the Brooklands Mosquito redesigned and renamed following Mr Brooks' death in March 1969. Regrettably, a further fatal accident brought production to a halt. Two additional aircraft (G-MIKE, G-BGEX) are believed to have been constructed using stored airframes.

Yearby, near Redcar

Barry Smith designed and built a small sporting aircraft, the Acro Advanced, which was first flown in October 1994 and was awarded the title of best new design at the PFA Rally at Cranfield in 1995. G-BPAA was built over a period of eight years as an affordable single-seat

G-MIKE is a Gyroflight Hornet, developed from the Brooklands Mosquito. (Author)

competition aerobatic aircraft using Barry Smith's own 2.1 litre fuel injected Acro Aerobatic Volkswagen conversion. The Acro Advanced is stressed to 8g and offers a cruise speed of 140mph at 3gph, and a maximum full throttle level speed of 170mph – exceptional performance on 68hp.

Greater Manchester

The following unitary authorities are included within the Greater Manchester area: Bolton, Bury, Manchester, Oldham, Rochdale, Salford, Stockport, Tameside, Trafford and Wigan.

Ashton-under-Lyne

A.V. Roe & Co. Ltd had production facilities at Whitelands Road, Ashton with more than 200,000 sq. ft capacity. These came into use in December 1938 and were mainly used for the production of Lancaster, York and Anson components and assemblies. There were additional stores facilities (greater than 50,000 sq. ft) at nearby Dukinfield.

Northern Aircraft & Engineering Ltd at Guide Bridge were purchased by Cornercraft Ltd in February 1939. The firm is believed to have been a component manufacturer.

Bolton

Dobson & Barlow of Radcliffe, near Bolton, assembled Bristol Blenheim wings in support of production by A.V. Roe & Co. Ltd, Rootes Securities and the Bristol Aeroplane Co. Ltd. The company continued with similar work on later types.

Failsworth

A.V. Roe & Co. Ltd: The Empire Works at Failsworth were used for component manufacture by the rapidly expanding A.V. Roe & Co. Ltd from the start of the First World War. The works were later to specialise in sheet metal work, and did not close until the end of October 1981 under **British Aerospace** ownership. Second World War activity included pipe manufacture for the York and Lancaster.

The Ivy Works at Failsworth came into use in April 1936 and covered more than 200,000 sq. ft. Six Avro 641 Commodore were built here from May 1934. The Commodore was an attractive cabin biplane whose design strongly suggested the influence of the American Waco design. Wartime usage of Failsworth included Blenheim components and assemblies for the Lancaster, York and Anson.

Manchester Area

The Manchester area has been dominated by the activities of the A.V. Roe & Co. Ltd and its successors. Throughout its existence A.V. Roe & Co. Ltd mainly based its production factories in Manchester, but carried out flight-testing elsewhere – often miles away from the factories. The main flight-test locations were (in approximate chronological order): Brooklands (1908), Lea Marshes, Wembley Park, Brooklands (1910), Shoreham, Hamble, Alexandra Park, Woodford, Ringway and Yeadon.

The main manufacturing locations were (also in approximate chronological order – several being in use simultaneously): Putney, Brownsfield Mills, Miles Platting, Newton Heath, Hamble, Chadderton, Woodford (assembly), and Yeadon, with (during the Second World War) dispersed component manufacture in the Manchester area including facilities at Ashton-under-Lyne, Failsworth, Royton, and Wythenshawe (refer to each of these entries for further details).

The presentation below presents the major Manchester locations of A.V. Roe & Co. Ltd in approximate chronological order. For each location, Avro and successor company activities are described chronologically, followed by a discussion of any non-Avro activities at each site.

Manchester – Brownsfield Mills

A.V. Roe & Co. was registered on 1 January 1910 at Everard Works, Great Ancoats Street. This was the Bullseye Braces factory, owned by H.V. Roe, elder brother of A.V. Roe, and from 1910 components of all early Avro designs (triplanes, etc.) were made in the basement here. Flying was conducted mainly at Brooklands and, from 1912, at the flying school at Shoreham. Early production included two Roe II, four Roe III and a single Roe IV triplane. Machines built under contract for third parties included:

- A single biplane of Farman 'boxkite' layout for the Edwards brothers of Bolton (see *British Aircraft Before the Great War*, p.22).
- A Curtis-type pusher for Capt. E.W. Wakefield that was later converted at Windermere to become the Lakes Water Bird.
- The biplane built for J.R. Duigan that was later purchased by the Lakes Flying Co. and modified at Windermere to become the Lakes Sea Bird.
- The monoplane constructed for Lt Burga of the Peruvian Navy that made its first flight at Shoreham, West Sussex on 12 November 1912.

Following his initial triplane series, A.V. Roe chose the tractor biplane as his preferred configuration. His initial biplane designs were the Type D (seven built); the Type E (later known as the Avro 500 and 502) eighteen of which were built; and the Type 503 (four built). These designs led directly to the immensely successful Avro Type 504 training aircraft. It was this series of aircraft that enabled A.V. Roe & Co. Ltd to advertise for many years with the slogan: 'The pioneer of the tractor biplane – the universally accepted type. A.V. Roe & Co. Ltd.' Additional details of A.V. Roe's earliest designs are provided under the entry for Brooklands, Surrey in Volume Three of this series.

A.V. Roe & Co. Ltd was registered on 11 January 1913. In January 1913, the Brownsfield Mills (Everard) works were reported to be full to capacity, the move to this factory having taken place during the production run of the Avro 500. Roy Chadwick, the famous designer

The Lakes Water Bird was adapted from a 'Curtis-type' biplane built by A.V. Roe & Co. Ltd at Brownfield Mills. It was first flown at Brooklands in July 1911, flying as a floatplane at Windemere in November of the same year. (Harry Holmes)

of many great Avro types joined the company in late 1911, working initially on the Avro 500, 504 and Avian. Chadwick was responsible for the Tutor, Anson, Manchester, Lancaster, York, Lancastrian, Lincoln, Tudor, Shackleton, and the conceptual design of the Vulcan (completed by Stuart Davies after Chadwick's death in the accident to the Tudor II at Woodford on 23 August 1947). Chadwick was surely one of the industry's giants.

The Brownsfield Mills works building survives (2004) and is at this time being renovated, probably for use as apartments.

Manchester – Miles Platting

A.V. Roe & Co. Ltd used works at Clifton Street, Miles Platting, Manchester from 17 March 1913. Miles Platting is particularly associated with the early production of the Avro 504 training aircraft. As demand for the type increased during the First World War, the company took over part of the Park Works of Mather & Platt Ltd, where large-scale production took place. See the entry for Newton Heath below.

The company telegraphic address was 'Triplane, Manchester' and early advertising slogans included 'Avro for quality' (1911-1912); 'First off land and first off water' (mid-1912); and 'Nothing better', which was used for an extended period from mid-1913. These slogans were sometimes combined with other phrases, for example, 'Nothing better for peace or war' used in October 1914. *The Aeroplane* archly notes that 'the works are situated in a district more noted for its manufactures, than its beauty'.

The Avro 504 was designed and built at Clifton Street, and became highly successful after the selection of the Avro 504J/K as the standard RFC training aircraft. The type was constructed by at least eighteen contractors during the First World War, with the 504K remaining in limited production until January 1927.

The entire site to the south-east of Lord North Street has been demolished, although one can still see the narrow strips of road surface that are all that remain after the clearance of the back-to-back houses which lay between Lord North Street and Clifton Street.

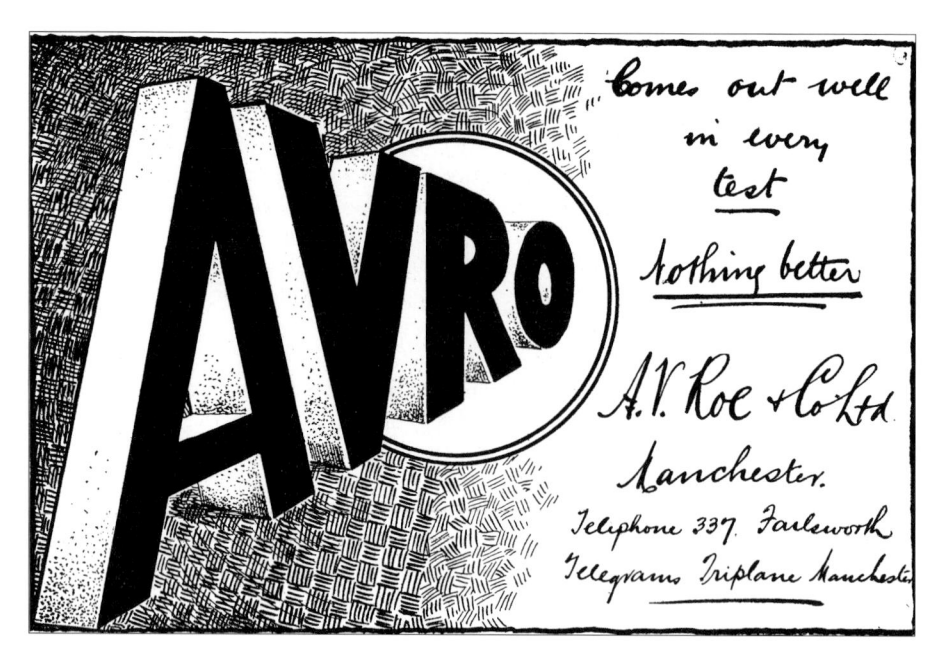

This page: *A selection of adverts from A.V. Roe & Co./A.V. Roe & Co. Ltd.*

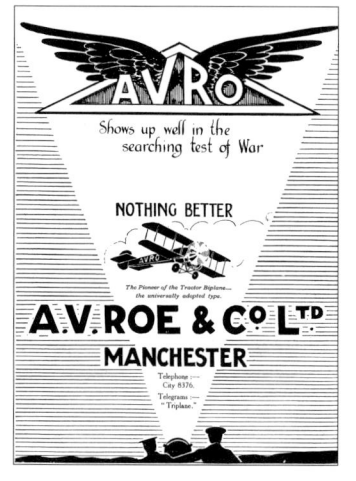

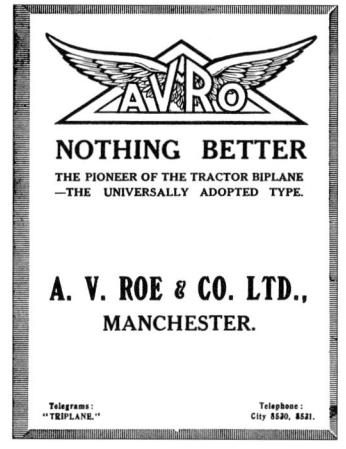

Manchester – Alexandra Park

This 110-acre airfield was opened during the First World War and was used by **A.V. Roe & Co. Ltd** for test flying from May 1918 up to 30 August 1924. The airfield was known at one stage as Didsbury, but took its name from the nearest railway station. An Aircraft Acceptance Park (No.15 (Manchester) AAP) also operated here from May 1918. Many surplus Avro 504 aircraft were stored at Alexandra Park after the end of hostilities and Avro 538 K-132, later G-EACR, made its first flight here in May 1919. In 1924, the landowner insisted that flying must stop and that all associated buildings be removed. As a result, A.V. Roe & Co. Ltd moved its test flying activity to Woodford.

The 1924 Ordnance Survey map shows that the airfield was sited to the south of Wilbraham Road, in the area now in use as Hough End playing fields. Although it is difficult today to imagine active test-flying just to the south of Manchester city centre, there is a small housing estate close by with street names such as Avro Close and Avian Drive.

The **Leeming Prince Wood** glider was built in 1924 from surplus Avro 504 parts. The machine was flown for the first time at Alexandra Park on 24 May 1924, but was badly damaged in an accident in September of the same year. An engine was subsequently fitted to the repaired machine, but it was never flown as a powered aircraft.

Manchester Aviation Co. Ltd converted a DH9 for civil use as DH9C G-EBDG at Alexandra Park in 1923.

Manchester – Newton Heath

A.V. Roe & Co. Ltd: Large-scale orders for the Avro 504 required additional production space and the use of three newly completed bays of the Mather & Platt Ltd Park Works (totalling 5,000 sq. ft) was obtained. Across Briscoe Lane, a new factory was built for Avro, which was occupied in 1918, becoming the company's Head Office on 23 August 1920. The company remained here until 1946, when work in this factory was transferred to Greengate, Chadderton. The Briscoe Lane factory was taken over by the CWS as a bacon factory, but is now (2004) used for general storage by a number of firms.

Much of the First World War production was delivered to one of the Aircraft Acceptance Parks by rail from the (then) London Road railway station (Manchester Piccadilly), having been transported by road to the station. Aircraft were sometimes delivered by air from a field near Trafford Park. The lack of experimental flight-test facilities close to the Manchester factories led directly to A.V. Roe selecting Hamble on the south coast for aircraft erection and test flying.

More Avro 504 aircraft were built during the First World War than any other British type. The total number constructed is quoted as 8,340 (4,644 by contractors), but this figure certainly includes some cancelled contracts. A.J. Jackson, in Putnam's *Avro Aircraft Since 1908* states that it is not possible to give a definitive production figure and that the above figures overstate the total. Whatever the exact figure, the production rate was phenomenal, and the Avro 504 was said by Lord Weir to have consumed one-third of the UK supply of silver spruce.

Contract production of the Avro 504 was undertaken by The Blériot & Spad Aircraft Works, The British Caudron Co. Ltd, The Brush Electrical Engineering Co. Ltd, Eastbourne Aviation Co. Ltd, The Grahame-White Aviation Co. Ltd, Harland & Wolff Ltd, The Henderson Scottish Aviation Factory, Hewlett & Blondeau Ltd, The Humber Motor Co. Ltd, London Aircraft Co. Ltd, Morgan & Co., Parnall & Sons, The Regent Carriage Co. Ltd, Frederick Sage & Co. Ltd, Savages Ltd, S.E. Saunders Ltd, and The Sunbeam Motor Car Co. Ltd.

After the First World War, many erstwhile constructors turned their hand to tuition and joy-riding. The ready availability, not to say glut, of Avro 504K aircraft available from the Aircraft Disposal Company meant that this was, for many such firms, the aircraft of choice.

Some idea of the rate of production of Avro 504 at Newton Heath can be gained from the number of fuselages awaiting collection from the factory. (JMB/GSL collection)

Civilian 504K aircraft were used by the following firms previously engaged in aircraft manufacture: Bournemouth Aviation Co. Ltd (five aircraft); Central Aircraft Co. Ltd (eight); C.L. Pashley; Eastbourne Aviation Co. Ltd; The Grahame-White Aviation Co. Ltd (twelve); Handley Page Ltd; Kingsbury Aviation Co. Ltd; London & Provincial Aviation Co. Ltd; Navarro Aviation Co. Ltd (three); and Vickers Ltd (four). A.V. Roe & Co. Ltd also entered this market in the form of the Avro Transport Company, with aircraft based all over England and Wales. Operating bases were dispersed around the coast like an itinerary for a British beach tour and included Blackpool, Southport, Fleetwood, Morecambe, Waterloo Sands (Liverpool) and Weston super Mare.

The vast supply of surplus Avro 504 airframes that were available from the Aircraft Disposal Company, and from Avro storage at Alexandra Park, formed the basis for a bewildering range of variants with different engines and passenger arrangements. The main types and their constructors included the following:

Avro type no.	Powerplant and configuration	Constructors	Location
504L	Seaplane	A.V. Roe & Co. Ltd (new and conversions)	Hamble
		Eastbourne Aviation Co. Ltd	Eastbourne
		The Aircraft Disposal Co. Ltd	Croydon
536	Bentley BR.1 rotary or Clerget rotary. Increased fuselage width for pleasure flying.	A.V. Roe & Co. Ltd	Hamble, Manchester
		Surrey Flying Services	Croydon
548	Various liquid cooled or 'V' engines: Curtiss OX-5 (Avro 545), 80hp Renault, 120hp Airdisco . (548A)	A.V. Roe & Co. Ltd	Hamble
		The Aircraft Disposal Co. Ltd	Croydon
		Surrey Flying Services	Croydon
		Henderson School of Flying	Brooklands
		Berkshire Aviation Tours Ltd	Witney

The Avro Rota (Cierva C.30A) was the final version of the Cierva Autogiro to enter production. Built in Manchester, the type was distributed from Hanworth. (Author)

552	Wolseley Viper	A.V. Roe & Co. Ltd	Hamble
		L.G. Anderson	Hanworth
		C.B. Field	Kingswood Knoll
504N & 504O	Radial engines, mainly Armstrong-Siddeley Lynx, but also ABC Wasp, Lucifer, Mongoose, Wright Whirlwind and 100hp Anzani. Featured a distinctive new undercarriage arrangement and other structural changes. New build aircraft and conversions from Avro 504K. Seaplane version was 504O	A.V. Roe & Co. Ltd (more than 500 new build aircraft) Royal Air Force – seventy-eight conversions from Avro 504K.	Manchester, Hamble
		Air Travel Ltd	Penshurt, Kent
		C.B. Field	Kingswood Knoll
		L.G. & L.J. Anderson	Hanworth
		The Aircraft Disposal Co. Ltd	Croydon
504Q	Lynx radial powered seaplane for Arctic use	A.V. Roe & Co. Ltd	Hamble
504R	'Gosport' with reduced structural weight. Engines included Gnome Monosoupape rotary and Alpha, Lynx and Mongoose radials	A.V. Roe & Co. Ltd – exported to Argentina, Peru and Estonia and 100 built under licence in Argentina	Manchester Hamble

By 1934, 250,000 sq. ft of factory capacity was available, building the Avro Avian, Avro Ten (fourteen licence-built Fokker F7/3m), Tutor, Prefect (192, widely exported), Cadet (129 Cadet/Club Cadet and variants), Cierva C30A (Avro 671), Avro 626, Audax (287 (also quoted as 244)), Blenheim (1,000), Anson (1,412), Manchester (157), York, and Lincoln.

Production of the Audax was followed by twenty-four Avro 674, an Audax airframe powered by an Armstrong Siddeley Panther radial engine, which was exported to Egypt in 1937-1938.

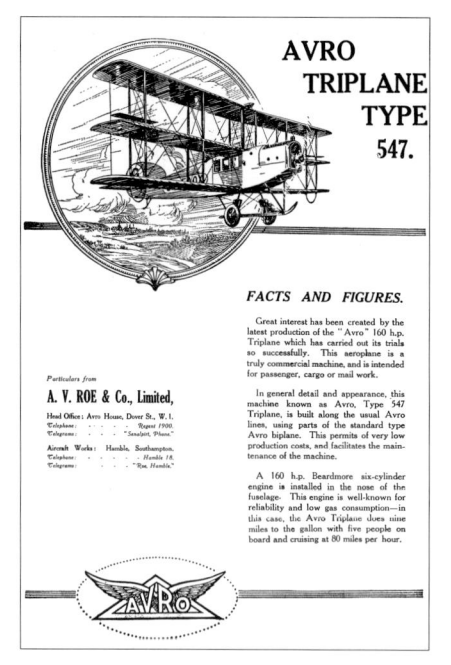

A.V. Roe & Co. Ltd advertising from the period immediately after the First World War.

Although the Avro Avian private and sporting biplane is eclipsed by the reputation of the de Havilland Moth, it was built in significant quantities. A total of 396 Avian were built, split between 194 wooden airframe Avian I to IV, and 202 metal airframe aircraft made up of 156 Avian IVM; sixteen Sports Avian; two long-range aircraft for Sir Charles Kingsford Smith; two Avian monoplanes; and at least twenty-six aircraft constructed under licence in Canada and the USA. Production was at Newton Heath, and the early aircraft were flown at Hamble, the Avian production run covering the period when A.V. Roe & Co. Ltd were purchased by Armstrong Siddeley Developments Ltd, which resulted in the withdrawal of Avro test-flying from Hamble.

In addition to the Avro Ten, other commercial transports were built in small numbers during 1929-1934, these being the Avro 619 Five (four built), Avro 624 Six (three built), Avro 642/2m Mailplane G-ACFV, and Avro 642/4m VT-AFM for the Viceroy of India. These aircraft, with their rather unimaginative designations and limited production quantities, are now almost footnotes in the history of the company. When first introduced, however, they were promoted as prominently as any other product of a major company. This is demonstrated by the following examples:

> *Avro 5: Businessmen are taking to the air. To cross London, the businessman uses his car and it is now just as practical for him to travel across Europe in his own Avro 5. … Its carpeted cabin contains chairs for four people. It is electrically lighted and comfortably ventilated. There is in fact everything necessary for convenient and pleasurable travelling. The Avro 5 can land in 330 yards, and can be left anywhere in all weathers. To own one is to be utterly independent of all public transport arrangements, and to be able to travel anywhere at any time with speed, safety and comfort.*
>
> *For the World's Airlines. The Avro 10 is gaining more and more the confidence and respect of the world's airlines. It is remarkably independent of climatic conditions, and the full weight of the tropic sun no more affects it than the frozen skies of the North.*

The AVRO 642 is now available with different combinations of Siddeley engines to suit all the varying requirements of commercial operators. It combines reliability, comfort, exceptional economy in service with speeds up to 190mph.

The Avro 621 Trainer was designed in 1929 to replace the Avro 504. The prototype was registered G-AAKT and, after a number of developmental changes, the type gave rise to the Avro Tutor and its derivatives. When first flown in late 1929, the type was advertised with the slogan 'Avro for training aircraft'. Contemporary reports describe the type as having large comfortable cockpits, good view, effective windscreens and a wide-track undercarriage.

Additional promotional material included:

The Avro Trainer is designed to give complete training, from beginning to end. It is built by a firm whose reputation is founded on the successful design of training machines during twelve years of highly specialised construction. The new machine is the result of that experience and will add to that reputation. Metal built and fabric covered, it is easily and economically maintained and repaired. In its dual cockpits every detail of every control is absolutely identical. Avro built the finest training machine before. Here they present a still finer machine for modern requirements in the same field of work.

795 Avro Tutor were built, comprising 436 military, forty-nine civil and no less than 310 engineless airframes. In addition, fifteen examples of a seaplane variant, the Avro 646 Sea Tutor were supplied to the RAF. Fifty-seven Tutor aircraft were built under licence in South Africa and three in Denmark. The combined production of the Tutor, the Avro 626 and Prefect (simplified versions of the Tutor) was nearly 1,000 airframes – all built in peacetime – making these types worthy successors to the Avro 504.

The Cadet was effectively a smaller Tutor intended for private and club use. Ultimately, it proved too expensive to operate, and the main user proved to be Air Service Training Ltd (AST)

Avro Tutor production underway at Newton Heath. In the background are major assemblies for the Avro Ten. (BAE SYSTEMS plc)

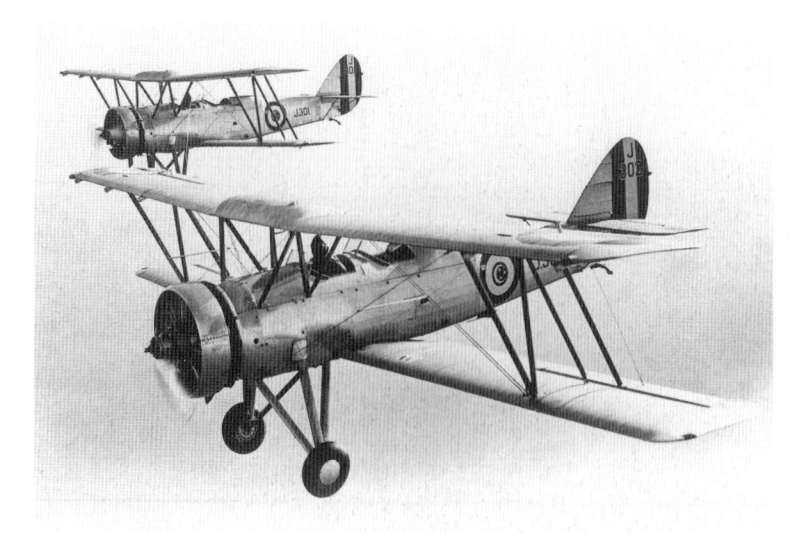

Left: *The Avro 626 was exported to a number of countries, including Egypt, whose first two aircraft are seen here flying in formation.* (BAE SYSTEMS plc)

Opposite above: *Newton Heath made a major contribution to production of the Anson during the Second World War. This Anson is under restoration for a museum in Australia.* (Author)

The Avro 638 Club Cadet was a simplified Tutor intended for flying club use. This aircraft is on its delivery flight to the Airwork School of Flying at Heston. (BAE SYSTEMS plc)

at Hamble (part of the Hawker Siddeley industrial group) who used a fleet of sixteen Avro 631 and twenty-three Avro 643 Mk II. Six versions of the Cadet were produced, the most numerous being the 631 Cadet (thirty-five), 638 Club Cadet (fifteen) and the 643 Mk II Cadet (sixty-one).

Pre-war and wartime expansion at Newton Heath added nearly 100,000 sq. ft to the production capacity between 1938 and mid-1943. Major components were taken by road to Woodford for assembly. Striking pictures exist of the wings and the complete fuselage of the prototype Anson K4771 loaded onto dollies for their journey to Woodford. The Anson entered production at Newton Heath, but this work was subsequently shared with the company's other Manchester factories, and with the shadow factory at Yeadon. The wartime responsibilities of Newton Heath included Lancaster and York wing manufacture, Lancaster centre section production, and machining facilities.

A.V. Roe & Co. Ltd also used the Heath Works in Newton Heath as a paint, dope and woodworking shop until it was destroyed by fire in May 1918. This activity was then transferred to the Evans & Co. (later Evans Bellhouse) timber yard, also in Newton Heath.

Manchester – Chadderton/Middleton

Chadderton has always been the preserve of A.V. Roe & Co. Ltd and its successors up to and including BAE SYSTEMS. The development of activity on the site is presented chronologically below. Note that the head office address of **A.V. Roe & Co. Ltd** was for many years Greengate, Middleton, Manchester, this being the location of the Chadderton plant.

On 6 May 1920, **Crossley Motors Ltd** purchased a controlling interest in A.V. Roe & Co. Ltd. In May 1928, **Crossley Motors Ltd** sold their share holding to **Armstrong Siddeley Development Co. Ltd**. A.V. Roe resigned at the end of October 1928, and moved on to take control of **S.E. Saunders Ltd**, to form **Saunders-Roe Ltd**. Mr John Siddeley (who controlled Armstrong Siddeley Development Co. Ltd) decided that the two aircraft manufacturing firms he now controlled (Sir W.G. Armstrong Whitworth Aircraft Ltd and A.V. Roe & Co. Ltd) should continue to run as separate concerns.

The next stage of industrial consolidation came in 1935, when A.V. Roe & Co. Ltd became, with Sir W.G. Armstrong Whitworth Aircraft Ltd, part of the Hawker Siddeley Group as a result of the merger between the Armstrong Siddeley Development Co. and Hawker Aircraft Ltd (which already controlled Gloster Aircraft Co.) to form Hawker Siddeley Aircraft Co.

Chadderton was a product of the expansion schemes prior to the Second World War, being built as a 'shadow' factory for production of the Blenheim, to be managed by A.V. Roe & Co. Ltd. Construction of the factory was begun in autumn 1938, the factory coming into production from April 1939. Chadderton provided no less than 750,000 sq. ft of production capacity and, with Woodford, has provided a major production facility for **Hawker Siddeley Aviation Ltd**, and **British Aerospace/BAE SYSTEMS**.

As with Newton Heath, major assemblies were taken by road to Woodford for erection. The main types manufactured at Chadderton were as follows: Anson, Manchester, Lancaster (3,076), Blenheim (250 Mk I – first example L6594, 750 Mk IV), Lincoln, Shackleton and Vulcan. Chadderton responsibilities included the main design office, tooling manufacture, machine shops and Lancaster and York fuselage production. The major types produced at Chadderton are summarised below:

- Manchester: The twin engine Avro 679 Manchester was only used operationally for fifteen months, but provided the basis for the outstanding four-engine Lancaster bomber.

Major assemblies for more than 3,000 Lancaster bombers were built at Chadderton; these were then moved by road to Woodford for final assembly and flight-test. (BAE SYSTEMS plc)

- Lancaster: The contribution of the Lancaster during the Second World War effectively established A.V. Roe & Co. Ltd as Britain's leading manufacturer of bomber aircraft. This is reflected in the following advertising material of 1946: 'From 1942 to 1945 two-thirds of all the bombs dropped by Bomber Command were dropped by Avro Lancasters – Superplanes by Avro'. The slogan 'a Superplane by Avro' was used during the late 1940s on most A.V. Roe & Co. Ltd advertisements. The total number of Lancaster aircraft built at all sites was 6,950 in the United Kingdom, with a further 430 Canadian-built Mk X. A.V. Roe & Co. Ltd built 896 Mk I and 2,774 Mk III Lancaster aircraft at Manchester and Yeadon, with a peak rate of 155 aircraft in a single month (August 1944).
- Anson: The total number of Ansons built was 10,996 (11,020 is also widely quoted – Harry Holmes discusses these numbers in *AVRO The History of an Aircraft Company*), for further details see Woodford and Yeadon.
- York: The prototype Avro York LV626 was built at Chadderton before being assembled and tested at Ringway in July 1942. Although the York can be regarded as an interim transport aircraft, this is not to overlook the hard work that it performed, often flying unglamorous cargoes on unglamorous routes. Skyways Ltd achieved very high utilisation rates, A.V. Roe & Co. Ltd advertising referring in particular to two Skyways aircraft – *Skyway* and *Sky Courier* – which achieved 2,177, and 2,402 hours utilisation, respectively, in 1947. Thus, 'By day and night, in fair weather and foul, Avro airliners are carrying their precious cargoes to the far corners of the earth'.
- Lincoln: 165 Lincoln bombers were built by Avro in Manchester, with others at Yeadon (six), Metropolitan-Vickers (seventy-nine), and Armstrong Whitworth, Coventry (299). In addition, fifty-four were constructed by the Australian Government Aircraft Factory, Melbourne, giving a grand total of 603 aircraft. The first Australian Lincoln B.Mk 30 built by the Beaufort Division of the Department of Aircraft Construction, flew on 17 March 1946.
- Shackleton: 181 Shackleton maritime patrol aircraft were constructed at Chadderton, comprising three prototypes, seventy-seven MR.1/1A, fifty-nine MR.2, thirty-four

One of many Lancasters, Lancastrians and Lincolns used for engine development, Lancastrian VM703 supported DH Ghost flight-testing at Hatfield. (BAE SYSTEMS plc)

MR.3 and eight aircraft for the SAAF. The Shackleton, in its AEW.2 form, was the last piston-engine powered front-line operational type in RAF service, not being replaced by the Boeing E-3 Sentry until 1991.

An overlooked, but important, role for the Avro heavy bombers was the part that they played in the development of the British gas turbine engine by providing flying test beds. Some of the resultant configurations were quite extraordinary in appearance, and possibly sounded even more remarkable! The Lancaster flew in this role in support of the Armstrong Siddeley Adder, ASX, Mamba, Python and Viper, the Metropolitan-Vickers F2 and the Rolls-Royce Dart. The Lancastrian supported the Armstrong Siddeley Sapphire, DH Ghost, and Rolls-Royce Nene and Avon programmes. The Lincoln acted as flying test bed for the Armstrong Siddeley Python, Bristol Phoebus, Theseus and Proteus, Napier Naiad and Rolls-Royce Derwent. The sound of a Lincoln (SX971) flying with its bomb bay mounted after-burning Derwent operating must have been quite unique. (For further details of test bed aircraft see Filton (Volume Two); Hatfield; (Volume Three); and Hucknall and Luton (Volume Four)).

Hawker Siddeley: On 25 June 1935, John Siddeley sold his shares of **Armstrong Siddeley Development Co.** to **Hawker Siddeley Aircraft Co. Ltd**, which also purchased half the shares of **Hawker Aircraft Ltd**. The new company controlled **Sir W.G. Armstrong Whitworth Aircraft Ltd**, **Armstrong Siddeley Motors Ltd**, **Air Service Training (AST)**, **A.V. Roe & Co. Ltd**, and 50 per cent of **Hawker Aircraft Ltd** and **Gloster Aircraft Co.** (the latter being already controlled by Hawker). The individual companies continued to trade under their original identities. For the later development of Hawker Siddeley into one of the UK's two major aerospace groups of the 1960s and 1970s, see the introductory chapters on the development of the industry.

Hawker Siddeley Aviation Ltd/British Aerospace/BAE SYSTEMS: HSAL/BAe/BAE SYSTEMS retained Chadderton for the manufacture of large assemblies, final assembly and flight-tests being conducted at Woodford. Chadderton therefore contributed major components for the HS748 and ATP, and the RJ/RJX series. Large assemblies such as complete fuselages were moved by road across the Manchester area from Chadderton to

Opposite: *The expanse of the production facility at Chadderton is evident from this aerial view.* (BAE SYSTEMS plc via Harry Holmes)

Left: *The Hawker Siddeley 748 fuselage production line at Chadderton.* (BAE SYSTEMS plc)

Below: *The first British Aerospace ATP fuselage being transported from Chadderton to Woodford in 1993.* (BAE SYSTEMS plc)

Woodford. In late 1998, it was announced that a major package of Tornado spares responsibility including the fin, canopy, tailerons, wing leading edge and engine bay doors was to move from Samlesbury to Chadderton. With the closure of Dunsfold, BAE SYSTEMS also transferred certain Harrier manufacturing work to Chadderton, including Harrier I tailplane and rudder repairs, and Harrier II/II+ work including speed brakes, undercarriage doors and rudders. The Chadderton unit also manufactured twelve Tri-Star large freight doors for **Marshall of Cambridge Aerospace Ltd**.

Under BAE SYSTEMS, Chadderton is responsible for the manufacture of the new Nimrod MRA.4 inner wing structure; on 23 August 2000 the first wing was moved by road from Chadderton to Woodford. In an operation reminiscent of many earlier operations cited elsewhere in this work, this involved a 46 tonne, 87ft-long trailer; police escort; removal of traffic bollards; and pruning of overhanging trees.

The Chadderton factory remains in active use as this is written in 2005, but now lacks the Avro company logo, flanked on either side by the name A.V. Roe & Co. Ltd, which used to grace its frontage.

Manchester – Ringway (now Manchester Airport)

This airfield was created following the compulsory purchase of the 664 acre site in 1934, and it was opened in 1938. The hangars used by A.V. Roe & Co. Ltd have now all gone following airport development. The original Municipal Hangar/Terminal and Bellman hangar were demolished as a result of development of the new terminal; the hangars on the south side used for York assembly were demolished in 1997 as a consequence of the second runway development.

Ringway was used by the experimental department of **A.V. Roe & Co. Ltd** for flight-testing from 1 May 1939, with a major expansion of assembly facilities (totalling more than 250,000 sq. ft) in January 1943. The facility at Ringway remained in use until November 1946, when all experimental flying was transferred to Woodford. After the departure of A.V. Roe & Co. Ltd, their assembly sheds and other facilities were taken over by BOAC.

The table below summarises first flights made from Ringway by aircraft built by A.V. Roe & Co. Ltd.

Type	**Registration/Serial**	**Date**
Manchester	L7246	25 July 1939
Lancaster	BT308	9 January 1941

The prototype Manchester L7246 photographed at Ringway in 1939. (BAE SYSTEMS plc)

York	LV626	5 July 1942
Lincoln	PW925	9 June 1944
Tudor 1	G-AGPF/TT176	15 June 1945

During the second half of 1940, A.V. Roe & Co. Ltd carried out conversion work on Douglas DB-7 aircraft to prepare them for RAF service as either Boston or Havoc. This activity was carried out at both Ringway and Woodford, the first Boston modified at Ringway flying on 11 February 1942.

The York was built both at Ringway and Yeadon. Some aircraft were also completed at Woodford, the last York from the production line at Woodford being PE108, in May 1948. A total of 258 (some sources 250) were built, comprising four prototypes, 208 aircraft for the RAF (five of which were diverted to BOAC), and new-build aircraft for BOAC (twenty-five), BSAA (twelve), Skyways (three), and FAMA (five); (one additional aircraft was built by Victory Aircraft Ltd in Canada). The type was the most effective British transport during the Berlin Airlift. Never glamorous, the York was widely used by a number of post-war airlines including BOAC, BSAA, FAMA, Skyways (a thirty-strong fleet), Dan Air, Lancashire Aircraft Corporation Ltd (twenty-eight aircraft), South African Airways, Air Charter Ltd, Eagle Aviation Ltd, Scottish Aviation Ltd, Hunting Air Transport, etc.

The Avro Tudor series provided a most unhappy saga for the company. Numerous variants were constructed with different engine installations and a succession of modifications to cure inadequate handling and stability problems. On 7 February 1947, BOAC announced that they were not satisfied with the Tudor 1 following flight trials on the route to Nairobi. The main concerns expressed were unacceptable buffeting at speeds significantly above approach speed, excessive swing on take off, and considerably worse fuel economy than expected.

Fuel consumption was such that BOAC would find difficulty in using the aircraft on the Atlantic route unless it could be considerably improved, due to the large reduction in payload that would be involved. One report indicates that the transatlantic payload would have to be reduced to only twelve passengers. There were also problems with cabin heater reliability, heater failure causing the aircraft to have to descend, often into adverse weather conditions. On their side, Avro also complained of the difficulties induced by BOAC's continual requests for modifications.

Despite the poor reception of the Tudor 1, Avro felt able to promote the Tudor 4 in 1948 as follows: 'For luxurious travel over long ranges at high speed. Avro Tudor IV – four Rolls-Royce Merlin engines'. The eventual main user of the Tudor was British South American Airways (BSAA) who used two 28-seat Mk 1 and six 32-seat Mk 4. Unfortunately, BSAA suffered tragic losses of the aircraft, and the type certification for passenger use was withdrawn in March 1949. The Tudor 2 was a stretched 60-seat version, which again proved to have performance problems. A total of thirty-seven Tudor aircraft were constructed of no less than seven variants, production consisting of Mk 1 (twelve), Mk 2 (four), Mk 3 (two), Mk 4 (twelve), Mk 5 (six), and Mk 7 (one). One Mk 1 was converted to a Mk 4, and subsequently fitted with four Rolls-Royce Nene engines to become the sole Tudor Mk 8, VX195.

The Fairey Aviation Co. Ltd erected a hangar at Ringway for assembly of the Fairey Battle, whilst the corporation airport was still under construction and had not yet been opened. Two additional hangars were built at Ringway, and were to be joined by two further

Above: *BSAA Avro Tudor 4 G-AHNK Star Lion. BSAA were the main user of the type.* (BAE SYSTEMS plc)

Left: *The Fairey test facilities at Ringway, photographed in 1946. Swordfish, Firefly, Barracuda and Halifax aircraft are parked outside.* (J.W.R. Taylor)

Avro proudly advertises the Tudor as 'A Superplane by Avro'. (© BAE SYSTEMS plc)

hangars moved from Barton. Fairey continued thereafter to use this site for the assembly and flight-test of aircraft built at their Stockport/Heaton Chapel works. The facilities at Ringway were further expanded as production of Halifax and Beaufighter aircraft built up from the Fairey-managed Errwood Park shadow factory alongside the Heaton Chapel works.

The Fairey Fulmar I N1854 first flew here on 4 January 1940. The first production Barracuda P9642 was flown at Ringway on 18 May 1942, to be followed by the prototype Barracuda Mk V (a converted Mk II) P9976 on 16 November 1944. Spearfish RN241 was flown on 29 December 1945. The Firefly T.1 trainer MB750 first flew at Ringway marked as F1 in July 1946.

By 1948, the main Fairey activities at Ringway comprised:

- Repair of York aircraft operating on the Berlin Airlift.
- Repair of Firefly aircraft, and their modification for the Royal Navy and the Royal Canadian Navy.
- Conversion of twelve Firefly aircraft to target tug configuration for export to Sweden. Two additional aircraft were delivered to Denmark.

Later Ringway activities are summarised below:

- On 12 May 1950, the diminutive F.D.1 VX350 undertook taxiing trials here, prior to its first flight from Boscombe Down. This research delta had a wingspan of only 19ft 6in, making it one of Britain's smallest jet aircraft.
- Fairey Aviation manufactured the de Havilland Vampire and Venom fighters, these aircraft being tested at Ringway. Fifty-one Vampire FR. Mk 9 and thirty-four Venom (FB.1 and FB.4) were built by Fairey.

- The first Firefly T.2 conversion was flown at Ringway on 12 August 1949. Firefly work continued with the conversion of pilotless U.8 and U.9 drones, the first of thirty-four U.8, WM810, flying on 30 December 1953. Additional information on the activities of the Fairey Aviation factories in Cheshire is presented under the entry for Stockport.
- A further 1950s activity was the overhaul of USAF Douglas Invader aircraft.

The Central Landing Establishment carried out experimental flying of the **Hafner** Rotachute at Ringway with around twenty prototypes being built by **F. Hills & Sons Ltd** and **Airwork Ltd**. **F. Hills & Sons Ltd** assembled and flight-tested a number of Percival Proctor aircraft at Ringway.

Manchester – Woodford Aerodrome

Woodford, previously New Hall Farm, was purchased by A.V. Roe & Co. Ltd in early 1925 to replace Alexandra Park for flight-testing. A contemporary description provides us with a view of the Woodford scene: 'A spinney in the centre of the flying field, coupled with a cunningly concealed pond, were among the hazards. The usual take-off run was up a gradient so steep that there was no hope of becoming airborne before the crest, on reaching which it was not uncommon to meet another aircraft previously hidden from view, taxiing back after landing. Take-off to the south offered a choice...an extremely short run towards the aerodrome road, or a longer run past the hangars involving a banked turn immediately after take-off to get through a gap in the trees'.

A.V. Roe & Co. Ltd: After the closure of Alexandra Park, many of the aircraft built in the Manchester factories of A.V. Roe & Co. Ltd were tested at either Woodford or Ringway (Manchester Airport). Avro Lancaster aircraft built by Metropolitan-Vickers were also flight-tested at Woodford. The table below summarises first flights made from Woodford by aircraft built by Avro, Hawker Siddeley and British Aerospace/BAE SYSTEMS.

Type	Registration/Serial	Date
Avro 618 Ten	G-AADM	Mid-1926
Avro 619 Five	VP-KAE	Autumn 1929
Avro 624 Six	G-AAYR	May 1930
Avro 638 Club Cadet	G-ACAY	May 1933
Avro 641 Commodore	G-ACNT	Spring 1934
Avro 652	G-ACRM	7 January 1935
Anson 1	K4771	24 March 1935
Blenheim (Avro built)	L8594	September 1938
Lancastrian	G-AGLF/VB873	17 January 1945
Tudor 2	G-AGSU	10 March 1946
Tudor 3	G-AIYA	27 September 1946
Tudor 4	G-AHNJ	9 April 1947
Tudor 7	G-AGRX	17 April 1947
Athena 1	VM125	12 June 1948
Athena 2 (Merlin)	VW890	1 August 1948
Tudor 8 (4 R-R Nene)	VX195	6 September 1948
Tudor 5	G-AKBY	24 September 1948
Avro 696 Shackleton	VW126	9 March 1949
Ashton Mk. 1	WB490	1 September 1950
Avro 698 Vulcan	VX770	3 September 1953
Avro 696 Shackleton MR. 3	WR970	2 September 1955

G-AHKX is an Avro XIX Anson. When owned by Kemps Aerial Surveys, it was one of the last to be operated in Britain and has been restored to flying condition by BAE SYSTEMS. (Author)

Avro Tudor 7 G-AGRX strikes an imposing pose at the SBAC show at Radlett in 1947. (BAE SYSTEMS plc)

Vulcan B.2 (development a/c)	VX777	31 August 1957
Vulcan B.2 (production)	XH533	August 1958
Avro 748	G-APZV	24 June 1960
HS.748 Srs 2	G-ARAY	6 November 1961
HS.748MF Andover	G-ARRV	21 December 1963 (aerodynamic prototype produced by modification of G-APZV)
Andover C.1	XS594	9 July 1965
HS.801 Nimrod (development a/c)	XV147	23 May 1967
Shackleton AEW. 2	WL745	30 September 1971
BAe ATP	G-MATP	6 August 1986
BAe 146	G-5-106	16 May 1988 (first Woodford-assembled example)

G-ARAY *is the prototype Avro 748 Srs 2, first flown at Woodford in November 1961.* (BAE SYSTEMS plc)

BAe (Avro) RJ85	G-ISEE	23 March 1992
BAe (Avro) RJ100	G-OIII	13 May 1992
BAe (Avro) RJ70	G-BUFI	23 July 1992
BAE SYSTEMS RJX-85	G-ORJX	28 April 2001
BAE SYSTEMS RJX-100	G-IRJT	23 September 2001
BAE SYSTEMS 146-300 Atmospheric Research Aircraft	G-LUXE	1 October 2003
Nimrod MRA.4 PA01	ZJ516	26 August 2004
Nimrod MRA.4 PA02	ZJ518	15 December 2004

Production flight-testing at Woodford also included the later versions of the Avian, the Tutor and Cadet, together with large numbers of Manchester-built Anson aircraft. The type (in its civil Avro 652 form) first flew at Woodford on 7 January 1935 and remained in production until 1952. The commercial origins of the type are reflected in the following advertisement from July 1935:

> SPEED! ECONOMY! *In commercial flying with the AVRO 652. Fuel consumption less than 1¼ pints per mile − Payload well over half a ton − Maximum speed nearly 200mph − Cruising at 165 − Ease of control − Avro 'service proved' construction − Ideal for feeder line or private charter work −* SUPPLIED TO IMPERIAL AIRWAYS LTD.

The first production Anson I K6152 flew at Woodford, on 31 December 1935. Including those built in Canada, nearly 11,000 were manufactured, the Manchester factories being responsible for around 4,700. The other United Kingdom factory was at Yeadon, where some 3,400 were built. The last RAF aircraft was retired from service in 1968, after some thirty-two years of operational service.

Woodford initially provided flight-test facilities, with two flight hangars opened in 1934, a third in April 1936 and a fourth in 1938. Major expansion came with the construction of some 690,000 sq. ft of assembly facilities which came into use in December 1939 and were to be used mainly for Lancaster assembly (from both A.V. Roe & Co. Ltd, and Metropolitan-Vickers factories). Further wartime expansion added a fifth flight hangar and a further 67,000 sq. ft assembly facility.

Overshadowed by the success of American-built transport aircraft designs, Avro's stop-gap Lancastrian nevertheless provided important capacity for a number of British airlines – eighty-two were built up to the end of 1946 (following six similar Canadian Lancaster XPP conversions). The Tudor (see also Ringway) followed the Lancastrian, and proved to be a commercial failure. The table above gives an inkling of the development problems, with prototypes of seven different variants (including the Tudor 1 at Ringway) flown in the space of barely three years. An even greater blow was the loss of Roy Chadwick, Avro's great Chief Designer, in the crash of the Tudor 2 prototype, as a result of a take-off with crossed aileron controls on 23 August 1947.

The Tudor 2 design was later adapted to produce the Ashton high altitude research aircraft, six of which were built and used for meteorological research and engine testing. Modifications to generate the Ashton included installation of four jet engines in podded pairs, and a reduction in fuselage length to that of the Tudor 1. The trial employment of these aircraft is summarised below:

- WB490, Ashton Mk 1: general navigation, engine and high altitude trials.
- WB491, Mk 2: first flown 2 August 1951, cabin pressurisation trials, converted by D Napier & Son Ltd for engine test use, including Conway, and Avon. First flown with Rolls-Royce Conway on 20 August 1955.
- WB492, Mk 3: first flown 6 July 1951, radar bomb sight development.
- WB493, Mk 3: first flown on 18 December 1951, Olympus engine test bed. Also flown with the Bristol Siddeley Orpheus (port side). Set a new altitude record of 63,668ft in 1962.

A fine photograph of Avro Ashton Mk.3 WB492. This aircraft was used for radar bomb sight development flying. (BAE SYSTEMS plc)

Left: *Avro Shackleton* (© BAE SYSTEMS plc)

Above: *Avro Vulcan* (© BAE SYSTEMS plc)

- WB494, Mk 4: first flown on 18 November 1952, instrumentation trials, bomb sight development and Conway testing, Sapphire icing trials and anti-ice system development for the Gyron Junior.
- WE670, Mk 3: first flown on 9 April 1952, bombing trials, Rolls-Royce Avon under-fuselage engine testing.

The Avro Shackleton maritime patrol aircraft was first flown on 9 March 1949, with the improved MR.2 WB833 following on 17 June 1952 and the MR.3, with its tricycle undercarriage configuration, flying as WR970 on 2 September 1955. The long endurance of the Shackleton was demonstrated at the 1960 SBAC Show at Farnborough, when, on each day of the show, an aircraft took off at the start of the flying display, to return a full twenty-four hours later. Like the Anson and the Vulcan, the Shackleton was destined to have an extremely long service life, the last AEW.2 aircraft being retired in 1991, forty-two years after the first flight of the prototype. Twelve Shackleton AEW.2 conversions were carried out at Woodford and Bittesnell, the first, WL745, flying on 30 September 1971. A grand total of 181 Shackleton aircraft were built. The only export customer was the SAAF, who operated eight MR.3, these aircraft not being retired from service until November 1984.

The long service life of the Shackleton was not unrelated to the failure of the Nimrod AEW.3, which was intended to replace the Shackleton AEW.2. The first Nimrod AEW development aircraft was a modification of Comet 4C XW626, this aircraft being flown for the first time on 28 June 1977. The first of three Nimrod-based development aircraft began flight trials in February 1980. The project was cancelled following technical difficulties encountered during development and the Shackleton AEW.2 was eventually replaced by the Boeing E-3 Sentry in 1991.

Twenty-two Avro Athena trainers were built at Chadderton and flown from Woodford. The prototype VM125 flew with Mamba power on 12 June 1948. VM129 (flown in September 1949) was Dart powered, but the limited production run of nineteen aircraft was given the designation Athena T. Mk 2, this version being powered by the Rolls-Royce Merlin piston

The ill-starred Nimrod AEW.3 displays its bulbous radomes at the SBAC Show. (Author)

Neither Avro's Athena, seen here, nor the Boulton Paul Balliol lived up to their promise as turbo-prop trainers for the RAF. (BAE SYSTEMS plc)

engine. The advertising may have sounded convincing at the time, but it now rather suggests wishful thinking: 'Avro Athena advanced trainer – a veteran before it left the drawing board. The Avro Athena embodies all Avro's thirty years' experience as builders of training aircraft.'

The incomparable Vulcan made its first flight (in the triangular shape of VX770) at Woodford on 3 August 1952. The Vulcan remained in operational service until 1984 in the tanker role, the last airworthy aircraft XH558 not being withdrawn from air display flying until 23 March 1993. Two prototypes, forty-five Vulcan B. Mk 1, and eighty-eight B. Mk 2 were built, for a grand total of 135 aircraft. In September 1954, the Vulcan was being advertised thus:

> *The Virtues of the AVRO VULCAN – Exceptional Safety.*
> *Simplicity of controlling the Avro Vulcan is due not only to the absence of high-lift devices, but also to smooth and progressive high Mach number effects. In addition, the low wing-loading ensures low stalling speed, while the docility of the stall and the most natural of stall warnings add to the safety of an aircraft fairly described as the most effective bomber in the world.*

1. *Aerodynamic Simplicity*
2. *Easy Landing*
3. *Exceptional Safety*
4. *Great Range*
5. *High Altitude Flight*
6. *High Speed Flight*
7. *Servicing Simplicity*
8. *Fighter-like Manoeuvrability*
9. *Large Carrying Capacity*
10. *Great Development Potential*

Another advertisement in the same series read:

The Virtues of the AVRO VULCAN – High Altitude Flight.
Low wing-loading and reduced drag are major factors in the unequalled high-altitude performance of the Avro Vulcan, the most effective bomber in the world.

The Avro 748 G-APZV first flew on 24 June 1960; the type continued in production until 1988, and is still in service today, more than forty years after its first flight. Never glamorous, the 748 was remarkably successful, and has been an effective DC-3 replacement in many inhospitable parts of the world. A total of 351 were built, including eighty-nine aircraft manufactured by Hindustan Aeronautics Ltd. In 1983, British Aerospace was advertising that the type was in service with seventy-nine operators in fifty countries around the world, with more than 300 aircraft having been exported. Significant users included Indian Airlines (Hindustan Aeronautics-built); Aerolineas Argentinas; VARIG; Phillipine Airlines; Thai Airways; LAN-Chile; Bouraq Airlines; the Indian Air Force (Hindustan Aeronautics-built);

The all-over camouflage of this Vulcan B. Mk2 demonstrates the low-level role of the aircraft during the latter years of its service career. (J.S. Smith)

G-BGJV *was British Aerospace's HS748 Srs 2B demonstrator.* (BAE SYSTEMS plc)

Brazilian Air Force; and the Royal Australian Air Force. The last Avro 748 to be built made its first flight at Woodford on 1 December 1988.

The military freighter derivative, the 748MF Andover flew in December 1963, this type being distinguished by its upswept rear fuselage with integral loading doors and ramp. Thirty-one Andover C. Mk 1 were built, the first production aircraft XS594 flying on 9 July 1965.

Very few products designed by other companies were contracted to A.V. Roe & Co. Ltd, although the company did build 287 Hawker Audax, a single Hawker Tornado (R7936, built at Yeadon and flown from Woodford), and, between 1953 and 1955, seventy-five English Electric Canberra B2.

Hawker Siddeley Aviation Ltd was formally created on 1 July 1963, merging its operating divisions from April 1965. After this date, Armstrong Whitworth, A.V. Roe & Co. Ltd, Blackburn, de Havilland, Folland, Gloster and Hawker ceased to exist as separately identifiable trading companies. During the Hawker Siddeley period, the main Woodford and Chadderton products were the HS.748, Vulcan and the Nimrod maritime patrol aircraft. The HS.801 Nimrod development aircraft XV147 first flew on 23 May 1967. The first production aircraft XV226 flew on 28 June 1968, with the first delivery to the RAF (XV230) taking place on 2 October 1969. A total of forty-six Nimrod were built for maritime patrol duties, together with a further three Nimrod R.1 aircraft (XW644–XW646) dedicated to electronic surveillance. Eleven Nimrod airframes were converted to AEW.3 standard, these being scrapped after some years of storage at RAF Abingdon. Thirty-four Nimrod MR.1 were upgraded to MR.2 standard with significant radar, acoustic and navigation system enhancements.

Handley Page Victor conversions from bomber to tanker configuration were carried out at Woodford following the collapse of Handley Page Ltd in 1969. Hawker Siddeley converted a total of twenty-nine Victor to K. Mk 2 configuration.

The Hawker Siddeley Andover is a military transport derivative of the Avro 748. The type features a kneeling undercarriage and rear loading ramp; a total of thirty-one were built. (Author)

The sole Avro-built Hawker Tornado R7936 is seen here whilst propeller testing at Hatfield. (BAE SYSTEMS plc)

British Aerospace: A developed version of the HS.748, the commercially disappointing ATP (Advanced Turbo-Prop), was announced in March 1984. The ATP featured a 748 fuselage stretched to provide a seating capacity of seventy-two passengers. Power was provided by PW126A turboprops driving five-blade propellers. The prototype G-MATP first flew at Woodford on 6 August 1986.

Hawker Siddeley's Nimrod anti-submarine aircraft was developed from the Comet. In the form of the Nimrod MRA.4, the type will see service for many years to come. (Author)

BAe Regional Aircraft Ltd, Avro International Aerospace Division (now BAE SYSTEMS, Regional Aircraft): Woodford was the production centre for the HS146, which was refined and re-launched as the Avro Regional Jet or RJ. The first Woodford-built BAe 146 flew in May 1988, and a total of 219 BAe/HS146 were delivered. Customer sales included thirty-four 146-100, 115 146-200 and seventy 146-300; one prototype was retained (G-LUXE later to become the Atmospheric Research Aircraft) and one unsold aircraft scrapped. The name Avro was initially revived in 1993, as the intended basis of a partnership agreement with Taiwan. Ultimately, the business was continued on a national basis, BAe Regional Aircraft being formed in 1996. **BAE SYSTEMS Aircraft Services Group** was created on 1 January 2001 as a result of the merger of BAE SYSTEMS Regional Aircraft and BAE SYSTEMS Aviation Services.

The first RJ85 G-ISEE flew on 23 March 1992, the first production example flying at Woodford in November 1992. By the time that production of the RJ series was completed, 170 Avro RJ had been sold, comprising twelve RJ70, eighty-seven RJ85 and seventy-one RJ100. One of the largest fleets is operated by Northwest Airlines who ordered thirty-six RJ85 aircraft. The 100th Avro RJ to be delivered formed part of this order, being the ninth RJ85 for Northwest Airlines' associate Mesaba Airlines. This aircraft was handed over on 30 January 1998.

The first RJ70 G-BUFI was flown on 23 July 1992 and seats seventy passengers in a five abreast cabin layout with 31in seat pitch, or eighty-two passengers in a six abreast configuration. Maximum range with full passenger load is 1,250nm. The intermediate RJ85 seats 85 to 100 passengers to the same cabin standards and can carry eighty-five passengers 1,570nm. The RJ100 is further stretched to increase passenger capacity to between 100 and 128 seats, carrying 100 passengers 1,220nm. All variants are cleared for steep approach paths, increasing operational flexibility and reducing noise exposure to surrounding communities. As indicated by the production totals given above, production concentrated on the RJ85 and RJ100 variants.

The ATP is a stretched and re-engined derivative of the Avro 748. The type was a commercial disappointment, with a combined total of sixty-seven ATP and Jetstream 61 being built. (Author)

The Avro RJ family was developed following transfer of BAe 146 production from Hatfield to Woodford. (BAE SYSTEMS plc)

Remarkable cost savings accompanied the transition of production of the RJ at Woodford. In 1998 assembly time and manpower required to produce an aircraft were eleven weeks and 12,500 man-hours, compared with a figure of twenty-nine weeks and 31,000 man-hours in 1991.

BAE SYSTEMS: In early 1999, British Aerospace announced a further development, the RJX, available like the RJ in 70, 85 and 100 seat configurations, the programme being formally launched by BAE SYSTEMS on 21 March 2000. The RJX married the RJ airframe to new engines, the Honeywell AS977-1A, for further improvements in operating economy. The first ground test of this new AS900 series engine was completed on 30 July 1999, and engine flight-testing began on a Boeing 720 test bed on 29 January 2000. Key RJX design targets included a 10–15 per cent reduction in fuel consumption, significantly reduced engine maintenance costs, lower noise levels and a 500lb reduction in aircraft empty weight. In mid-2000, the type received its first order, two RJX-85 being ordered by Druk Air of Bhutan. The first flight of the RJX-85 prototype G-ORJX was completed on 28 April 2001, with RJX-100 G-IRJT following on 23 September 2001.

The RJX was to be a further enhancement of the RJ series. In the event, only three airframes were built before the programme was abandoned. (BAE SYSTEMS plc)

Following the significant downturn across the commercial aerospace sector after the attack on the New York World Trade Center on 11 September 2001, BAE SYSTEMS reviewed its exposure to this sector. As a result, it was announced on 27 November 2001 that the company was closing both the RJ and RJX programmes with the loss of 1,669 jobs. This decision has brought to an end the construction of complete aircraft for the civil market by BAE SYSTEMS. At the time that the programme was cancelled, the RJX order book stood at two RJX-85, and twelve RJX-100, with a further fourteen RJX-100 delivery options.

When the 170 Avro RJ orders are combined with the 219 BAe 146 that were delivered, the type can be considered to be the most successful British jet airliner ever produced. A total of 394 aircraft of this family were built, broken down as follows:

- BAe 146: 221 built, including the prototype G-SSSH/G-LUXE and the first 146-200; these development aircraft not being delivered to airline service. G-SSSH was modified to become the first BAe 146-300 G-LUXE, and subsequently further modified to become the Atmospheric Research Aircraft (ARA), flying for the first time in this form on 1 October 2003.
- Avro RJ: 170 built, with 166 delivered and four aircraft remaining unsold in mid-2002. The last RJ to be built (RJ85 constructors number E2394) was flown for the first time on 26 April 2002, and left Woodford for Filton to await sale on 24 June 2002. This final aircraft was delivered to Blue 1 (formerly Air Botnia) of Finland on 26 November 2003.
- Avro RJX: three flown, comprising the two development aircraft and one RJX-100 (G-6-391, constructors number E3391), which was intended to be the first aircraft for British European. One RJX-85 (constructors number E2395) was substantially complete when the programme was cancelled, but remained unflown.

Eighteen of the remaining twenty-seven Nimrod MR.2 aircraft were expected to be converted to Nimrod MRA.4 by BAE SYSTEMS. Airframe final assembly was to take place at Woodford. The Nimrod MRA.4 programme has proved difficult for BAE SYSTEMS, and on 19 February 2003 it was announced that the programme was being re-shaped to reduce risk. Rather than move directly to the production of eighteen aircraft as originally

The Atmospheric Research Aircraft G-LUXE photographed making its maiden flight on 1 October 2003. (BAE SYSTEMS plc)

anticipated, the programme is to focus on the completion of three development aircraft. Production of the remaining fifteen aircraft would resume once the development activity had shown sufficient progress toward maturity to allow the price of the remaining aircraft to be set with confidence. On 21 July 2004, the Minister of Defence, Geoff Hoon, indicated in a statement to Parliament that the number of Nimrod MRA.4 to be procured would be further reduced to twelve. The first flight of PA01 (ZJ516), the first development aircraft for the Nimrod MRA.4, took place on 26 August 2004. The first flight lasted some two hours and was used to re-position the aircraft to Warton, from where further development flying is to be conducted. PA02 (ZJ518) followed suit on 15 December 2004.

BAE SYSTEM's Woodford factory is set in a leafy suburb on the very edge of Manchester, with its million square feet of production facilities providing a strange counterpoint to the neighbouring garden centres and detached houses.

Metropolitan-Vickers Electrical Co. Ltd: The Avro Manchester aircraft, and the majority of the Avro Lancaster aircraft that were built by Metropolitan-Vickers at Mosley

Nimrod MRA.4 PA01 (ZJ516) lifts off for its first flight from Woodford to Warton on 26 August 2004. (BAE SYSTEMS plc)

Road, Trafford Park, were assembled and tested at Woodford. The first Metropolitan-Vickers-built Lancaster was flown at Woodford on 5 January 1942. At the end of the Second World War, some twenty-two of these aircraft were assembled and tested at the Vickers-Armstrongs shadow factory at Chester.

Royton

The **A.V. Roe & Co. Ltd** Laurel Works at Royton was used for the manufacture of components for the Lancaster and York. These works were used from February 1941, and covered an area in excess of 220,000 sq. ft.

Shaw

'The American aircraft factory at Shaw, near Oldham is for sale by private treaty. Six acres of land. Brick buildings with concrete floors and timber roofs. Sidings connect to the Lancashire and Yorkshire Railway.' – Advertisement in *Flight*, August 1919. This referred to the plans made for the assembly of the Handley Page O/400 from American-made components using disused mills. The Lilac Mill at Shaw, and Gorse Mill No.2 at Chadderton were taken over, and a new factory was constructed alongside Gorse Mill 'in the area known as White Gate, alongside Broadway' (to quote Barry Abraham). In the event, no aircraft had been completed before the Armistice brought an end to these plans. The factory was to have been managed by the **Alliance Aeroplane Co. Ltd**.

Stockport (Heaton Chapel and Errwood Park)

Crossley Motors Ltd: Crossley, founded in 1867, was a well-established machinery and engineering firm in the Manchester area and was well known for its gas engines prior to the setting up of Crossley Motors Ltd for motor car manufacture. (Crossley had built a number of vehicles from 1905 onward and a separate business was felt to be justified by 1910).

Prior to the First World War, Crossley Motors Ltd had constructed an engine factory parallel to the railway line at Heaton Chapel. During the First World War, the company gained the contract to manage the **National Aircraft Factory** (NAF) **No.2** Heaton Chapel. This factory, which was operational by November 1917, was set up from scratch in nine months, specifically to build AIRCO DH9 aircraft and Beardmore engines. Crossley also built the ABC Dragonfly engine and the Bentley BR2 rotary. The National Aircraft Factory buildings ran at an angle to the original Crossley factory, away from the line of the railway.

Crossley Motors delivered 326 DH9 aircraft from an order for 500 (serials were allocated to a total of 384). The first aircraft, D1001, was delivered on 16 March 1918. Production was then switched to the DH10. 200 DH10 aircraft were ordered from this factory, with perhaps as few as eight aircraft having been completed. The first DH10 to be built by the factory was F351. Aircraft were test flown from a field next to the site.

After the Armistice, the company was able to purchase the site, although it lay empty until 1923 when Willys Overland Crossley Ltd was formed to assemble the American Willys car, unfortunately without success. This failure led to the ex-NAF part of the site being sold to **The Fairey Aviation Co. Ltd** in late 1934 for use as their Heaton Chapel works (see below).

Difficulties within Crossley Motor's car and bus businesses meant that the remainder of the site was mainly under-utilised, until the rearmament and shadow factory schemes started to accelerate from 1936 onward. The upshot was that part of the site (that not already sold to Fairey Aviation), was sold to the Government for aircraft manufacture, with its next-door neighbour, The Fairey Aviation Co. Ltd, being appointed to manage the factory. As a result, additional buildings were erected, filling in the area between the original Crossley factory and

The adjacent factories of Heaton Chapel and Errwood Park in Stockport. (J.W.R. Taylor)

the Fairey Aviation Heaton Chapel Works. This factory was maintained as a separate organisation, and was known as Erwood Park works.

The Fairey Aviation Co. Ltd: The two factories which lie side-by-side here are known as Heaton Chapel (Fairey's western half of the site), and Errwood Park (the Second World War shadow factory managed by Fairey). The sites are separated by a private road, Sir Richard Fairey Road. The Heaton Chapel works became known as **Stockport Aviation Co. Ltd**, this company having been registered on 11 February 1936. During the Second World War, Heaton Chapel was used for Fairey Aviation's own products, whereas the Errwood Park shadow factory produced the Beaufighter and then the Halifax.

Aircraft built by The Fairey Aviation Co. Ltd at Stockport are tabulated below; these aircraft were normally flight-tested at Ringway.

Type Comments

Hendon   Fourteen Hendon bombers, flight-tested at Barton. The Hendon was Britain's first monoplane bomber and was characterised by its thick wings and large trouser-faired fixed undercarriage. The type was rapidly superseded by the Hampden, Whitley and Wellington.

Battle   Light day bomber. Fairey Battle production was made up of the prototype and 2,184 Battle I, 1,029 of which were built by Austin Motors. Included in this total are the 266 aircraft built as Battle Trainers – 200 at Stockport and sixty-six at Longbridge, and the 200 examples built as target tugs by Austin Motors. An additional sixteen aircraft sets of components were built by Fairey at Stockport for assembly in Belgium. Other production figures can also be found.

Fulmar   Naval fighter. Two prototypes and 600 production aircraft 250 Mk I and 350 Mk II, all at Heaton Chapel. The Fulmar was the Royal Navy's first monoplane

The Battle day bomber proved to be obsolescent by the time it was used in anger during the Second World War. This is the Heaton Chapel production line. (J.W.R. Taylor)

	fighter and served with some distinction before being replaced in service by the Seafire and Sea Hurricane.
Barracuda	1,190 out of a total of 2,600 production aircraft – all the Fairey-built aircraft except the two prototypes were built at Heaton Chapel with final assembly and flight-test at Ringway. The first production aircraft P9642 was flown at Ringway on 18 May 1942. The 1,000th Stockport (Heaton Chapel)-built Barracuda was completed in August 1945. This impressive aircraft was also built by Westland Aircraft Ltd (18), Blackburn Aircraft Ltd (700) and Boulton Paul Aircraft Ltd (692).
Firefly	Late-mark Firefly aircraft (forty-one AS. Mk 7) and pilotless conversions (thirty-four U.8 and forty U.9). Trainer conversions from F.1 were also carried out at Heaton Chapel, in a programme that included thirty-four T.1, fifty-seven T.2 and an unknown number of T.3 conversions.
Spearfish	The second prototype Fairey Spearfish RN241 was built at Heaton Chapel and flown at Ringway. A second Heaton Chapel-built example, TJ175, was not flown.
Beaufighter	Errwood Park: 500 aircraft – twenty-five Beaufighter Mk IF, 300 Mk IC, 175 Mk VIC.
Halifax	Errwood Park: 662 aircraft – 326 Mk III, 246 Mk V and ninety Mk VII.
DH Vampire /Venom	Stockport-built: Fairey Aviation manufactured the de Havilland Vampire and Venom fighters, these aircraft being tested at Ringway. Fifty-one Vampire FB Mk 9 and some thirty-four Venom (FB.1 and FB.4) were built by Fairey.
Gannet	Early production AS.1 and AS.4 from 1954, the first example being AS.1 WN370. Eighty-eight Gannet were built at Stockport.
Fairey F.D.1	Built at Stockport, but flown from Boscombe Down.

The Fairey Aviation Co. Ltd managed repair facilities at Burtonwood, Warrington (ex-shirt factory), Reddish, Parrs Wood and Stretton. The Avions Fairey designer E.O. Tips was

Manager and Chief Engineer of the Burtonwood Repair Depot from 1940 to 1943, and was subsequently head of the Fairey Aviation Experimental and Research Department. The following summary of Fairey Aviation activities at their Cheshire factories is based on an article published in *The Aeroplane* in November 1948:

> *Stockport is used for repair, maintenance, overhaul and conversion in parallel to its production activities. By May 1945, more than 5,000 aircraft (including their equivalent in spares) had been produced from Heaton Chapel, Errwood Park, Ringway, Reddish and Warrington. The peak employment of this group of factories was 15,000. 500 Beaufighter and more than 600 Halifax had been constructed at Errwood Park. Since VE Day, in three years 591 aircraft have been built, modified, repaired, overhauled or converted.*
>
> *Immediate post-war activity included repair of Firefly reconnaissance fighters; conversion of the Firefly I to operational trainer configuration; new production Halifax aircraft; the conversion of sixty-four Halifax to trooping duties; and the overhaul and modification of a large number of Mosquito aircraft for Turkey, Dominica and Sweden.*

At the end of the war, the site reverted to Crossley Motors under lease. This proved to be an unsuccessful venture, and production at Errwood Park ceased in 1958. After operation as a box-making factory by Hugh Stevenson Ltd until 1993, the site was sold and is now operated as an industrial park, with units let out to a number of companies. The Heaton Chapel half of the site is operated by Williams Fairey Engineering, producing military amphibious craft, portable bridging units and the like.

Trafford Park and Barton

Trafford Park Industrial Estate was the home of the British Ford Motor Company Ltd car operation from late 1911, Ford taking over the electrical works of Dick, Kerr & Co. (see Preston). Trafford Park was first used for aviation on 7 July 1911, when Mr Henry Melly landed his Blériot monoplane on Trafford Park Golf Course, on completion of the first flight between Liverpool and Manchester. A ninety-one acre aerodrome was established adjoining Ashburton Road in Trafford Park, it being used until around 1914 by The Manchester Aero

Beaufighter production at the Fairey-managed Errwood Park shadow factory. (J.W.R. Taylor)

Fairey Hendon aircraft built in Stockort were flight-tested at Barton from September 1936 until March 1937. (Ken Ellis collection)

G-ANYV is a civil conversion of Proctor IV NP308, built at Barton by F. Hills & Sons. (Via Author)

Hills & Sons modified Hurricane L1884 as the F.H.40 Mk.1 for testing of the 'slip-wing' concept. (BAE SYSTEMS plc)

Club. The aerodrome directors were based at 22 Booth Street, Manchester. The municipal aerodrome at nearby Barton was opened on New Year's Day 1930, and still operates today as the home of the Lancashire Aero Club.

During the First World War, **A.V. Roe & Co. Ltd** made limited use of Trafford Park for flight-test and occasional delivery flights. Experimental flying was subsequently moved to Hamble. One type that made its first flight at Trafford Park was the Avro 521, a single bay variant of the Avro 504, in late 1915 or early 1916.

The Fairey Aviation Co. Ltd used Barton airfield for flight-test of the Hendon and Battle, taking over the municipal hangar for this purpose. Subsequently the flight-testing of Stockport-built Fairey aircraft was carried out at Ringway. Fairey Hendon flight-testing was undertaken at Barton from September 1936 to March 1937.

F. Hills & Sons Ltd: Hills & Sons were a long-established woodworking company that obtained a licence in 1936 to produce the Praga E.114 Air Baby, as the Hillson Praga, the Praga engine being built by Jowett Cars Ltd. The company was re-structured as F. Hills & Sons Ltd from 22 April 1936.

The first British-built aircraft was exported to Australia as VH-UVP. In all, some twenty-eight Praga aircraft were built, twenty-five being registered in the United Kingdom and three exported to Australia. Registrations were allocated for seven additional aircraft, which were not completed. The characteristics of the type are indicated by contemporary advertisements which emphasised the low costs of the type: 'The Hillson Praga – Praga B 40hp, £385 cabin two-seater, dual control, 33mpg.' 'The Hillson Praga – Economy with Safety. Low price and low flying costs of the Praga, with its fine performance, special safety features. 33mpg, 80mph cruising speed. £385.'

In September 1936, a more commercial tone appeared: 'The Hillson Praga two-seater aeroplane now with Certificate of Airworthiness. Increased price of £435. Our machine has now passed the tests at Martlesham Heath, and we can now supply the machine with full C of A, enabling it to be used for flying for hire and reward.'

Perhaps it is worth recording the unlikely feat of Mr H.L. Brook who succeeded in flying a Czech-built Praga from Lympne to the Cape in sixteen days (135 flying hours) in May 1936. The first British-registered Hillson Praga was G-AEEU.

F. Hills & Sons' first aircraft was a Flying Flea G-ADOU completed in October 1935 at Barton. The company designed and built two light aircraft designs of their own, their development being stopped by the outbreak of the Second World War. These were:

- The Hillson Pennine G-AFBX of 1938, which resembled a cross between an Aeronca and a Praga, having a stubby, deep fuselage and an unconventional spoiler control system without rudder or ailerons.
- The Hillson Helvellyn G-AFKT, a mid-wing tandem two-seat monoplane powered by a 90hp Cirrus Minor. The Helvellyn was overtaken by the onset of the Second World War and did not fly until the spring of 1940, thereafter being used by the company as a communications aircraft.

One of seventy-nine Lincoln bombers built by Metropolitan-Vickers Electrical Co. Ltd. (Ken Wixey)

The 1936 announcement from F. Hills & Sons that the Hillson Praga is now available with a full C of A.

During the Second World War, F. Hills & Sons were mainly occupied in the manufacture of the Percival Proctor, building 812 aircraft. In December 1941, the company was advertising 'Aircraft and Aeronautical Plywood'. The company also came up with the 'slip-wing' concept, which consisted of fitting a monoplane design with an upper biplane wing that could be released in flight. The intention was to allow an increased take-off weight and/or the use of a shorter take-off run as a result of the much increased wing area. The upper wing was to be released in flight to allow increased performance for combat.

A small-scale experimental aircraft, the Hillson Bi-Mono was built and flown in both biplane and monoplane configuration. A release of the upper wing in flight was successfully carried out in July 1941, the Bi-Mono flying from Blackpool Airport, see entry for which for further details.

Development continued with the manufacture of a releasable upper wing for a Hawker Hurricane. The trial aircraft was known as the Hillson F.H.40 Mk 1. This aircraft was a modification of L1884, which flew at Barton in (modified) monoplane configuration in April 1943. It was moved to RAF Sealand for further trials, including testing in biplane configuration, in which form it first flew on 26 May 1943.

Metropolitan-Vickers Electrical Co. Ltd, Mosley Road Works, Trafford Park, Manchester operated an important shadow factory during the Second World War. It was reported in December 1938 that work had started on the construction of a thirty-acre factory for Metropolitan-Vickers Electrical Co. Ltd at Trafford Park, under the technical direction of A.V. Roe & Co. Ltd, who were, themselves, erecting a new factory at Chadderton.

Metropolitan-Vickers built a large number of Lancasters. Production numbers given by different sources vary, but the general consensus is around 944 Lancaster Mk I and 136 Lancaster Mk III, for a total of 1,080 aircraft. Metropolitan-Vickers also manufactured seventy-nine Lincoln bombers.

Initial production consisted of forty-three Avro Manchester, which were the initial part of an order for 100, the remaining fifty-seven aircraft from this order being completed as Lancasters. Aircraft built by Metropolitan-Vickers were assembled and flight-tested at Woodford, with a small number of the Lancasters (about twenty-two) being assembled at the Vickers-Armstrongs factory at Chester.

The initial Manchester order encountered significant difficulties in building up the production rate. The reasons cited included a new and partially equipped factory; using untrained personnel; and attempting to produce the aircraft before the actual designers of the type had yet produced a production aircraft. Success rose out of this adversity, as is illustrated by the following report: 'The many setbacks, caused by modifications, changes in policy, and, not the least, the extreme damage to the factory by enemy action in December 1940, which practically destroyed the first production aircraft, and numerous major components of succeeding aircraft, produced the fighting spirit and things were made to move.'

Many of the Mosley Road buildings in Trafford Park have now been demolished. The site to the east of Mosley Road and south of Westinghouse Road is occupied by Hotpoint and GEC Alstholme.

30,000 Rolls-Royce Merlin engines were built by the **Ford Motor Co. Ltd** at Trafford Park during the Second World War. This production was managed under the shadow factory scheme.

David Rosefield Ltd were responsible for the repair Hurricane and Corsair aircraft during the Second World War. Individual aircraft repaired included Z2484, Z2489, Z2515 and Z2565. After the end of the Second World War the company broke up large numbers of Fairey Swordfish aircraft.

Wythenshawe

A.V. Roe & Co. Ltd had a 100,000 sq. ft facility at Wythenshawe, which was used for Lancaster and York fuel tank manufacture. The buildings were intended as a bus depot, but were taken over before completion for that purpose. These buildings still survived in 2002.

Lancashire

Accrington

Bristol Aeroplane Co. Ltd: A shadow factory was established in 1939 at Clayton-le-Moors, close to Accrington, controlled by Bristol, and primarily associated with Bristol Hercules engine manufacture. The factory was taken over by **The English Electric Co. Ltd** in 1952 and used for the production of Canberra components. Production initially was of rear fuselages, but later included control surfaces, fin, tailplane and engine nacelles and parts for both the Lightning and TSR.2. The 200,000 sq. ft site passed to GEC in 1968, being used by GEC Engineering (Accrington) Ltd for a wide range of engineering work. Aerospace contracts included work on Jetstream, BAe 125, Hawk, Tornado, Shorts SD360 and Fokker 100. The site is now in use as the GEC Alstholm Clayton Business Park, and is a large factory complex divided between a wide range of industrial users.

Entwistle & Kenyon Ltd carried out the manufacture of Airspeed Horsa wing centre sections under sub-contract from **Waring & Gillow**.

The shadow factory at Accrington was created to manufacture engines, but was subsequently used by The English Electric Co. Ltd for the manufacture of aircraft components and assemblies. (BAE SYSTEMS plc)

The Hawker Hunter factory at Blackpool (centre right) was originally a Vickers-Armstrongs Wellington factory. (Author)

Blackpool

Early flying meetings (including the first officially recognised British flying meeting in 1909), which did much to popularise aviation, were held at Blackpool in Stanley Park, now the site of Blackpool Zoo, and at Squires Gate, the site of the present Blackpool Airport. Most of the major manufacturing activity described below took place at Squires Gate. Stanley Park was used for civil flying after the First World War, with G-AACJ, the last Armstrong Whitworth Argosy, being used by United Airways for joy rides as late as 1936.

A.V. Roe & Co. Ltd, like other manufacturers facing hard times after the First World War, supplemented their income with a fleet of joy-riding machines. An aerodrome for pleasure flights was operated in 1919 on Blackpool South Shore opposite the Star Inn. Twelve Avro 536 (Bentley rotary powered Avro 504) were built at Manchester specifically for use at Blackpool.

Hawker Aircraft Ltd: the Vickers-controlled Squires Gate shadow factory, covering some 2.25 million sq. ft, was re-opened in the 1950s to meet the priority need for Hunter production as **Hawker Aircraft (Blackpool) Ltd**. The first contract for Blackpool production was dated 15 August 1953, the first aircraft built being WW599. Production included twenty-six F. Mk 1, 177 F. Mk 4 and ninety-six Mk 50 for Sweden. After the 1957 Defence White Paper, production of the two-seat variants of the Hunter (the first forty-five of which had been intended to be completed at Blackpool) was brought back to Kingston. As a result, the Blackpool factory was then closed.

F. Hills & Sons Ltd constructed a small experimental aircraft, the Hillson Bi-Mono, so named because it was configured as a biplane for take off, but could release the top wing in flight to improve performance. The Bi-Mono was a small-scale (20ft span) proof of principle demonstrator to provide evidence to support a subsequent test programme using a modified Hawker Hurricane. The Bi-Mono aircraft flew from Squires Gate on 16 July 1941 and was filmed (from a Hudson) releasing its upper wing whilst flying over the sea. The release took place at 4,500ft at 4 p.m. whilst five miles due west of Blackpool Tower. There was no significant change in trim upon release, although there was a gentle and controlled sink.

On test in its biplane configuration, the aircraft had such a low wing-loading that it could fly at very low speeds, where there was very inadequate elevator control authority available. This caused some concern over how to recover should the aircraft be thrown into the air by a bounce on landing.

The related 'slip-wing' Hurricane L1884 (known as the Hillson F.H.40 Mk 1) was test-flown from RAF Sealand.

Lancashire Aircraft Corporation Ltd: During the Second World War, this company repaired several hundred Beaufort and Beaufighter aircraft. It had a number of associated companies, including Samlesbury Engineering Ltd (see below, and Samlesbury), and Yeadon Engineering Ltd. The company is best known for its post-war freight operations using Halifax and Halton aircraft. In mid-1947, a fleet of more than twenty aircraft was in operation, including (in addition to the Halifax/Halton) Rapide, Consul, Proctor and Auster aircraft. The company also operated the last de Havilland DH86 Express in airline use. Operating bases included Stanley Park, Squires Gate, Stansted, Yeadon (where the company leased the terminal building and a hangar from 24 May 1947) and Bovingdon.

Samlesbury Engineering Ltd purchased **Edgar Percival Aircraft Ltd** in 1958, acquiring the rights to the Edgar Percival E.P.9 Prospector light utility aircraft, and a number of incomplete airframes. The company name was changed to **Lancashire Aircraft Co. Ltd**, this company setting up a facility at Blackpool Airport for the assembly of the type, which was marketed as the Lancashire Prospector. Two aircraft, G-APWX and G-APWY, were flown at Squires Gate before production was transferred to Samlesbury in 1960 (see also Samlesbury).

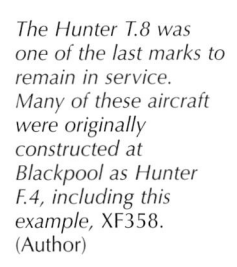

The Hunter T.8 was one of the last marks to remain in service. Many of these aircraft were originally constructed at Blackpool as Hunter F.4, including this example, XF358. (Author)

Vickers-Armstrongs Ltd: The major shadow factory at Squires Gate (Blackpool Airport) was a product of the pre-war expansion schemes and was managed by Vickers-Armstrongs using a large number of local sub-contractors for component supply. A total of 3,406 Wellington aircraft were built at Blackpool, in seven marks ranging from the Mk IC to the T.XVIII. The main Blackpool production variants were the Mk III (780), Mk X (1,369) and the Mk XIII (802). The first Wellington from this factory (a Mk IC) was delivered in August 1940; the last (Mk X RP590) was delivered on 25 October 1945.

Burnley

Earnshaw & Booth of Burnley has been identified by Barry Abraham as a sub-contractor to **Waring & Gillow**, manufacturing Horsa wing centre-section components.

Burtonwood

Burtonwood was used by an RAF Maintenance Unit (No.37) that specialised in American types. In the period up to 1942, the RAF MU handled an extraordinary range of American types including Martin Maryland (first aircraft assembled on 29 June 1940), Brewster Buffalo, Curtiss Mohawk, Douglas Boston conversions to the night fighter Havoc, Martin Baltimore, B-17C Fortress Mk1, Curtiss Cleveland, Vought-Sikorsky Chesapeake, Fairchild Argus and Vultee-Stinson Vigilant. After 1942, the Repair Depot became the main British centre for repair of American-built airframes and engines, handling virtually every American type in operation in the UK.

The Fairey Aviation Co. Ltd: The Avions Fairey designer E.O. Tips was manager and chief engineer of the Burtonwood Repair Depot from 1940 to 1943, and was subsequently head of the Fairey Aviation Experimental and Research Department. The Fairey civilian factory site, which began operations in 1940 as Burtonwood Aircraft Repair Depot, was on the opposite side of the airfield to the RAF MU. From July 1942, **The Fairey Aviation Co. Ltd** and **The Bristol Aeroplane Co. Ltd** jointly managed this site as **Burtonwood Repair Depot Ltd**.

Wellington T.10 MF628 was originally built as a B.X at the Squires Gate shadow factory. It is now displayed in the RAF Museum. (Author)

The Moss M.A.1 G-AEST prepares to take part in the 1950 King's Cup Air Race. (Alec Brew)

Chorley

Moss Brothers Aircraft Ltd: The origin of the company was the paint manufacturer H.G. Moss Ltd of Chorley. W.H. Moss, of that company, formed a new company for the purpose of aircraft manufacture, known as Moss Brothers Aircraft Ltd (but also sometimes referred to as **Mosscraft Ltd** (see *The Aeroplane*, June 1950) on 1 January 1936 with his four brothers. The company built two attractive low-wing monoplanes, the Pobjoy Niagara powered M.A.1 G-AEST flown on 6 September 1937, and the Cirrus Minor powered M.A.2 G-AFMS. The M.A.1 was initially flown in a cabin configuration seating two in tandem, and then converted (as the Mosscraft Sports) to open cockpits. In 1949 it was further converted into a single seater. The M.A.2 was flown in 1939 in open cockpit form and subsequently converted to a cabin configuration. Both aircraft continued to fly into the 1950s. Regrettably, the M.A.1 was destroyed in a fatal accident during the 1950 King's Cup Air Race, killing W.H. Moss.

Barnoldswick and Clitheroe

The Rover Co. Ltd: Rover operated a shadow factory at Waterloo Mill, Clitheroe from the end of 1940 that was actively involved in the development of the Whittle jet engine. Rover built the Whittle W.2B/26, which ran in March 1942, and was destined to enter production as the Rolls-Royce Derwent. Waterloo Mill has now been replaced by a housing estate, one of its roads being named Whittle Close. Rolls-Royce took over the Rover Co. factory at Barnoldswick in April 1943, thus creating the Jet Engine Division of Rolls-Royce.

Darwen (Near Blackburn)

Snellings Light Aircraft Service, 404 Blackburn Road, Darwen. This company was advertising in 1936: 'Flying Flea: all parts and materials in stock. Distributors of the famous Anzani engine. Place your order now for early delivery. We invite you to visit our works and inspect a number of machines in various stages of construction.' A single Flying Flea G-AEDM was built by Snellings.

Heysham

Mr J.G.A. Kitchen constructed an annular winged tractor biplane in 1910, which was hangared at Famine Point, and tested on Middleton Sands. Although it was not flown successfully, the machine was purchased by Mr Cedric Lee, who continued experimenting with this and subsequent annular wing designs (at Shoreham, West Sussex). Mr Kitchen also tested an annular winged biplane glider from Sellet Bank, near Kirkby Lonsdale, tests continuing throughout 1912.

Preston, Lancashire (Strand Road)

This site has been dominated by the activities of Dick, Kerr & Co. and The English Electric Co. Ltd and their successors, which are discussed chronologically below.

Dick, Kerr & Co. of Strand Road Preston was registered as a public company on 31 May 1890. The company works were situated on both sides of Strand Road, a disused factory on the eastern side of the road being acquired in 1897, and a new factory being built on the western side of the road. The western factory was the property of The English Electric Manufacturing Co. Ltd (which had itself been incorporated in November 1899). The company also had a slipway and hangars on the Ribble estuary at Lytham St Annes (rented from The Admiralty, which had requisitioned the land from the estate of Squire Clifton), and a seaplane assembly facility at South Shields. The main types manufactured by Dick, Kerr & Co. included the Felixstowe F.3 and F.5 flying boats. Contradictory data are available for the production quantities for these types.

- Felixstowe F.3: fifty aircraft from N4230, some of which were stored without engines. This order is believed to have been made up of thirty-five F.3 built by Dick, Kerr & Co. and tested at South Shields, with an additional fifteen aircraft stored there unflown. A second order for fifty F.3 from N4100 was completed as a mixed order of F.3 and F.5 (see below).
- Felixstowe F.5: an order for fifty F.5L aircraft from N4730 was cancelled. The second order for fifty F.3 was modified to become a mixed order for eighteen F.3 and thirty-two F.5 of which only eleven F.3 and two F.5 were actually delivered.
- N.4 Atalanta – serial number N119. For discussion of the history of the N.4 class, refer to the entry for the **Phoenix Dynamo Manufacturing Co. Ltd** at Bradford, West Yorkshire. N119 Atalanta Mk I used a hull built by **May, Harden & May**,

The Preston factories of The English Electric Co. Ltd had their origins with Dick, Kerr & Co. and continued in use by BAC and British Aerospace before their closure in 1993. (BAE SYSTEMS plc)

A Dick, Kerr & Co.-built Felixstowe F.3 photographed at Preston in 1918. (BAE SYSTEMS plc)

Only one English Electric Ayr was built, its unusual configuration without wing-tip floats proving to be unsuccessful. (JMB/GSL collection)

which was moved by a circuitous route to Lytham, for assembly in the sheds on the Ribble estuary. Although the aircraft was completed in 1921, it was not flown until 4 July 1923, having been taken, again by road, to the Isle of Grain.

The aviation department of **The English Electric Co. Ltd** was formed by combining **Dick, Kerr & Co.** (of Preston), **Phoenix Dynamo Manufacturing Co. Ltd**, and **Coventry Ordnance Works** in December 1918. Following the merging of these companies, the aviation activity was carried out at Preston.

The English Electric Co. Ltd continued to use the Lytham hangars of Dick, Kerr & Co. until 1926 for flying boat assembly and testing; aircraft being built at Strand Road, Preston. English Electric built two types of flying boat of their own design, the Ayr and the P.6 Kingston. Work on the Ayr began in 1921, the type being intended for use in fleet gunnery spotting. The Ayr used the wing roots of its lower wings to provide lateral stability on the water, rather than fitting the more usual wing-tip float. The single example built (N148) was not launched until 1925, and then proved to be unsuccessful. A planned second example was cancelled.

Still flying at Old Warden, the Wren motor glider achieved a remarkable performance, but was not the basis for a practical light aeroplane. (Author)

The complex structure of a Kingston flying boat hull was hardly suitable for mass production. (BAE SYSTEMS plc)

The first English Electric design to be completed and flown was the Wren motor glider, which was designed to enter the 1923 Motor Glider Competition. The first example (J6973) was flown for the first time at Ashton Park, Preston (just north-west of the factory) on 5 April 1923. After three flights, testing continued from 8 April at Lytham sands. The Wren was designed to meet an official specification (S1) for an ultra-light training machine and could hardly have been more different from the large flying boats that Dick, Kerr & Co. had previously built at Preston. With its 398cc motorcycle engine and empty weight of only 232lb, the Wren achieved the quite remarkable performance figures of a maximum speed of 64mph and an economy of 87.5 miles per gallon. Three Wren motor gliders were built, two of which competed in the Lympne trials.

The last and numerically most successful design of this period was the English Electric P.6 Kingston, which was powered by two Napier Lion engines, each of 450hp. Instructions for the construction of a single prototype Kingston were given on 20 January 1923, under contract AM/333124/22 and the first example N168 was moved by road from Preston to Lytham for assembly in April 1924, followed by initial testing in May 1924. Unfortunately, this prototype hit a submerged timber during these first taxiing trials on 22 May 1924, tipping vertically nose down and being further damaged during its salvage. Five additional Kingston were built, the penultimate aircraft N9712 being completed with a duralumin hull as the Kingston II. The last aircraft N9713 was flown from Lytham for delivery to RNAS Felixstowe on 16 March 1926, after which the aviation department was shut down.

The designer W.O. Manning left English Electric at this time, moving on to Simmonds Aircraft Ltd. During the 1920s and 1930s, English Electric at Preston built power stations, electric rolling stock, trams and bus bodies for use all around the world. The English Electric hangars at Lytham were used from 1932 until 2001 by Cooksons Exhibition Bakery.

Aircraft manufacture was re-started at Preston in 1939, following conversion and expansion of the factory for aircraft manufacture when The English Electric Co. Ltd was included in Scheme L of the shadow production scheme to expand the RAF. The main types manufactured by English Electric at Preston were as follows: Hampden, Halifax and Vampire. English Electric went on to build aircraft at additional factories at Samlesbury and Warton (including the Canberra and Lightning), these facilities remaining in use under BAC, BAe and BAE SYSTEMS.

In 1939, 225 Hampden aircraft were ordered, this marking the return of English Electric to aircraft construction. In all, 770 Hampden and 2,145 Halifax aircraft (of Marks II, III, VI and VII) were manufactured at Preston (Strand Road), before being assembled and test flown at Samlesbury. The initial Halifax order was received on 30 April 1940. A number of other local sites (a foundry, a car showroom, a cotton mill and a bus depot) were taken over in support of aircraft production. The peak production rate for the Halifax was eighty-one aircraft in a single month, this being achieved in February 1944.

English Electric received an order for 120 de Havilland Vampire in June 1944, setting up a design office in the offices and showroom of Barton Motors in Corporation Street, Preston. At around the same time, W.E.W. Petter joined English Electric from Westland, and work began on what was to become the most successful English Electric design, the Canberra.

The first Preston-built Vampire flew in April 1945, one year after the transfer of production from Hatfield. English Electric subsequently built the majority of the single-seat Vampires, production including F.1 for the RAF (174), Sweden (seventy) and Switzerland (four), F.3 for the RAF (117), RCAF (eighty-five), India (three) and Norway (four), and large numbers of FB.5, including aircraft exported to Italy and South Africa. Components were manufactured at Strand Road, with assembly and flight-test at Samlesbury. Total Vampire production extended to 1,359 aircraft.

The company's most successful design was the twin-engine Canberra. A total of 1,376 Canberra were built from 1949 to 1959; 925 of these aircraft were built in Britain by the following companies: The English Electric Co. Ltd (631), Short Bros. & Harland Ltd (144), A.V. Roe & Co. Ltd (seventy-five) and Handley Page Ltd (seventy-five). Forty-eight Canberra were constructed in Australia, and a total of 403 Martin B-57 were built in the United States of America. Twenty-three countries operated the type and it remains in service in 2004.

The Canberra was followed by the supersonic English Electric P.1A. The P.1A, after completion of its development, entered service with the RAF as the Lightning. Development aircraft were built at Strand Road and assembled at Samlesbury, the first P.1A WG760 flying at Boscombe Down on 4 August 1954. Details of Lightning production are provided under the entry for Warton.

Lightning centre and rear fuselage join at Preston. (BAE SYSTEMS plc)

English Electric Aviation Ltd was formed on 9 January 1959, following the announcement that the Government would not award contracts against GOR.339 (for TSR.2) other than to a consortium. As a precursor to the formation of the British Aircraft Corporation, The English Electric Company Ltd created English Electric Aviation Ltd to separate its aviation and non-aviation assets. The English Electric Co. Ltd (the 'electric' part of the business) retained the western part of the Strand Road site, and the Accrington production facility, passing the eastern part of the Strand Road site, together with Warton and Samlesbury on to English Electric Aviation Ltd.

The English Electric Aviation Ltd part of the Strand Road site at Preston has now been demolished and is awaiting re-development, although the GEC-Alstholm site on the western side of Strand Road remains in use.

British Aircraft Corporation (BAC): See Warton.

British Aerospace: The Strand Road site (previously used by English Electric and transferred to BAC) was closed in 1993 as a result of re-structuring announced in November 1990, and the eastern part of the site was demolished.

Fishers of Preston was identified by Barry Abraham as a sub-contractor to **Waring & Gillow**, manufacturing Horsa wing centre-section components.

Samlesbury Airfield (near Blackburn)

Samlesbury was used as a wartime factory of **The English Electric Co. Ltd**, continuing with **English Electric Aviation, British Aircraft Corporation (BAC), British Aerospace (BAe)** and **BAE SYSTEMS**. The site came into use to provide flight-test facilities following the re-start of aircraft production at Preston, with hangars being constructed at Samlesbury from April 1939, followed in the summer of the same year by the construction of tarmac runways. Aircraft were manufactured at Strand Road and then assembled and test flown at Samlesbury. The first type to be built was the Hampden, followed by the Halifax. In all, English Electric built 770 Hampden and 2,145 Halifax, all of which were test flown at Samlesbury. The first Hampden P2062 was moved by road from Preston to Samlesbury on 31 December 1939, flying for the first time on 22 February 1940; production continued until 15 March 1942. Peak production rate for the Hampden was fifty-three aircraft per month, this being achieved in April 1941. The first English Electric-built Halifax V9976 flew at Samlesbury on 15 August 1941 and the last on 30 November 1945.

Samlesbury was also used to carry out a range of engineering modifications to the Avro Lincoln, 200 aircraft being processed through Samlesbury up to the end of 1948.

Samlesbury was subsequently used for Vampire testing, more than 1,350 of these aircraft being test flown here. The first example TG274 was flown on 20 April 1945. The Vampire was followed by Canberra production test flying, and Lightning assembly and first flight. All English Electric-built Canberra aircraft, with the exception of the first prototype, were built and flown from Samlesbury. Manufacture of the Lightning was continued under **English Electric Aviation** and the **British Aircraft Corporation** (BAC). Production Lightning aircraft were first flown at Samlesbury but, being unable to land there, were flown directly to Warton to continue their flight-test programme from there. Details of Lightning production are provided under the entry for Warton.

Under **BAC**, Samlesbury was used in the main for:

- Lightning production and component manufacture.
- TSR.2 wing and centre fuselage work prior to the cancellation of this programme.
- Manufacture of the wings for the SEPECAT Jaguar programme (between 1972 and 1985).
- Significant Canberra overhaul, repair, modification and refurbishment for export was carried out at Samlesbury throughout the 1960s and early 1970s.

British Aerospace/BAE SYSTEMS: The Samlesbury site has produced major airframe components for a range of products, including T-45 Goshawk sub-assemblies and Tornado fin, and forward and rear fuselage production. Samlesbury also made a major contribution to the Harrier programme, with the supply of components for the Harrier II Plus, FA.2, T. Mk 10 and GR. 7 variants. In late 1998, it was announced that a major package of Tornado spares responsibility including the fin, canopy, tailerons, wing leading edge and engine bay doors was to move from Samlesbury to Chadderton.

Samlesbury was used by English Electric and BAC for production flight-testing. The site is now a major manufacturing facility for the Eurofighter. (Author)

The return of English Electric to aicarft production came with pre-war expansion contracts, initially for Hampden. The first aircraft P2062 emerges into the snow at Salmesbury prior to its first flight in February 1940. (BAE SYSTEMS via Ken Ellis)

Halifax II W1048 is an English Electric-built example, preserved in the RAF Museum at Hendon. (Author)

Under BAE SYSTEMS, Eurofighter Typhoon major components are being manufactured at Samlesbury in the Eurofighter Machining Centre. The construction of the Machining Centre has required some 3,700 tonnes of concrete and twenty-eight miles of steel reinforcing bar. This facility is used for the manufacture of light alloy structural details such as fuselage frames, including over 100 major structural components for Eurofighter. Construction for the civil

Vampire completion in No.2 shed at Samlesbury in October 1945 with Halifax aircraft in the background. (BAE SYSTEMS plc)

The peerless Lightning was built at Samlesbury with production test-flying at Warton. (Author)

TSR.2 fuselage mate-up at Samlesbury. (BAE SYSTEMS plc)

Canberra refurbishment at Samlesbury. (BAE SYSTEMS plc)

The E.P.9 Prospector was built at Stapleford and, by Lancashire Aircraft Corporation, at Blackpool and Samlesbury. (J.S. Smith)

aircraft industry includes an extensive range of leading and trailing edge components for the Airbus series, and the supply of engine mounting struts for all Rolls-Royce powered Boeing 747 aircraft. In 2002, BAE SYSTEMS announced that they were investing in a 5,000 sq. ft production and assembly facility for JSF structures at Samlesbury.

Samlesbury Engineering Ltd purchased **Edgar Percival Aircraft Ltd** in 1958, acquiring the rights to the E.P.9 Prospector, together with a number of unassembled aircraft. A facility was set up at Blackpool to assemble these aircraft, which then became known as the

Lancashire Prospector. From 1960, production was moved to Samlesbury, ceasing in July 1961 after a further five aircraft had been assembled there. Samlesbury Engineering Ltd also built the hull of Donald Campbell's famous jet-powered speedboat *Bluebird*.

The activities of the company prior to its manufacture of the Lancashire Prospector were summarised in contemporary advertising: 'Samlesbury Engineering Ltd. Main constructors of Mr Donald Campbell's record breaking *Bluebird*. Specialists in aircraft conversions, repairs, modifications and all types of overhauls. Manufacturers of major assemblies and components for the famous Vickers Viscount. Samlesbury, Squires Gate, Stansted.'

Samlesbury was one of several operational bases of the **Lancashire Aircraft Corporation Ltd** (see also the entry for Blackpool).

Warton

Warton airfield was constructed in 1940, as a satellite of RAF Squires Gate. Its major Second World War role was, however, as USAAF Base Air Depot No.2, Warton airfield handling the maintenance and repair of vast numbers of Mustang and Liberator aircraft. At its peak, more than 10,000 personnel were stationed on what became the second largest US maintenance facility in Britain, the site being handed over to the control of the USAAF on 17 July 1943. More than 14,000 aircraft passed through Warton, including 4,372 P-51 Mustang, 2,894 B-24 Liberator, 711 A-26 Invader, 360 B-17 Flying Fortress and 338 P-47 Thunderbolt. The other Base Air Depots were No.1 at Burtonwood and No.3 at Langford Lodge, Northern Ireland.

The English Electric Co. Ltd and **English Electric Aviation Ltd**: The first use of Warton by English Electric occurred from August 1947 to July 1948, English Electric being responsible for high altitude and high Mach number trials using Gloster Meteor IV EE545, operating from Warton. From May 1948, the Canberra design team began to move onto the site.

The English Electric Canberra, designed by W.E.W. (Teddy) Petter was, to quote Don Middleton, '…a jet-age Mosquito', produced in large numbers in a huge variety of marks for

Warton, the primary military flight-test centre for English Electric Aviation, BAC and BAE SYSTEMS, lies immediately to the north of the Ribble estuary. (Author)

RAF and export use. The prototype VN799 was first flown at Warton on 13 May 1949. Advertising copy in 1950 included: 'Canberra B. Mk 1 designed and built by The English Electric Co. Ltd. Designers and Constructors of Aircraft since 1911'. The prototype of an interdictor version, the B(I). Mk 8 was flown on 23 July 1954. The B(I). Mk 8 is distinguished by its tandem seat canopy offset to the port side of the fuselage.

A similar arrangement was adopted for the high-flying photo-reconnaissance Canberra PR.9. The PR.9 also featured an increase in wing area and span, together with more powerful engines to maximise operating altitude. This variant was built by Shorts at Belfast, the prototype flying on 8 July 1955.

As I write (in 2005), the English Electric Canberra (PR.9) is still in service with the RAF in a front-line operational role, fifty-six years after the type's first flight. The type is expected

A Canberra line-up at Warton comprising T.4 prototype WN467, B.5 prototype VX185 (later the B(I).8 prototype), production PR.3 WE135 and second prototype B.2 VX169. (BAE SYSTEMS plc)

A classic collection of BAC's most famous products, the Canberra, Lightning and TSR.2. (BAE SYSTEMS plc)

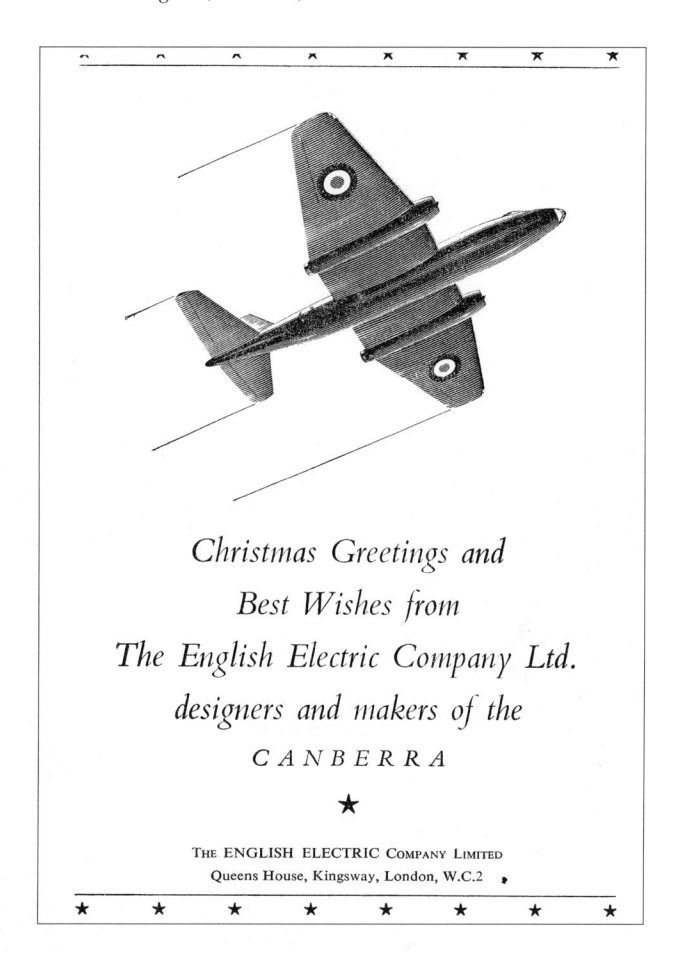

English Electric Canberra (© BAE SYSTEMS plc)

to remain in service until around 2006. Canberra upgrades and modifications are still undertaken to ensure that the PR.9 continues to meet the needs of its operational deployments (over the Gulf and Bosnia, for example). In August 1999, the five remaining RAF Canberra PR.9 aircraft received upgraded defensive aids systems, these being installed by DERA at Boscombe Down. In addition to its evident military reconnaissance role, the Canberra PR.9 has contributed to humanitarian efforts. For example, twenty-four sorties were flown in 1996 to establish the precise location of Rwandan refugee groups in eastern Zaire. The air forces of Peru and Chile were also long-standing Canberra users.

British Aircraft Corporation (BAC) Military Aircraft Division: The formation of the British Aircraft Corporation was announced on 1 January 1960, with ownership split as follows: 40 per cent English Electric Aviation Ltd, 40 per cent Vickers-Armstrongs (Aircraft) Ltd, and 20 per cent Bristol Aircraft Ltd. The appointment of company directors was announced on 18 May 1960, and the company legally came into being and began trading on 1 July 1960. In September 1960, BAC also obtained a controlling interest in Hunting Aircraft Ltd of Luton. The Warton, Preston and Samlesbury production facilities were passed from English Electric Aviation to BAC in 1963. The various entities within BAC were fully consolidated by 1 January 1964, at which point the individual parent company trading names effectively disappeared.

BAC at Warton is, perhaps, best known for the impressive Lightning interceptor, which was dramatic both in appearance and performance. Lightning production was carried out at Samlesbury. The Lightning was the production version of the English Electric P.1A and featured many unusual design features. These included: a twin engine configuration with the engines installed one above and to the rear of the other in a deep, narrow fuselage; a low thickness chord ratio wing of sixty degrees sweep; ailerons installed across the wing tips; and (due to the low volume available in the wing) flaps sealed to act as fuel tanks. The P.1B prototype XA847 was first flown at Warton on 4 April 1957; the first F.1 was flown on 29 October 1959; the T.4 on 6 May 1959; the F.2 on 11 July 1961; the F.3 on 16 June 1962; and the T.5 on 29 March 1962.

Different figures can be found for total Lightning production. A reasonably consistent listing (excluding conversions between marks) is a total of 340, broken down as follows: two P.1A (WG760, 763), one test airframe, three P.1B prototypes, twenty P.1B development aircraft, a further test airframe, twenty F.1, twenty-eight F.1A, fourteen F.2, thirty F.2A, sixty-three F.3, two T.4 prototypes, twenty T.4, twenty-two T.5, sixty-two F.6, forty-five F.53 and seven T.55. The last Lightning flight was made from Warton in December 1992. The author can attest to the excitement of seeing the last of these aircraft flying at Warton, even at the very end of their career.

Test flying of the TSR.2 was transferred to Warton from 22 February 1965. At this time, the aircraft had completed fourteen flights and had already flown supersonically. Early undercarriage and engine vibration problems had been solved, and the aircraft was demonstrating excellent performance and outstanding handling. A total of only twenty-four flights had been completed when the programme was cancelled in April 1965.

English Electric P.1, P.1B (© BAE SYSTEMS plc)

English Electric's thoroughbred Lightning (in this case F.6 XS901) is seen flying from Warton. (BAE SYSTEMS plc)

The Jet Provost Mk 5 was developed by BAC at Warton, following closure of the Luton site. (Author)

The Jet Provost line was transferred to Warton following cancellation of the TSR.2 programme, resulting in closure of the Luton site. BAC then developed and produced the Jet Provost Mk 5, and its armed derivative the BAC 167 Strikemaster at Warton. 110 production Jet Provost T. Mk 5 were built for RAF use with the first of two prototypes (converted from the last two production T. Mk 4 aircraft) being flown at Warton on 28 February 1967. Five Jet Provost Mk 5 were built for Sudan. The production of other marks of Jet Provost included 185 T.4 and 201 T.3; total production of all marks for the RAF and six export countries was 588 aircraft.

The first BAC 167 Strikemaster G-27-8 was flown on 26 October 1967. The Strikemaster had a more powerful engine and eight weapon stations. The aircraft proved to be an export success with some 144 aircraft ordered by Saudi Arabia, South Yemen, Oman, Kuwait, Singapore, Kenya, New Zealand and Ecuador. Data from the BAE SYSTEMS North West Heritage Group indicate that a total of 266 Jet Provost and Strikemaster aircraft were built at Warton.

BAC formed part of the **SEPECAT** team producing the Anglo-French Jaguar, the initial agreement enabling this activity being signed very shortly after the TSR.2 cancellation. SEPECAT was formed in May 1966, and produced 403 Jaguar, supplemented by ninety-four

Left: A spirited display by a BAC167 Strikemaster, photographed at Old Warden in 2003. (Author)

Below: The Tornado has been produced in large numbers by BAE SYSTEMS as part of the Panavia Aircraft Gmbh. consortium. This example was photographed at Yeovilton. (Author)

Opposite: The Tornado Air Defence Variant was developed as a long-range stand-off fighter and serves with the RAF and the air forces of Saudi Arabia and Oman. (BAE SYSTEMS plc)

export aircraft, and aircraft manufactured by Hindustan Aeronautics Ltd (HAL). The first of three British-built Jaguar development aircraft S-06/XW560 was flown at Warton on 12 October 1969. The first production Jaguar GR. Mk 1 XX108 was flown on 11 October 1972.

RAF orders comprised 165 single-seat and thirty-five two-seat aircraft. Export sales included thirty-five single-seat and five two-seat aircraft for India, followed by licensed production of more than 100 aircraft in India. Sales were also made in Ecuador, Nigeria and Oman. In late 1998, upgrade programmes were underway in the UK, Oman and Ecuador. The Indian fleet is in excess of 120 aircraft, with the HAL production line having been re-opened to produce a new batch of fifteen single-seat aircraft. In late 1998, HAL were about to commence construction of a further seventeen two-seat aircraft.

In 1973, BAC signed a major contract, taking over responsibility for the provision of equipment, ground support and facilities to the Saudi Arabian Air Force, which had ordered the Strikemaster and Lightning in 1968. This contract and those that have followed under BAe and BAE SYSTEMS have been of great commercial significance to the company. In addition to the ground support and infrastructure elements, Saudi Arabia has operated the Lightning, Strikemaster, Tornado, HS125, Hawk and Pilatus PC9. A large workforce remains employed in Saudi Arabia and a key element has been the training of Saudi nationals to take on an increasing role in this programme. The various contracts are managed by a dedicated team in Warton.

British Aerospace (BAe)/BAE SYSTEMS: BAE SYSTEMS participates in the Tornado programme as part of the tri-national (UK, Germany, Italy) **Panavia Aircraft Gmbh** consortium, and in Eurofighter 2000 as part of the four-nation (UK, Spain, Italy, Germany) **Eurofighter Jagdflugzeug Gmbh** consortium. The BAE SYSTEMS share of the Munich-based Panavia is 42.5 per cent. Panavia was formed on 28 March 1969, and the first Tornado (D-9591) flew on 14 August 1974 at Manching. The first United Kingdom aircraft XX946 (P-02) flew at Warton on 30 October 1974, with the first UK production aircraft ZA319 (BT-001) following on 10 July 1979.

Production of bomber variants for the RAF has comprised four prototypes, three pre-series aircraft (one of which was later brought up to full production standard) and 228 GR.1 (thirty-six as dual control GR.1T), plus fourteen GR.1A. Sixteen GR.1 were also converted to GR.1A. On 29 July 1994, the MoD contracted BAe to modify 142 Tornado GR.1/1A aircraft to GR.4 mid-life update standard. This features an improved avionics system, cockpit displays and enhanced low level night capability. The first production Tornado GR.4 flew for the first time on 4 April 1997 and was delivered on 31 October 1997. The final aircraft in the programme was delivered to the RAF on 10 June 2003.

Saudi Arabia has been the main (non-partner) export customer for the Tornado, purchasing an initial batch of forty-eight bomber and twenty-four fighter versions. A further Tornado buy of forty-eight additional bomber variants extended production of the type at Warton into 1998.

The EAP experimental aircraft supported technology developments for the Eurofighter. (Author)

The impressive Eurofighter is a product of quadripartite collaboration, and is a cornerstone of the European defence industry. (Author)

The Tornado F.2 and F.3 or Air Defence Variant (ADV) were developed as long-range stand-off fighter aircraft. The prototype ZA254 was rolled out on 9 August 1979, making its first flight on 27 October 1979; it was followed by two further development aircraft and eighteen production F.2. This version was superseded in production by the F.3, 147 of which were built for the RAF, plus twenty-four for Saudi Arabia and eight for Oman. The F.3 first flew on 20 November 1985. The Tornado F.3 is the subject of a Capability Sustainment Programme, which will introduce compatibility with the AMRAAM and ASRAAM air-to-air missile systems.

Including production by MBB (later DASA/EADS) and Alenia, the programme has seen the construction of a total of 992 aircraft of all variants.

The EAP experimental aircraft ZF534 was built in support of the Eurofighter programme and first flew at Warton on 8 August 1986.

BAE SYSTEMS makes up 33 per cent of the **Eurofighter Jagdflugzeug Gmbh** consortium, which was formed in June 1986 and is based in Munich. Eurofighter is responsible for the development and production of the Eurofighter Typhoon. The first of seven EF2000 development aircraft (DA1 98+29) first flew at Manching on 27 March 1994. The first British aircraft (DA2) ZH586 flew at Warton on 6 April 1994. By September 2001, the seven development aircraft had completed 1,750 flights with a total flight time in excess of 1,400 hours. The seven development aircraft were followed by three instrumented production aircraft, prior to the start of full series production.

Current production plans envisage a total of 620 aircraft, 232 for the RAF, 180 for Germany, 121 for Italy and eighty-seven for Spain. For the RAF and in export markets, the type is designated Eurofighter Typhoon, the first export order announced being for sixty aircraft for Greece, with the potential that this order may be increased to ninety in due course. This order has not, as yet, been confirmed, the final decision being delayed in a decision announced on 29 March 2001 'for at least three years'. On 23 November 2004, there were reports in the media that the Greek government intends to cancel this order and open a new procurement competition during 2005. Another order has been received from the Government of Austria for eighteen Eurofighter Typhoon aircraft, confirmation of this order being announced on 22 August 2003. The type is being offered to a number of other nations, including Saudi Arabia, Singapore and Norway, although it was reported in April 2005 that the Typhoon had been dropped from consideration in Singapore.

The main BAE SYSTEMS Eurofighter responsibilities are the ECR 90 radar, and the following airframe elements: cockpit, front fuselage, canard surfaces, centre fuselage spine, inboard wing control surfaces, rear fuselage and vertical fin. The twenty-one minute first flight of BT001, the first British series production aircraft, took place at Warton on 14 February 2003. First flights took place near simultaneously in the partner nations, with GT001 (Germany) flying on 13 February, IT001 (Italy) flying, like the British aircraft on 14 February with ST001 (Spain) following on 17 February. The first single-seat series production aircraft PS001 was flown at Getafe on 27 February 2004. The first British single-seat production aircraft (IPA 5) made its first flight from Warton on 7 June 2004.

The Typhoon Batch 2 procurement contract was signed on 17 December 2004. This covers a procurement of 236 aircraft across the partner nations, eighty-nine of these for UK use.

Hawk assembly and test was moved to Warton from Dunsfold in 1989, with the design and structural work being carried out at Brough. The first Hawk Mk 127 Lead-In Fighter (LIF) for the Royal Australian Air Force flew at Warton during December 1999. The aircraft is designed to have significant cockpit similarity to the RAAF F/A-18, thereby reducing conversion training for the latter type. Thirty-three LIF aircraft have been ordered, with the first twelve aircraft undergoing final assembly in the UK.

A new demonstrator aircraft for BAE SYSTEMS, the Hawk New Development Aircraft ZJ951, was flown for the first time on 5 August 2002. In all, the company has built six Hawk demonstrator aircraft. The first of these, ZA101, flew in 1976 and remains in use. ZJ100, which flew in 1992 also remains active, configured as a Mk 127, but due to be updated to RAF Mk 128 standard.

Sales success continues, with the most recent orders being summarised below. In July 2002, Bahrein announced their intent to order the Hawk under a contract that was signed on 28 January 2003, becoming effective on 28 March 2003. Whilst the number of aircraft ordered has not been made public, it is reported in the trade press to be six, with options for a further six. The designation for these aircraft is Hawk Mk 129. On 30 July 2003, the UK Ministry of Defence announced that it would be ordering twenty Hawk Mk 128 aircraft from BAE SYSTEMS, with an option to order a further twenty-four aircraft. Entry into service is expected in 2008, and these aircraft will support the fast-jet training requirement to provide RAF pilots for the Eurofighter Typhoon and F-35 JSF. On 3 September 2003, BAE SYSTEMS announced that the Indian Government had selected the Hawk for service with the Indian Air Force as its Advanced Jet Trainer (AJT). This contract was signed on 26 March 2004, and covers no less than sixty-six aircraft, the first twenty-four to be built at Brough and flight-tested at Warton. The remaining forty-two aircraft will be built by Hindustan Aerospace in Bangalore. Details of the Hawk order book can be found under Dunsfold, Surrey in Volume Three of this series.

An air-to-air photograph of BAe's single-seat and two-seat Hawk demonstrators. (BAE SYSTEMS plc)

The Harrier T.10 was manufactured at Warton, the prototype T.10 ZH653 being first flown at Warton on 7 April 1994. The Harrier GR.9 upgrade programme, to fit RAF aircraft with improved avionic and weapon systems capability (including the carriage of Brimstone), is also being carried out at Warton. The first Harrier GR.9 development aircraft ZD320 was flown for the first time at Warton on 30 May 2003. In December 2003, BAE SYSTEMS were awarded a further upgrade contract known as 'Capability C2', which will integrate a range of additional weapons and systems (including IR and TV variants of Maverick; Precision Guided Bomb carriage; and improved IFF) on the Harrier GR.9. This programme will also upgrade the Harrier T.10 to become the Harrier T.12 with equivalent capabilities to the GR.9.

The Warton site is also participating in the Nimrod MRA.4 programme, a substantial re-design of the Nimrod airframe and mission system. The Nimrod MRA.4 contract was placed with BAe in July 1996. MRA.4 work is carried out across the whole of the BAE SYSTEMS organisation, the main programme activities being as follows:

- Warton: overall management and completion including mission system installation.
- Brough: fuselage manufacture (front fuselage, centre fuselage, rear fuselage and unpressurised portion).
- Chadderton: inner wing manufacture.
- Farnborough: design of front and unpressurised section of fuselage; design (with Prestwick) of assemblies – tailplane, elevators, rudder, bomb bay.
- Prestwick: centre fuselage design; manufacture of assemblies; outer wing manufacture; manufacture of wing trailing edges and flaps.
- Filton: design integration of the new BMW/RR engines and overall wing design.
- Woodford: inner wing structural testing and airframe assembly.
- Boeing: mission system main supplier.
- BMW/Rolls-Royce: engine supply.

The prototype Harrier T.10 was flown at Warton in April 1994 and transferred to Dunsfold for its flight-test programme. (J.S. Smith)

One non-military aircraft to be flown for the first time at Warton was Practavia Sprite G-BCWH, in February 1979. (Author)

- Dassault: sub-contract design work on rear fuselage.
- AS&T: design work on wing trailing edges and flaps.
- Westland: sub-contract design activity on outer wing.

The Nimrod programme has proved difficult for BAE SYSTEMS, and on 19 February 2003 it was announced that the programme was being re-shaped to reduce risk. Rather than move directly to the production of eighteen aircraft as originally anticipated, the programme is to focus on the completion of three development aircraft. Production of the remaining fifteen aircraft would resume once the development activity had shown sufficient progress toward maturity to allow the price of the remaining aircraft to be set with confidence. On 21 July 2004, the Minister of Defence, Geoff Hoon, indicated in a statement to Parliament that the number of Nimrod MRA.4 to be procured would be further reduced to twelve.

Two non-military types to have their first flights at Warton were Practavia Sprite G-BCWH in February 1979, and Procter Petrel G-BACA in June 1979, the latter having been built by BAC apprentices at Strand Road, Preston.

Merseyside

The following unitary authorities are included within the Merseyside area: Knowsley, Liverpool, St Helens, Sefton and Wirral.

Aintree

Aintree Racecourse was the scene of Liverpool's first flight, made by S.F. Cody on 15 November 1909. The **National Aircraft Factory No.3** was located at Aintree and managed by the **Cunard Steamship Co. Ltd**. The factory was built at the Government's expense and managed by Cunard, work on its construction beginning on 4 October 1917. All building work was completed within nine months, by which time aircraft were already being completed. This was a significant undertaking, the largest buildings measuring some 700ft by 500ft. In addition, a six-mile power cable had to be laid and a new siding constructed to connect the site to the Lancashire & Yorkshire Railway. A 370ft-deep well supplied water for the factory.

Contracts included the production of some 120 Bristol F.2B Fighter from an order for 500 aircraft. The first aircraft was handed over on 7 June 1918 some eight months after the start of construction of the factory. A further contract to build 500 Sopwith Snipe was cancelled. The NAF employed a workforce of some 2,600, more than 1,000 of whom were women. The factory passed to Government control on 17 October 1918.

In this general area, **Waring & Gillow Ltd** undertook production of propellers and DH9 structure (wings and fuselages) using workshops at Liverpool and Lancaster. Whilst the details were, at the time of writing, still being researched by Barry Abraham and Nick Forder, the Waring & Gillow output was potentially used by a number of concerns, these including NAF.3 at Aintree, Vulcan Motor & Engineering Co. (1906) Ltd at Crossens and Alliance Aeroplane Co. Ltd at Acton.

The Planes Ltd biplane was built by Handley Page Ltd at Barking, where this photograph was taken. The machine was flying at Freshfield Sands by September 1910. (JMB/GSL collection)

A view across Cunard National Aircraft Factory. (J. & C. McCutcheon)

Interior of the Cunard Factory. (J. & C. McCutcheon)

Freshfield (between Southport and Crosby)

Compton Paterson, Freshfield Sands: The first Compton Paterson biplane was built by **Liverpool Motor House Ltd** in 1910 and was first flown on 14 May 1910, proving to be a highly successful design. This machine was described as 'a Curtiss-type biplane' and initially featured an Anzani three-cylinder engine, this being replaced in due course by a more powerful Gnome engine. The type used a pusher propeller and a tricycle undercarriage. It was used for a mail service between Freshfield and Southport in October 1911, being flown by Mr G. Higginbotham.

The second machine, built for Compton Paterson by **Lawton's Motor Body Works** of Cricklewood, was more in the Farman/Boxkite style. This aircraft was distinguished from the normal Boxkite by the ability readily to remove the outer wings for ease of transport. It was built in 1911, flying for the first time on 18 October; it was then taken to South Africa, where it later crashed.

Planes Ltd/Mersey Aeroplane Co. of Freshfield had offices at 6 Lord Street, Liverpool, and works at Duke Street and Cleveland Street, Birkenhead. Planes Ltd was formed by W.P. Thompson. A large biplane with two pusher propellers was constructed in 1909 by Handley Page at Barking, to Mr Thompson's design. This machine was flying successfully at Freshfield from September 1910 until early December of the same year.

Freshfield aerodrome was reported in 1910 as having five hangars, the locally based machines being a Curtiss biplane belonging to Mr Paterson, two Blériots, a Henry Farman biplane, and the biplane constructed by Planes Ltd, which was flown by Mr Fenwick. In July

The sweep of sand at Freshfield now seems an unlikely site for pioneer flying activity. The flat firm sand, space and lack of obstacles were, however, a significant advantage. (Author)

1911 G. Higginbotham gained his Royal Aero Club certificate (No.96) flying 'his 50hp Gnome biplane'. This was probably the original Compton Paterson machine, which was purchased by Mr Higginbotham. Another local flier was Mr Melly, who was to set up the Liverpool Aviation School at Waterloo Sands, Bootle in 1911. In August 1911, the aerodrome was advertising 'flying rights over several miles of hard smooth beach, very broad (probably the best flying ground in England)' and had hangars available for rent.

In November 1911, Mr Fenwick was test flying the Planes Ltd monoplane at Freshfield. By February 1912, it was reported that this aircraft had now flown a distance of 100 miles without defect. Entered for the 1912 Military Trials, this unconventional monoplane crashed during the trials, fatally injuring R.C. Fenwick. The monoplane featured a nose-mounted engine, with an extended drive shaft to a pusher propeller mounted behind the wings, the tail being supported by (visually) very flimsy tail booms. In May 1912, Planes Ltd sold their monoplane and licence thereto to **Mersey Aeroplane Co**. Thereafter, the aircraft was known as the Mersey monoplane.

Freshfield Sands remain an impressive sight, with high sand dunes backing the miles of beach – one can readily imagine the attraction to a pioneer aviator of such a natural aerodrome.

Liverpool Area

J. Blake & Co. of 22 Rodney Street was advertising capacity at its Aircraft Works, South Hunter Street, Liverpool in December 1916. South Hunter Street is a narrow cobbled street in central Liverpool. There are a number of buildings in the vicinity that could have been used by Blake & Co.

The Liverpool Aviation Co. of 68 Victoria Street, Liverpool was advertising war surplus AIRCO DH6, DH9, Avro and Armstrong Whitworth aircraft for sale in January 1920.

Rootes Securities Ltd operated shadow factories at Speke and at Blythe Bridge, Staffordshire for Halifax, Blenheim I/IV/V and Beaufighter production. The purpose-built

Rootes factory at Speke included an impressive assembly hall 1,440ft long and initially 400ft wide, initially used for Blenheim construction. This factory, on which work was started in February 1937, achieved production relatively quickly, and featured a single straight production line with material and parts delivery at one end, and aircraft delivery at the other. The first Blenheim I to be built at Speke, L8362, was delivered in October 1938, some eighteen months after the commencement of the factory build. As production built up, the factory was enlarged; a number of outlying sites were brought into use to support the effort. Nos 2, 3 and 7 factories were in the local area, No.6 Factory at Burtonwood, No.8 at Meir, Staffordshire, No.9 at RAF Shawbury and No.10 at Blythe Bridge.

The precise split of Blenheim production between Blythe Bridge and Speke is not clear. Production of 250 Blenheim I, and the majority of 2,230 Blenheim IV was undertaken at Speke. Some of the last batch of Blenheim IV were manufactured at Speke, with final assembly and test flying conducted at either RAF Shawbury, or at Blythe Bridge (assembly) and Meir (test flying). The company built 942 Blenheim V, of which the majority were built at Blythe Bridge. Barry Abraham and Phil Butler, writing in *Air Britain Aeromilitaria*, Volume 30, Issue 118, indicated that two Rootes-built prototypes and fifty production Blenheim Vs were built at Speke. (Two further prototypes had been constructed by Bristol at Filton). 1,070 Halifax were manufactured by Rootes at Speke, comprising twelve Mk II, 279 Mk III, 658 Mk V and 121 Mk VII. Beaufighter production (at Blythe Bridge) included 260 aircraft from serial KV896.

The origins of the Rootes Group was with the Rootes brothers, who were Maidstone garage owners and car builders. During the 1930s Rootes acquired Sunbeam, Talbot, and 60 per cent of Humber, which owned Hillman and Commer; Rootes acquired Singer after the Second World War. The Rootes Group vehicle manufacturing business was acquired by Chrysler, and then Peugeot in the late 1970s.

Lockheed Hudson aircraft were assembled at Speke in a programme set up by **Lockheed Overseas Corporation**, facilities at Speke being taken over from February 1939. The first Hudson (N7205) arrived by sea at Liverpool on 15 February 1939, and a substantial activity followed, being subsequently expanded with additional facilities at Renfrew, and at Langford Lodge and Sydenham in Northern Ireland. The Lockheed Overseas Corporation facility at Speke was taken over by the Ministry of Aircraft Production in May 1940 as No.1 Aircraft Assembly Unit, a wide range of types being handled, including Hudson, Boston, Wildcat, Avenger, Hellcat, Corsair, Bermuda, Kingfisher, Argus, Reliant, Seamew and Helldiver.

1,070 Halifax were built at Speke in the Rootes Securities Shadow Factory, this example being photographed in November 1942. (Ken Ellis collection)

John Gaunt flying Baby Biplane of his own design and construction, at Southport, Aug. 23rd, 1911.

JOHN GAUNT,
Constructor-Aviator,
SOUTHPORT.

BABY BIPLANE
(All British)
30 h.p. Alvaston Engine.
208 sq. ft. area.
7 ft. × 4 ft. Gaunt Propeller.
Weight 600 lbs.
Speed 35-50 m. per hour.

J. BLAKE & CO.
Aircraft Works,
South Hunter Street,
LIVERPOOL

will be glad to receive communications from firms producing A.G.S. Parts, etc., to R.A.F. Specifications.

Above: *John Gaunt flying a plane of his own construction at Southport, 23 August 1911.*

Left: *J. Blake & Co. of South Hunter Street, Liverpool, parts manufacturer.*

Southport

Southport aerodrome was established during the summer of 1910, by Messrs Woodhead and Gaunt 'at the top end of Hesketh Road'. A hangar was erected, and the aerodrome boasted of '40 square miles of hard sand'.

Gaunt Aircraft built the 1911 Gaunt Baby, which was reportedly originally flown as a monoplane, and later as a biplane. In mid-1911 Mr Gaunt was making regular trips from Southport aerodrome on the 'Baby' biplane that he had made. Flying was reported regularly in *Flight* during 1911, the machine being a diminutive, unequal span biplane powered by a 30hp Alvaston engine. A two-mile flight was reported on 8 July 1911 and the machine remained in use until 22 August 1912.

Vulcan Motor & Engineering Co. (1906) Ltd of Crossens undertook sub-contract aircraft manufacture during the First World War. The main aircraft types built by Vulcan were the DH4 (100), DH9 (100), DH9A (225), and BE2C/D/E (300). Vulcan also manufactured the ABC Dragonfly engine. In this general area, **Waring & Gillow**

One of the 225 AIRCO DH9A built by Vulcan Motor & Engineering Co. (1906) Ltd at Southport. (Ken Wixey)

Ltd undertook production of propellers and DH9 structure (wings and fuselages) using workshops at Liverpool and Lancaster. Whilst the details were, at the time of writing, still being researched by Barry Abraham and Nick Forder, the Waring & Gillow output was potentially used by a number of concerns, these including NAF.3 at Aintree, Vulcan Motor & Engineering Co. (1906) Ltd at Crossens and Alliance Aeroplane Co. Ltd at Acton.

Post-war, Vulcan became part of the Bean conglomerate (A. Harper Sons & Bean Ltd) – a far-reaching group set up for large-scale vehicle production and including interests in a number of firms which, like Vulcan, had manufactured aircraft (e.g. The Regent Carriage Co., ABC Motors Ltd) or were suppliers of car components. This group acquired 60 per cent of Vulcan's car and commercial vehicle factory at Crossens. Production exceeded demand, however, and the enterprise had to be massively restructured. Vulcan continued in existence with a relationship with Lea-Francis, unhappily marred by the unreliability of the Vulcan engine.

Crossens contains a large brick-built factory site, whose entrance is dated 1907; this is the previous Vulcan Motor & Engineering Co. (1906) Ltd factory. It was, in 1997, used by Dorman Traffic Components Ltd and by Phillips Components.

Waterloo Sands, Bootle

The Liverpool Aviation School, of Sandheys Avenue, Waterloo, Liverpool was set up in March 1911 by Mr Henry Melly, previously of Freshfield, and was equipped with one single-seat and one two-seat Blériot. Two hangars were erected, and a third, Anzani powered, Blériot was subsequently assembled here by Mr Melly.

Northumberland and Tyneside

The following unitary authorities are included within Northumberland and Tyneside: Gateshead, Newcastle-upon-Tyne, Sunderland, North Tyneside and South Tyneside.

Boldon Flats, Northumberland (East of Gateshead)

The **Welford** monoplane, built at Mansion House, North Hylton, Sunderland, was flown here in May 1910. The aircraft had features resembling those of both the Blériot and Antoinette monoplanes, but used ailerons rather than wing warping for lateral control.

> SIR W. G. ARMSTRONG, WHITWORTH & CO., LTD.,
>
> AIRCRAFT WORKS, NEWCASTLE-ON-TYNE.
>
> DESIGNERS AND MANUFACTURERS OF
> HIGH CLASS AIRCRAFT.
>
> CONTRACTORS TO H.M. ADMIRALTY AND WAR OFFICE.
>
> Telephone: 500 Gosforth.   Telegrams: Armstrong Aviation, Newcastle-on-Tyne.

Left: *Sir W.G. Armstrong, Whitworth & Co. Ltd (Gosforth).*

Below: *BE2C production at Gosforth, with the FK1 visible to the left.* (Ray Williams)

Cramlington

Sir W.G. Armstrong, Whitworth & Co. Ltd: The Armstrong Whitworth F.M.4 Armadillo was test flown from RAF Cramlington in September 1918.

Gosforth

Sir W.G. Armstrong, Whitworth & Co. Ltd: This company came into being with the merger between the engineering firm Sir W.G. Armstrong & Co. Ltd and the Manchester firm Sir Joseph Whitworth & Co. Ltd in 1897. The first aircraft built was a Farman constructed in 1912 at the Elswick works and sold to A.V. Roe at Brooklands. The main types produced at Newcastle by Sir W.G. Armstrong, Whitworth & Co. Ltd included:

- Royal Aircraft Factory BE2: eight BE2A, twenty-five BE2B and about fifty BE2C.
- FK.3 – an improved BE2C with simplified structure (150 by Armstrong, Whitworth, with an additional 350 ordered from Hewlett & Blondeau, of which at least 225 were completed).
- FK.8 (prototype (FK.7), plus orders for 1,652 FK.8, 702 from Armstrong Whitworth & Co. Ltd, and 950 ordered from Angus Sanderson & Co. Ltd. Not all these aircraft were necessarily completed and some were delivered as spares).
- 250 Arab-powered Bristol F.2B Fighter.

The aircraft department was formed in 1913, with components initially manufactured in the Elswick sawmills at Scotswood on the River Tyne. When the involvement of the company in aircraft manufacture was first announced, it was stated that the aviation department was developing at Selby. 'Aircraft are to be built at Gosforth until manufacture can be transferred to Selby, where the company has a flying ground.' Aircraft manufacture never moved to Selby, however, which remained the province of the company's airship activity. (The main airship

The FK.2 was an improved version of the BE2C that led directly to the FK.3, some 500 of which were ordered. This aircraft was photographed at C.F.S. Upavon and shows the BE2C fin and rudder and separate cockpits which distinguish the FK.2 from the FK.3. (JMB/GSL collection)

An RFC FK.3 A8103 undergoing camouflage trials at Orfordness, photographed on 26 June 1916. (JMB/GSL collection)

shed at Barlow, three miles south east of Selby was 700ft long and boasted a door opening that was 150ft wide and 100ft high. It was dismantled during the 1920s).

The chief designer, F.W. Koolhoven, came from the British Deperdussin Co. and designed a clean and attractive tractor biplane, the FK.1, which was flown in September 1914 but did not enter production. The first Government contract was for two BE2A, which were built in one of the Elswick sawmills' shops in April 1914, with BE2B aircraft being manufactured from August of that year. Owing to inadequate space, larger premises (a disused skating rink) were taken over at Gosforth on the outskirts of the city. The BE2A/B/C was then built. BE2C production ran at four to six per week, and, as elsewhere, aircraft production increased apace throughout the First World War.

An improved version of the BE2C was then developed. First came the FK.2, which was essentially a cleaned-up BE2 with improvements intended to ease its manufacture and an

The FK.9 was a clean quadruplane design, but did not enter production. (JMB/GSL collection)

Angus Sanderson Ltd were a major contractor for the Armstrong Whitworth FK8. (JMB/GSL collection)

oleo-sprung undercarriage; seven were built. The FK.3 was effectively a production version of the FK.2, although it differed in that the pilot and observer positions were reversed from those of the BE2. The two crew were also placed closer together in a linked cockpit for better communication and the type featured a more angular fin and rudder than the FK.2. At its peak, FK.3 production built up to twenty to twenty-five per month. The crew arrangement of the FK.3 was retained in the FK.8, which used the large Beardmore water-cooled engine. The FK.8 was an Armstrong, Whitworth design that was comparable to the Royal Aircraft Factory RE8; although successful, it was not built in as large numbers as the RE8. The FK.8 first flew in May 1916. The FK.3 and FK.8 were known, respectively, as the 'Little Ack' and the 'Big Ack'.

Not all Mr Koolhoven's designs were as successful. The bizarre FK.5 triplane featured twin lateral gunner's pulpits to allow an arc of fire outside the propeller. The design was to re-emerge as the FK.12. The FK.9 quadruplane was a clean design, but it also failed to enter production. An enlarged quadruplane, the FK.10 reached limited production with prototypes constructed by Armstrong, Whitworth, five production machines from Angus Sanderson and three more from Phoenix Dynamo of Bradford. It is not clear whether all these aircraft were completed, however. The 250 Bristol F.2B fighters, referred to above, were constructed after the departure of Koolhoven to BAT in 1917.

Initially, flying was conducted from the west end of Duke's Moor, part of Newcastle's Town Moor. This was considered not sufficiently safe, and a new aerodrome was set up in June 1916 in the north-east corner of the main Town Moor. Town Moor was also used as **No.9 Aircraft Acceptance Park**. In November 1915, the company was advertising as 'Designers and Manufacturers of High Class Aircraft. Contractors to HM Admiralty and War Office'.

By the end of 1917, the Armstrong, Whitworth works were reported to be building 80–100 aircraft per month (some 423 aircraft were in fact built during 1917, and 429 during 1918, rather less than is suggested by the previously quoted construction rates). The aircraft department at Newcastle built a total of 1,275 aircraft before it was closed down in October 1919.

Sir W.G. Armstrong, Whitworth & Co. Ltd purchased the shares of the **Siddeley-Deasy Motor Car Co. Ltd** in February 1919. A parent company, **Armstrong Whitworth Development Co. Ltd**, was set up as a result in May 1919. Two subsidiary companies were created in mid-1920, these being **Armstrong Siddeley Motors Ltd** and **Sir W.G. Armstrong Whitworth Aircraft Co. Ltd**.

In December 1926, the **Armstrong Whitworth Development Co. Ltd** (including **Sir W.G. Armstrong Whitworth Aircraft Co. Ltd** and **Armstrong Siddeley Motors Ltd**) was sod to Sir John D. Siddeley. The holding company was renamed **Armstrong Siddeley Development Co. Ltd** in March 1927. The aircraft business conducted its operations at Parkside, Coventry, with other works being developed at Whitley Abbey, Baginton and Bitteswell.

The **George & Jobling** 1910 biplane made several successful flights at Gosforth and was exhibited at the 1910 Olympia Show. The design appears to have been Farman inspired.

Sir Wm. Angus, Sanderson & Co. Ltd of St Thomas Street, Newcastle was originally a coachbuilder, and later a motor manufacturer. The factory is now occupied by part of Durham University. Aircraft production contracts comprised:

- 250 Bristol F.2B Fighter from E2651, many delivered to store.
- Orders for 900 Armstrong Whitworth FK.8, the first being C3507. Some 788 of these aircraft were delivered, Angus Sanderson sharing production of this type with Sir W.G. Armstrong, Whitworth & Co. Ltd.
- Up to five Armstrong Whitworth FK.10 Quadruplanes from an order for fifty. The FK.10 was unsatisfactory in service and those built were allotted for use as targets. In

G-BEBO is a rare two-seater development of the Currie Wot, known as the Turner Super Wot (TSW 2). (Author)

addition to those constructed by Angus Sanderson, three were ordered from the Phoenix Dynamo Manufacturing Co.

Angus Sanderson also built car bodies for Armstrong Siddeley Motors Ltd.

Heaton

The **Lowe** HL(M)9 Marlburian, G-EBEX, was designed and constructed by F. Harold Lowe in 1921, but crashed in November 1922. This side-by-side, two-seat, shoulder wing monoplane with a 50hp Gnome, bore a passing resemblance to a Morane monoplane. A company, **Northern Aerial Transport Co.**, was set up to market the type, which was one of Britain's first post-First World War homebuilt aircraft.

Hunday (Newton Hall, Northumberland)

The **Turner** Super Wot is a two-seat derivative of the Currie Wot. The first aircraft G-BEBO was flown in markings advertising Hunday Farm Museum. G-BEBO was first flown in June 1979 and was based at Usworth. The type first attended a PFA Rally in 1985.

Newcastle-upon-Tyne

John Dawson & Co. (Newcastle-on-Tyne) Ltd had a number of works and offices in the Newcastle area. These included Victoria Works, City Road, Newcastle; offices at 2 Collingwood Street; further works at St Lawrence Road; and also Wallsend Aircraft Works. The company advertised using the slogan 'Aircraftsmen', with the telegraphic address 'Dependable, Newcastle on Tyne'. In 1919, the company announced its return to the furniture business thus: 'Contributory to the Nation's need for aircraft during the War, they now contribute to the Nation's need in furniture in the re-establishment of England's homes – in the firm conviction that war shall be no more'. In January 1920, John Dawson & Co. was in liquidation, with its stock to be sold on 6–8 January.

The **Northern Aircraft Co. Ltd** of Saville House, Saville Row, Newcastle upon Tyne was registered in February 1914 and took over the **Lakes Flying Co.**, Windermere, Cumbria, which see for further details.

South Shields

Dick, Kerr & Co. established a number of seaplane and flying boat sheds at South Shields, these being ready for use by February 1918. Felixstowe F.3 flying boats were moved across country from Preston by steam-driven lorry for testing at South Shields. It took some three days (of what must have been very hard work) to traverse the route, passing from Preston through Skipton, Harrogate, Thirsk, Stockton and Sunderland. A total of thirty-five F.3 were tested here, the last on 28 February 1919. Six of the F.3 aircraft that had been tested here, and a further fifteen unflown aircraft, were stored at South Shields, the Dick, Kerr facility having been taken over as a Marine Aircraft Acceptance Depot. The buildings were eventually passed to the Royal Air Force in December 1919.

Usworth (Sunderland)

Kendal Mayfly: An entrant in a PFA design competition, the Mayfly G-PFAK is a high-wing T-tail pusher homebuilt, which was built in Sunderland and was first flown at Usworth in June 1981.

The **Turner** Super Wot G-BEBO first flew in June 1979 and is based at Usworth (see also Hunday).

The site at Usworth has been redeveloped as a Nissan car factory.

East Yorkshire

Brough Aerodrome

Brough has been almost exclusively the preserve of the Blackburn Aeroplane & Motor Co. and its successor companies, the evolution of which is described below.

The **Blackburn Aeroplane & Motor Co.** began activity at Brough during the First World War to support seaplane production contracts. The company used sheds on the Humber for the erection and testing of Leeds-built Sopwith Baby seaplanes. Phoenix Dynamo also used these same sheds for the erection of their Bradford-built Short 184 aircraft. 186 Sopwith Baby were built by Blackburn in Leeds and tested at Brough. The Admiralty commandeered the hangar and slipway in 1916 as No.2 Marine Acceptance Depot.

In February 1921, the company was advertising, 'Blackburn Aircraft – Pioneers since 1909. Specialists in Torpedo Aircraft'. A common First World War slogan used by Blackburn was: 'Always at the Front'. The principal Blackburn-designed types included the following (it should be noted that other production figures can be found for some of these types):

- Kangaroo twin-engine maritime patrol bomber, later adapted as a civil transport. Twenty were built, the first B9970 flown at Brough at the end of December 1917.
- Swift carrier-borne torpedo bomber – prototype N139 and some seven export demonstration examples. Led to the successful Dart.
- Dart carrier-borne torpedo bomber, 117 built. Prototype N140 flown in October 1921.
- The modestly successful but curiously named Blackburn Blackburn entered service in 1923; sixty-two were built.
- Ripon – general-purpose coastal patrol and torpedo landplane or seaplane. Prototype N203 was first flown at Brough on 17 April 1926. Four prototypes were built, followed by twenty Ripon II, forty Ripon IIA and thirty-one Ripon IIC for the Fleet Air Arm. Blackburn built a single Ripon IIF for Finland, which was followed by an additional twenty-five manufactured in Finland (*Blackburn Aircraft since 1909*).

Aircraft under construction at Brough in the early 1920s including a civil Kangaroo conversion; Dart fuselage; and the towering incomplete fuselage of a Blackburn Cubaroo in the background. (BAE SYSTEMS plc)

- Baffin torpedo bomber – a Pegasus-powered version of the Ripon, initially flown as B-5 on 30 September 1932. Most late production Ripon were converted to Baffin. Twenty-nine new-build aircraft were supplemented by sixty-eight Ripon conversions.
- Shark general-purpose shipboard reconnaissance and torpedo bomber – prototype first flown as B-6 (later K4295) at Brough on 24 August 1933. 270 built, comprising the prototype, 237 for Fleet Air Arm service (sixteen Shark I, 126 Shark II and ninety-five Shark III), six Shark II for Portugal and a total of nine aircraft exported to Canada (seven Shark II and two Shark III). A further seventeen Shark III were built in Canada by Boeing Aircraft of Canada at West Georgia Street, Vancouver, BC.
- Bluebird – civilian light aircraft – for further details, see below.
- B-2 side-by-side, all metal, biplane training aircraft first flown (G-ABUW) on 10 December 1931 – forty-two built. The one preserved example, G-AEBJ, is still capable of smooth and graceful aerobatics as testimony to the fine handling of the type.
- Skua carrier-borne dive bomber – two prototypes built plus 190 production aircraft. Prototype K5178 was first flown at Brough on 9 February 1937.
- Roc naval fighter with gun turret, equivalent in concept to a naval Defiant – the first aircraft L3057 was flown for the first time on 23 December 1938, the type being put into production at Boulton Paul, Wolverhampton. A total of 136 Roc were built.
- Botha twin-engine torpedo bomber and reconnaissance aircraft – 380 built at Brough and 200 at Dumbarton, see further details below.
- Firebrand – a gloriously rugged naval torpedo strike aircraft whose development was delayed by slow engine development and low priority for the engines that were available. For further details, see below.

The Blackburn "SHARK" combines the duties of a Torpedo Plane – a Medium Bomber – a Reconnaissance aeroplane and a Gunnery Fleet Spotter · It can be fitted with float or land undercarriage and represents the most efficient form of COASTAL DEFENCE

A 1936 advertisement for the Blackburn Shark for torpedo operations and general duties (© BAE SYSTEMS plc)

The Shark was a very successful general-purpose shipboard reconnaissance and torpedo bomber. This is RCAF 525, the first of two Shark Mk. III (Canada) to be built by Blackburn, photographed on 31 December 1938, whilst undergoing trials at Brough in floatplane configuration. (BAE SYSTEMS plc)

The first Blackburn Bluebird side-by-side two-seat biplane had its origins as an intended entry in the 1924 Lympne two-seat light aeroplane trials. The design began to gain acceptance after it was fitted with the Genet engine for the 1926 Lympne trials, flying in this form on 4 June 1926. This aircraft was subsequently registered as the Bluebird I G-EBKD. Thirteen wooden Bluebird II and seven Bluebird III were built before the type was effectively redesigned with an all-metal structure as the Bluebird IV.

The prototype Bluebird IV G-AABV was flown on 23 February 1929. Fifty-eight were built (fifty-five by Saunders-Roe), but by the time that the Bluebird had reached this fully developed state, the de Havilland Moth was too firmly established to be displaced. In May 1930, Blackburn were competing hard with the Moth, and did not disguise their opinions of their more successful competitor in their May 1930 advertising: 'Fly as you drive: side-by-side. ... It had to come, of course. I mean, take this plane with its all-metal construction, side-by-side seating, baggage locker, self starter and compare it with the old bus where you shouted into telephones, and one of you looked at the other's back all the time.'

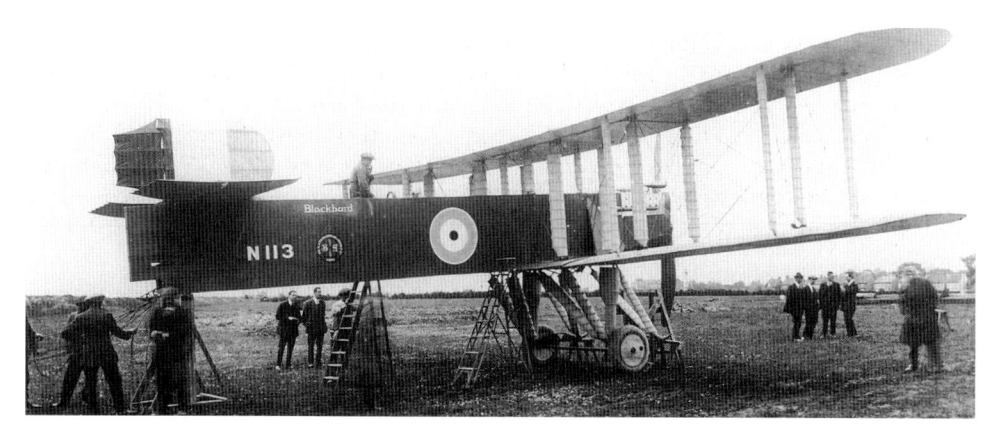

The Blackburn Blackburd was described by Harald Penrose as 'unspeakable ugly'. This is the first of three to be built. (BAE SYSTEMS plc)

The type was used for long-distance flying as the mount of The Hon. Mrs Victor Bruce, who used Bluebird IV G-ABDS for a solo flight around the world, starting from Heston on 25 September 1930, returning to her point of departure in February 1931.

The Blackburn Dart was described, reasonably accurately, as 'functional rather than aesthetic'. In my opinion, however, it did not even come close to the unlovely Blackburn Blackburd in this regard! The late Harald Penrose clearly shared this view, describing the Blackburd as 'uncompromisingly ugly'. Three Blackburd were built, the prototype N113 flying from Brough at the end of May 1918. As if vying for the title of least complimentary description of an aircraft, it is worth noting a further Blackburn contender, the Napier Cub-powered Cubaroo, N166. This was a single-engined aircraft of nearly 90ft wingspan, which was described by C.G. Grey as 'looking like a docile cow in a field'. Only two were constructed.

The Blackburn Iris all-metal biplane reconnaissance flying boat first flew from the Humber in June 1926, being succeeded by the Iris III (three built), which first flew in November 1929. Although, with its three Rolls-Royce Condor engines, the Iris was undeniably impressive in appearance, only nine were built in five different marks. The Iris was followed in 1933 by the equally dominant Perth.

During the late 1920s and early 1930s, contracts were few, and Blackburn, like the rest of the industry, produced a series of prototypes more in hope than expectation. Some examples include:

- The F.1 Turcock single-seat fighter built as a private venture against a possible Turkish contract and flown on 14 November 1927.
- The RB.2 Sydney, an all-metal monoplane flying boat for reconnaissance and coastal patrol powered by three Rolls-Royce F.XIIMS and first flown (N241) on 18 July 1930.
- The Nautilus two-seat Rolls-Royce F.XIIMS-powered fighter reconnaissance biplane N234, which flew in May 1929 and competed unsuccessfully against the Osprey.
- The Beagle, a Jupiter-powered day bomber (or torpedo and coastal patrol aircraft) N236, which was first flown on 18 February 1928.
- The Blackburn C.15 'Civil Monoplane' G-ABKV and the closely related 'Civil Biplane' G-ABKW. These aircraft were ordered for comparative trials for monoplanes and biplanes designed to meet the same requirements.

The Sydney featured a pylon-mounted wing with an upswept tail with three rudders having no fixed fin surfaces. At the time of its first flight, the Sydney was the largest monoplane flying boat to have flown in Britain. Other unsuccessful designs included the Airedale, Nautilus, Sprat, M.1/30 and F.7/30.

In spring 1928 Blackburn produced the Lincock I 'mini-fighter' – a 22ft 6in span biplane G-EBVO powered by a 240hp Lynx engine and noted for its aerobatic capabilities. All-metal versions were built, these being the civil Lincock II G-AALH (flown in autumn 1929), and Lincock III G-ABFK flown in 1930. Four additional Lincock III were exported for military use, two to China and two to Japan. The Lincock was the subject of glowing advertising as follows:

Blackburn Lincock – metal single seat fighter and two seater advanced training machine. Adopted for foreign service.

A quote from a pilot who had recently tested the aircraft followed:

Having flown a number of single-seaters, I can think of none to compare with this remarkable little aeroplane. I was immediately struck by its incomparable manoeuvrability and lightness of control,

The Blackburn Lincock had 'amazing performance' and 'phenomenal manoeuvrability'. (BAE SYSTEMS plc)

which combined with its sturdy construction, gives one an amazing sense of security. The pilot's position is extremely comfortable, while the vision is exceptionally good for an aeroplane of this type. With its astounding performance, simplicity and freedom from vice, I consider the 'Lincock' to be the perfect single-seater.

Among other contemporary reports one finds descriptions such as 'amazing performance' and 'phenomenal manoeuvrability', suggesting that the advertising material was not far from the truth.

Blackburn produced a metal fuselage derivative of the Segrave Meteor as the Blackburn Segrave, following the accidental death of Sir Henry Segrave in his speedboat *Miss England II*. Three aircraft of this type were built by Blackburn, the first (G-ABFP) flying on 9 February 1931. Blackburn built the fuselages for all these aircraft, wings for the first two being supplied by Saunders-Roe Ltd. The final aircraft had an experimental wing with a tubular spar designed by Mr F. Duncanson, which offered considerable saving in weight compared with the original design. This third aircraft (G-ACMI) was designated the Segrave II and first flew on 2 February 1934.

The Shark was advertised in February 1936: 'The Blackburn Shark combines the duties of a Torpedo Plane – a Medium Bomber – a Reconnaissance Aeroplane and a Gunnery Fleet Spotter. It can be fitted with float or land undercarriage and represents the most efficient form of COASTAL DEFENCE.'

The company name was changed on 2 April 1936 to **Blackburn Aircraft Ltd**, the authorised capital being £630,000. Blackburn's flying boat activity was moved to Dumbarton in 1937 as a result of agreements with William Denny & Bros. The main types produced at Dumbarton were the Botha and Sunderland.

The Botha was designed for general reconnaissance and torpedo bomber duties, but proved to be a disappointment. The prototype L6104 was first flown on 28 December 1938. Underpowered and criticised at Martlesham for its poor handling and high landing speeds, the Botha had only a short service life (due, in part, to no less than 169 aircraft being destroyed in accidents). The type was used, in the main, for the operational training of bomber crews.

The N.11/40 Firebrand prototype DD804 first flew at Leconfield with the Sabre III engine on 27 February 1942, but protracted development meant that its production version, powered by the Centaurus engine, did not see wartime operational service. Production comprised:

- Three prototypes.
- Nine Firebrand I.
- Twelve Firebrand II, first flown (NV636) 31 March 1943.
- Twenty-nine Firebrand III, prototype (converted Firebrand II) DK372 flown on 21 December 1943.
- 102 Firebrand IV, prototype EK601, first flown on 17 May 1945.
- Sixty-eight Firebrand V (some sources give a total of seventy Firebrand V).

Another spectacular, but little known, Blackburn naval aircraft was the YA.1 Firecrest to specification S.28/43. One notable feature of the Firecrest, apart from the aircraft's awesome

Above: EK726 *is a late production Firebrand Mk.IV, one of the most imposing naval aircraft of its day. Like the later Westland Wyvern, the type suffered from protracted development problems.* (BAE SYSTEMS plc)

Left: An advertisement for the impressive *Blackburn Firebrand IV.* (© BAE SYSTEMS plc)

appearance, was its adoption of an unusual double fold in its wing structure to achieve carrier compatibility. The first Firecrest RT651 was flown on 1 April 1947, only one other prototype (VF172) being built.

Types manufactured under sub-contract at Brough included eighteen DH9A, forty-two Armstrong Whitworth Siskin IIIA, 635 Fairey Barracuda, 125 Percival Prentice, thirty Boulton Paul Balliol T.2, and a single Handley Page HP88, an experimental aircraft used in support of Victor development (see Carnaby). Substantial production of the Fairey Swordfish was undertaken at Sherburn-in-Elmet, which see for further details. Gaps in production were filled by sub-contract component manufacture. Examples of such work by Blackburn included, in 1927, fifty Duralumin wing-tip floats for the Stranraer.

During the Second World War, Blackburn carried out modifications to substantial numbers of Chance Vought Corsair and Grumman Avenger, Wildcat (Martlet) and Hellcat aircraft for RN use. Robertson's *British Military Aircraft Serials 1878-1987* lists a block of 605 Corsair from JT100, which were delivered to Blackburn for subsequent modification. To meet these needs, additional modification depots were set up under Blackburn's control at Kirkbymoorside, Leeds, Keighley and Hammersmith, in addition to the work at the Blackburn production sites and at Prestwick and Abbotsinch. Another Second World War contract was the modification of Lysander II P9105, a special Steiger high-lift wing of rectangular planform being fitted.

At the end of the Second World War, there was a degree of enforced diversification, including light alloy roof trusses, baking tins, market stalls and agricultural implements (as The Humberside Agricultural Products Co. Ltd). The Dumbarton factory, like many others, built aluminium bungalows. In mid-1947, Blackburn listed their capabilities as including, 'More than a dozen different concerns ranging from aircraft and aero engines to prefabricated houses, over 1,500,000 sq. ft of factory space, some 500 acres of flying fields for aircraft testing, 65,000 sq. ft given over to research plant...'. At this time the Firebrand featured heavily in the company's advertising, an example being, 'Blackburn Firebrand V – the Navy's Strike Aircraft', accompanied by a suitably impressive photograph or artist's impression.

The company name was changed on 1 January 1949, to **Blackburn & General Aircraft Ltd**, Robert Blackburn taking a less active role from that time due to ill health. Blackburn & General Aircraft is best known for the production of the Beverley four-engine transport aircraft, and the development of the Buccaneer naval strike aircraft. The Beverley was built by Blackburn as the productionised version of the General Aircraft Universal. The GAL.60 Universal WF320/G-AMUX was first flown at Brough on 20 June 1950. The prototype Beverley (originally styled the Blackburn and General Aircraft GAL.65 Universal Freighter) WZ889 was first flown on 14 June 1953. The first production aircraft (XB259) was flown on 29 January 1955. Forty-seven production aircraft were constructed, in addition to the aforementioned prototypes. The Beverley served with the RAF from 1956 until 1968. In 1953, Blackburn still foresaw a civilian role for the type; their advertising ran, 'The Blackburn Universal is designed and destined for the worldwide carriage of military or civil freight and passengers'.

An unsuccessful product of this period was the Blackburn YB.1, which was a competitor to the Fairey Gannet. The Double Mamba-powered YB.1 was preceded by Griffon-engined prototypes, the YA.7 (WB781, flown on 20 September 1949) and YA.8 (WB788, first flown on 3 May 1950). The YB.1 WB797 was first flown on 19 July 1950, and made its first deck landing on HMS *Illustrious* on 30 October 1950.

The Blackburn NA.39 became, in its production form, the famous Buccaneer, adoption of this name being announced on 20 August 1960. First flown on 30 April 1958, production comprised twenty NA.39 development aircraft, forty Gyron Junior-powered Buccaneer S. Mk 1, eighty-four Spey-powered S. Mk 2, sixteen S. Mk 50 for South Africa and forty-nine new production S. Mk 2B for the RAF. The NA.39 prototype XK486 was first flown at RAE

The Aircraft Manufacturers of Northern England, Scotland, Wales and Northern Ireland   151

Right: *The load carrying ability of the Blackburn & General Aircraft Beverley.* (© BAE SYSTEMS plc)

Below: *Beverley production at Brough photographed on 6 January 1955, shortly before the first flight of the first production aircraft.* (BAE SYSTEMS plc)

Bedford on 30 April 1958. The first Buccaneer S. Mk 1 XN922 was flown on 26 January 1962, with the prototype S. Mk 2 XK526 being first flown on 17 May 1963.

Blackburn & General Aircraft were absorbed into **Hawker Siddeley Aviation Ltd** (HSAL) in 1960, but continued to trade under its original identity. From 1 July 1963, a divisional structure was created, with Blackburn becoming part of the Hawker Blackburn Division; from this date onward, all products were styled as Hawker Siddeley types, rather than under the name of their original parent firm. From 1 April 1965, the company was managed through a more unified organisation and reference was no longer made to the legacy concerns from which the company had developed. HSAL acted as sister design authority for the McDonnell F-4K and F-4M Phantom and continued development and production of the Buccaneer. Buccaneer and Phantom test flying was conducted at Holme-on-Spalding Moor a few miles to the north-west of Brough.

British Aerospace (BAe)/**BAE SYSTEMS**: The Military Aircraft Division of **British Aerospace Defence Ltd** continued to support the Phantom and Buccaneer at Brough, and completed fifty Pilatus PC9 for export to Saudi Arabia under the Al Yamamah programme. The PC9 aircraft were flown into Brough and the work conducted there was limited to modifications to meet specific customer requirements and final painting.

Hawk design leadership transferred to Brough in 1988, with final assembly and test flying transferring to Warton from Dunsfold in 1989. Brough has led the development and production of the T-45, Hawk 100 and Hawk 200. Hawk aircraft are manufactured, assembled and undergo systems testing up to and including engine running at Brough. Routine flight operations ceased at the end of 1992 and aircraft are taken to Warton for flight-test, final painting and customer acceptance. In the case of the T-45 Goshawk, Boeing

Brough's post-war masterpiece, the Buccaneer S.2 is seen here in production. (BAE SYSTEMS plc)

A recent photograph of the BAE SYSTEMS factory at Brough. (BAE SYSTEMS plc)

(previously McDonnell Douglas) are responsible for manufacture of the forward fuselage up to the rear cockpit bulkhead and conduct final assembly, test and delivery of the type. All remaining structural components are manufactured at Brough. In mid-2004, the Hawk variants that were then in development and manufacture were the South African Mk120; the Mk115 for the NATO Flying Training College in Canada; the RAF Mk128; the Mk129 for Bahrain; and the Indian Mk132. Further information on Hawk production and sales can be found under the entry for Dunsfold in Volume Three of this series and under the entry for Warton in this volume.

Other activity has included new-build, and return-to-works conversions of Sea Harrier FA.2 aircraft. The last new-build FA.2 rear fuselage (NB18) was completed in 1997, and Harrier II Plus rear fuselage assembly was then transferred to Brough, with a production rate of one per month. This programme has also now been completed. Brough has also conducted Sea Fury and Swordfish rebuilds for the Royal Navy Historic Flight.

On 30 November 2002, the merger of BAe with Marconi Electronic Systems (MES) was marked by a change of identity to BAE SYSTEMS plc. In 2002, BAE SYSTEMS announced that they were establishing JSF structural test facilities at Brough in addition to those at Samlesbury.

The **Clarke Cheetah**, G-AAJK, was a light aircraft designed by J. Clarke. The Cheetah was flown as a parasol monoplane (using DH53 wings), and also as a biplane, by use of the discarded lower wings of the Halton Mayfly G-EBOO following its conversion to parasol form as the Halton Minus. The Cheetah was first flown at Brough as a biplane in 1929. Components from the Clarke Cheetah were later used in the construction of the Martin Monoplane of 1937.

Carnaby (near Bridlington)

Handley Page Ltd: The Handley Page HP88 was an experimental design built in support of the Handley Page Victor programme. The HP88 was made up from a Supermarine-designed fuselage (the Supermarine Type 521, which closely resembled a Supermarine

The experimental Handley Page HP88 VX330 was intended to support the Victor programme. This photograph was taken on 23 May 1951, just under a month before the aircraft's first flight. (BAE SYSTEMS plc)

510/Attacker), fitted with a low wing of crescent planform and a new empennage with high-set tailplane. General Aircraft Ltd initially carried out the wing and tail design, and manufacture, the work being transferred to Brough following the formation of **Blackburn & General Aircraft Ltd**. At Brough the project gained a new designation as the Blackburn YB.2. The sole aircraft, VX330, was first flown at Carnaby on 21 June 1951. The HP88 was destroyed at Stansted on 26 August 1951, after just twenty-eight flights.

Blackburn & General Aircraft Ltd: Carnaby was also used for a small number of the early development flights of the GAL.60 Universal WF320 in 1950-1952. Although the main test activity was centred on Brough, *Balloons to Buccaneers – Yorkshire's Role in Aviation since 1785* reports the use of other local airfields including Carnaby, Full Sutton and Holme-upon-Spalding Moor on various occasions between October 1950 and May 1952.

Holme-on-Spalding Moor (north east of Goole)

Blackburn & General Aircraft Ltd: Holme-on-Spalding Moor airfield was leased to support Buccaneer development, with testing of the NA.39 (twenty pre-production Buccaneer) commencing in July 1958. Aircraft to be flown at Holme-on-Spalding Moor were towed to the airfield by road from Brough on their own wheels.

Hawker Siddeley Aviation Ltd continued the development of the Buccaneer from the Blackburn NA.39. The first Gyron-powered Buccaneer S. Mk 1 XN922 was flown on 26 January 1962, to be followed by the prototype of the Spey-powered S. Mk 2 XK526 on 17 May 1963. For production details, see Brough. In September 1966, Hawker Siddeley Aviation became sister design authority to McDonnell Douglas for the United Kingdom F-4 Phantom programme. Many Phantom aircraft were tested here, but following the closure of the airfield, this activity was moved to RAF Scampton.

British Aerospace: Phantom and Buccaneer in-service support was continued at Holme-on-Spalding Moor after the formation of BAe. The last Buccaneer flight at Holme-on-Spalding Moor took place in December 1983, following which the airfield was closed and the runways were broken up and removed. The Buccaneer was phased out from RAF operations on 27 March 1994 after thirty-three years in service; SAAF aircraft had already been retired, going out of service during 1991.

A Buccaneer photographed at high speed and low-level. (BAE SYSTEMS plc via Ken Ellis)

Holme-on-Spalding Moor in its heyday. (BAE SYSTEMS plc)

Hull (Hedon)

The airfield was originally a racecourse, and was opened by HRH Prince George as (*Flight* reported) the first British municipal airfield on 10 October 1929. In fact, as reported in *Aviation in Manchester*, Manchester Council had already opened a municipal aerodrome at Wythenshawe (which was licensed on 22 April 1929), whilst completing the construction of Barton Aerodrome, which was officially opened on 1 January 1930.

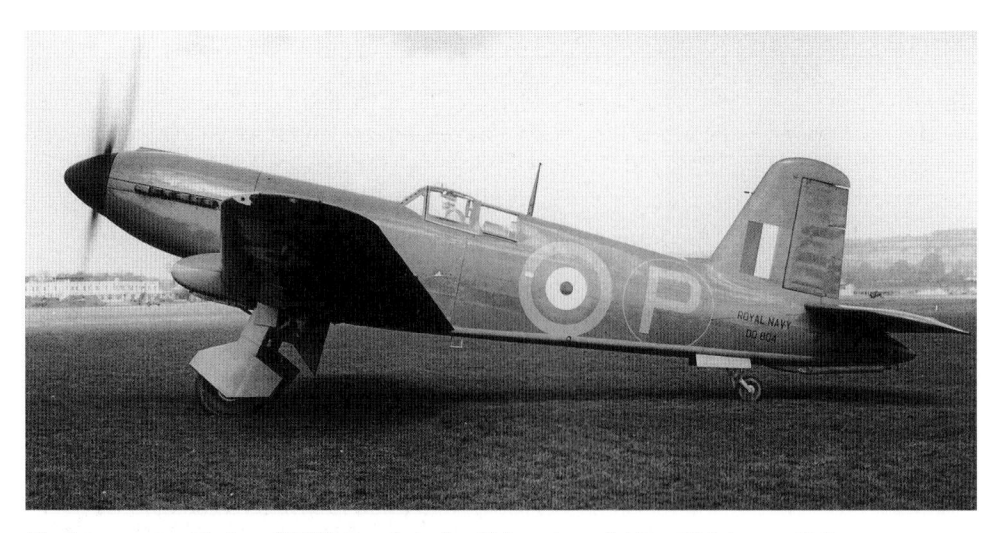

The first prototype Firebrand DD804 made its first flight at Leconfield on 27 February 1942, some twenty-five days after this photograph was taken. (BAE SYSTEMS plc)

The **Camsell** Monoplane was one of a number of amateur-built aircraft built and flown without official sanction during the inter-war years. (The interested reader is referred to Mr Ord-Hume's excellent *British Light Aeroplanes 1920-40* for comprehensive coverage of this subject). The Camsell Monoplane was a light parasol monoplane built by Mr H.N. Camsell at his home, 1 National Avenue, Hull, and flown from Hedon aerodrome. The aircraft made its first flight on 5 March 1939 and remained in use until the outbreak of the Second World War.

The Civilian Aircraft Co. Ltd, Airport of Hull, England: The Civilian Coupé was produced at Hedon from 1931 to 1933, but only five aircraft were built. The 1930 sales price was £650 fully equipped. The last surviving aircraft G-ABNT was restored to flying condition in the 1980s, flying at Biggin Hill in 1985.

RAF Leconfield

Blackburn Aircraft Ltd: The Blackburn N.11/40 Firebrand prototype DD804 first flew at Leconfield with the Napier Sabre III engine on 27 February 1942, Brough airfield then being unserviceable.

North Yorkshire

RAF Clifton (near Rawcliffe, York)

Handley Page Ltd managed a repair depot at Clifton/Rawcliffe during the Second World War. Two main sites were in operation, the first of these being close to Rawcliffe Village (to the west of the airfield), with further facilities at Water Lane to its south. Operations began in July 1941. One source indicates that some 320 Halifax were rebuilt here, together with other modification work; another refers to 2,000 aircraft being repaired and/or overhauled by this depot. Work continued after the Second World War with some 1,000 aircraft being scrapped on this site. Aircraft modification work continued until the middle of 1947.

Dishforth (East of Ripon)

Slingsby Sailplanes Ltd: The Slingsby Hengist glider DG570 first flew at Dishforth in January 1942, towed behind Whitley Z6640. Only eighteen Hengist were built, comprising four prototypes (DG570–573) and fourteen production Hengist I.

Filey Sands (between Bridlington and Scarborough)

Robert Blackburn used Filey Sands for his early flying in 1910 and 1911, renting a hangar above the slipway down to the beach. After unsuccessful trials of his initial monoplane at Marske-by-the-Sea in April 1909, the second Blackburn monoplane was flown successfully at Filey on 8 March 1911. This aircraft was followed by the series of Mercury monoplanes,

Renault-powered Blackburn Mercury I monoplane at Filey in 1911. (BAE SYSTEMS plc)

The Blackburn 1912 Monoplane operated by the Shuttleworth Trust is seen here at Old Warden in mid-2003. (Author)

production comprising a single example of the Mercury I, two Mercury II, followed by six Mercury III. These aircraft were flying at Filey, Brooklands and Hendon from mid-1911 until mid-1912.

Other early machines included two military monoplanes in 1912; and a single-seat design for Mr Cyril Foggin – this aircraft surviving in flying condition with The Shuttleworth Trust. Note that the precise identity of this machine is of some debate. Whereas most sources identify this as the aircraft built for Cyril Foggin, A.J. Jackson, in *Blackburn Aircraft since 1909*, suggests that this identification may not be correct. The case remains unproven.

Two Type I monoplanes were built in 1913, the first (for Dr Christie) being flown for the first time at Lofthouse Park, Leeds on 14 August 1913. The second aircraft, which had originally flown in landplane form on 14 December 1913, was tested unsuccessfully on floats at Lake Windermere by W. Rowland Ding. A further two-seat monoplane, the Improved Type I was built in 1914, this also being fitted with floats and flown (successfully) from Lake Windermere from 26 October 1915 until April 1916. This aircraft is also known as the Land/Sea monoplane. Note that this account reflects the information provided in *British Aircraft Before the Great War*, but differs in some respects from that presented by A.J. Jackson in *Blackburn Aircraft since 1909*. It does not appear possible to readily resolve the discrepancies between two such apparently authoritative sources.

Mr Blackburn lived in a small bungalow he had rented at Low Cliffs, nearby. B.C. Hucks (later well known for his aerobatic display flying, being the first Englishman to complete a loop) joined Robert Blackburn here to assist in test flying the Mercury monoplane. Hucks gained his Royal Aero Club certificate on the Mercury monoplane – the final glide landing was marked by the (un)timely loss of the propeller at the end of the preceding figure of eight manoeuvre! Other early fliers also flew from the beach, including the Blériot monoplane owned by the Mr Tranmer who had alerted Robert Blackburn to the suitability of this site.

In September 1912, Robert Blackburn moved his flying school to Hendon and in October advertised the Filey site for sale or let. 'Filey aeroplane shed – well constructed, 42ft by 36ft with workshop adjoining and charming three room bungalow. Fine shed with concrete floors specially built for aviation, concrete slipway to three-mile stretch of fine sandy beach and an ideal bay for hydroplane flights. (Sale £150, let £28 per annum).'

Kirkbymoorside

Kirkbymoorside is mainly known for the manufacture of Slingsby gliders and sailplanes. The firm itself has had a number of changes in identity, including the following: **Slingsby, Russell & Brown Ltd**; **Slingsby Sailplanes Ltd** (formed July 1939); **Slingsby Aircraft Ltd** (formed in 1967, following Mr Slingsby's retirement); **Vickers-Slingsby Division of Vickers Ltd** (formed 1969 after the collapse of Slingsby Aircraft following the disastrous fire of 1968); **Slingsby Engineering Ltd**; and **Slingsby Aviation Ltd**. The company is now a subsidiary of Cobham plc.

The origins of Slingsby Sailplanes were in Mr Slingsby's woodworking and furniture works at Queen Street, Scarborough. Although initial manufacture was at Scarborough (in redundant Corporation tram sheds), new premises were opened at Kirkbymoorside in September 1934.

For much of its life, the company has been famous for its gliders, including the Kite, Kadet, Tutor, Sedbergh (first flown 1944, 218 T21B built), Petrel, Swallow (106 built, first flown October 1957), Skylark (201 built, first flown March 1953), Capstan (thirty-two built, first flown November 1961), Dart (first flown November 1963), T53 (first flown on 9 March 1967), Kestrel and Vega (first flown June 1977).

The Second World War activities of Slingsby Sailplanes Ltd included the manufacture of Anson parts, and thirteen Hotspur and eighteen Hengist gliders. Slingsby were also the United Kingdom design authority for the Waco Hadrian glider. The company's main

G-AWDA *is a Slingsby T66 Nipper Series III.* (Author)

Slingsby T61F XZ564 *photographed at Kirbymoorside* c. *December 1981.* (Slingsby Aviation Ltd)

wartime production was of gliders for the Air Training Corps (ATC). The Kirby Kadet (Cadet Mk1) and the Tutor (Cadet Mk 2) were built in quantity, not only by Slingsby, but also by such firms as **Ottley Motors Ltd** (thirty), **Papworth Industries** (seventy-two), **S. Fox & Sons** and **A. Davies Ltd** (thirty), **Enham Industries**, and **Martin Hearn Ltd** (at Hooton Park). Well over 100 Grasshopper primary gliders were also built. Glider production continued post-war, and was supplemented by light aircraft activity in the form of Nipper production on behalf of **Nipper Aircraft Ltd** of Castle Donnington. The Slingsby-built T66 Nipper Mk III aircraft were significantly modified from the Tipsy-built aircraft, and can be identified by their neatly cowled engine installation.

Two Type 29B Motor Tutor powered glider conversions were constructed, the first G-AKEY flying in June 1948. A later venture into the realm of the motor glider was the single powered Capstan G-AWDV, which used a pylon mounted 45hp Nelson engine driving a pusher propeller. This aircraft was first flown on 15 February 1968.

Six Currie Wot-based SE5A scale replicas designated Slingsby T56 were built for film use, together with three non-flying replicas. The flying versions were built and delivered in the space of twelve weeks, the first example G-AVOT flying at Welburn on 20 June 1967. Slingsby also built two Tiger Moth-based Rumpler C.IV replicas G-AXAL and G-AXAM for film use, the first of these being flown at Rufforth on 24 March 1969.

The factory was severely damaged by fire on 18 November 1968 leading to a takeover by Vickers Engineering Ltd. The Slingsby T57 Camel replica G-AWYY first flew at White Waltham during March 1969. Slingsby subsequently built some thirty-five Scheibe SF25 Motorfalke motor gliders under license as the T61 from around 1970, with a further forty for the Air Training Corps, this variant being known as the T61E Venture T. Mk 2. The T61E was flown in April 1977.

Slingsby took over the production rights to the Fournier RF6B two-seat aerobatic trainer and assembled ten aircraft from French-built components, these being completed as the wooden T67A. The first example G-BIOW flew on 15 May 1981. The type was then completely re-engineered for composite construction, being produced with a range of engines as the T67B, C, M, M-MkII, M200 and M260-T3A.

The T67B (116hp Lycoming) was specifically aimed at the civilian market; the T67M (160hp Lycoming) at the military market (hence M). This version was developed with a 200hp Lycoming as the T67M200 and finally evolved to the T67M260-T3A (260hp Lycoming). The non-USA variant is known as the T67M260 and this is the current production type. The T67M was 'downgraded' for the civilian market as the T67C (although this type has also been sold to Canada for military pilot training'.

The T67M Firefly has been selected for pilot training in a number of countries. Its most notable success was the 113 T67M260-T3A delivered to the United States Air Force for use as the Enhanced Flight Screener. This success has been somewhat tarnished by the early withdrawal of the type from service following a series of accidents. No specific cause has been found, although the investigation has focused on engine and fuel system performance.

The Netherlands Government has ordered nine Slingsby T67C for use by its Civil Aviation Flying School. 281 T67 Firefly aircraft have been delivered, operating in Belize, Canada, Germany, Hong Kong, Japan, Netherlands, New Zealand, Norway, Switzerland, Turkey, UK and USA (delivered from new) and Belgium, Russia, Slovenia and Sweden (second-hand sales). In 2001, an order was received from the Royal Jordanian Air Force for sixteen T67M260 Firefly aircraft to be delivered from mid-2002. In March 2002, it was announced that three T67M260 were to be supplied to the Bahrein Amiri air force, these being delivered by March 2003. There is the possibility of a further three to be ordered by Bahrein.

As part of its desire to achieve a more diverse product base, Slingsby undertook the design and development of a wide range of composite products, including submersibles; gondolas,

The Slingsby T-67M Firefly is an all-composite development of the Fournier RF6. This photograph shows T67M200 G-BLUX, which was used as a demonstrator aircraft. (Slingsby Aviation Ltd)

Ivan Shaw's hugely successful Europa is represented here by G-EUXS, the prototype Europa XS. (Europa Aircraft Ltd)

control surfaces, propulsors and other components for the Skyship 600 airship; wind turbine blades; and some twenty-five SAH 2200 hovercraft. Slingsby took over the type certificate for the Skyship 500 and 600 following the collapse of Airship Industries in 1990. Slingsby also manufactured the major structural components for the second **CMC** Leopard G-BRNM.

The Europa light aircraft was built (in kit form) by **The Europa Aircraft Co.**, Dove Way, Kirkby Mills Industrial Estate, which, after a management buy-out became **Europa**

Management (International) Ltd on 1 August 2001. The Ivan Shaw-designed Europa single-engine, low-wing monoplane offers outstanding performance and is a two-seater of composite construction, featuring a central retractable single main wheel. Its performance figures of 150mph cruise speed on an 80hp Rotax 912 engine, 500nm range, 50mpg, and 620lb useful load truly represent unparalleled efficiency. Designed for the homebuilt and kit construction market, the Europa first flew in September 1992.

In 1997, a new model, the Europa XS, was introduced with 115hp Rotax 914T engine and increased wing aspect ratio. By November 1998 no less than 550 kits had been sold in twenty-nine countries, with more than seventy aircraft already flying. By the end of 1999, sales had exceeded 750 kits in thirty countries. On 24 November 2003, Europa Management (International) Ltd announced that the total number of kits sold had passed the significant total of 1,000 in thirty-four countries. The Europa is well on the way to becoming Britain's most successful post-war light aeroplane.

Following financial difficulties, the company was re-launched as **Europa Aircraft (2004) Ltd** 'to continue to develop and sell the Europa range of aircraft'.

Scarborough

Blackburn Aeroplane & Motor Co. Ltd: The last Blackburn type to be flown before the First World War was the Type L hydro-biplane, which was originally built for the 1914 Circuit of Britain. This was the first machine to be constructed in the Olympia Works at Leeds. The Type L was taken over by The Admiralty and tested at Scalby Mills, north of Scarborough.

Slingsby: The origins of Slingsby Sailplanes Ltd were in Mr Slingsby's woodworking and furniture works at Queen Street, Scarborough. Although initial manufacture was at

Airspeed Ferry G-ABSI first flew from Sherburn-in-Elmet in April 1932, shortly before the company moved to Portsmouth. (BAE SYSTEMS plc)

162 Sopwith Cuckoo were built under contract at Sherburn-in-Elmet by the Blackburn Aeroplane & Motor Co. Ltd. (JMB/GSL collection)

Scarborough (in the redundant Corporation tram sheds), new premises were opened at Kirkbymoorside in September 1934. See Kirkbymoorside for further details.

Selby (between Leeds and Hull)

When the involvement of **Sir W.G. Armstrong, Whitworth & Co. Ltd** in aircraft manufacture was first announced, it was stated that the aviation department was developing at Selby. 'Aircraft are to be built at Gosforth until manufacture can be transferred to Selby, where the company has a flying ground.' In practice Selby became associated with Sir W.G. Armstrong, Whitworth airship manufacturing activities at Barlow, south-east of Selby. The aircraft department remained at Gosforth, which see for further details.

Sherburn-in-Elmet Airfield (east of Leeds)

Airspeed Ltd: The Airspeed Ferry was towed on its wheels at night from York to Sherburn-in-Elmet to be test flown. The first flight of the prototype, G-ABSI, took place on 5 April 1932. Four Airspeed Ferry were built – for further details of Airspeed production, see Portsmouth and Christchurch.

The **Baynes** Bat was a one-third scale prototype (RA809) for a tank-carrying tailless glider known as the Baynes Carrier Wing. The Bat was built by Slingsby to the design of L.E. Baynes and flown at the Airborne Forces Experimental Establishment at Sherburn-in-Elmet in July 1943.

During the First World War Sherburn-in-Elmet was used as an Aircraft Acceptance Park, with twenty-one storage sheds and eight hangars in use in 1918. During the First World War, **The Blackburn Aeroplane & Motor Co. Ltd** built 162 Sopwith Cuckoo at Sherburn-in-Elmet (including thirty of a batch originally ordered from Pegler & Co.). The first of these aircraft, N6950, was first flown in early May 1918.

British Built Aircraft – Northern England, Scotland, Wales and Northern Ireland

This Royal Navy Historic Flight Swordfish is one of many built by Blackburn Aircraft Ltd at Sherburn-in-Elmet. (Author)

The experimental Alula-winged DH6 was assembled and flown at Sherburn-in-Elmet. (JMB/GSL collection)

During the Second World War, **Blackburn Aircraft Ltd** built a new shadow factory at Sherburn-in-Elmet, which took a major role in Fairey Swordfish production. This was carried out between 1940 and 1944, Blackburn building a total of 1,700 aircraft, the first example flying at the end of 1940. Many local contractors were used in support of this effort, which achieved a peak production rate of sixty aircraft per month. Significant repair and modification activity was carried out during the Second World War; 1,215 aircraft passed through the Blackburn repair organisation, most of these being repaired at Sherburn-in-Elmet.

Two examples of the **Crosby** BA-4B, G-BEBS and G-BEBT were constructed at Sherburn-in-Elmet by Dave Fenton, trading as Hornet Aviation. These aircraft were a British version of the Swedish Andreasson BA-4 biplane.

The first of the homebuilt **Practavia** Sprite aircraft to fly was G-BDDB, flown at Sherburn-in-Elmet on 16 June 1976 (see also High Wycombe in Volume Three of this series).

The Airborne Forces Experimental Establishment conducted tests of the **Hafner** Rotabuggy/Rotajeep at Sherburn-in-Elmet in late 1943 and 1944.

The **Shackleton-Murray** S.M.1 G-ACBP was a pusher parasol monoplane designed by Mr W.S. Shackleton and built in 1933 by Airspeed Ltd. The S.M.1 was an all-wood design, whose layout offered excellent view, good handling and reasonable performance. G-ACBP ultimately came to grief with a forced landing off the Isle of Wight in 1937. W.S. Shackleton had originally designed the ANEC I and II, the Beardmore Wee Bee and the giant Beardmore Inflexible. For further details of Mr Shackleton's career, see Dalmuir.

Three **Tipsy** Belfair aircraft (the edibly registered 'POD, 'PIE and 'OXO) were shipped over from Belgium in a partially finished state and erected at Sherburn-in-Elmet in 1957.

The Varioplane Co. Ltd/The Commercial Aircraft Wing Syndicate test flew a DH6 fitted with the Holle/Alula wing here, the aircraft being modified by Blackburn at

Airspeed's first factory was the Piccadilly Works, a disused bus garage in York. (Ken Ellis collection)

Construction of the Airspeed Ferry at York, with a Tern glider suspended from the rafters in the background. (BAE SYSTEMS plc)

Sherburn-in-Elmet. This aircraft, G-EAWG, was first flown on 2 January 1921 powered by a 200hp Bentley BR2 rotary.

York

Airspeed Ltd was founded on 13 March 1931 by Hessel Tiltman and Nevil Shute Norway, following the demise of the R100 airship project, on which they had both worked. Airspeed's first factory was the Piccadilly Works, a disused bus garage in York (which still survives (2004)), the office address being 10 Piccadilly Chambers, York. Its first product was the Tern glider, which was used to publicise the capabilities of the firm by breaking gliding records. Production of the three-engine Airspeed Ferry for Alan Cobham's National Aviation Displays followed in 1932, before the Company was attracted south to the new Municipal Airport at Portsmouth. Four Airspeed Ferry aircraft were built, and the prototype Airspeed Courier was also built at York, being flown from Portsmouth in April 1933. The Airspeed Ferry aircraft were flight-tested at Sherburn-in-Elmet. See Portsmouth (in Volume Two of this series) for the further development of Airspeed Ltd and its products.

The **London & North East Railway (LNER)** were responsible, among many other dispersed contractors, for the manufacture of Horsa components, including 450 sets of outer wing and aileron components, split between works at York and Doncaster.

South Yorkshire

The following unitary authorities are included within South Yorkshire: Barnsley, Doncaster, Rotherham and Sheffield.

Doncaster

Doncaster has a place in British flying history as the site of the first (unofficial) British flying meeting on 15 October 1909. This was held on the St Leger racecourse, but was badly affected by poor weather. This meeting was held effectively in competition with the first officially recognised event at Blackpool, which ran from 18–23 October 1909.

Brooklands Aviation Ltd assembled repaired Vickers Wellingtons at Doncaster, making use of the factory that had been previously occupied by Phillips & Powis (Aircraft) Ltd for the production of Miles Master aircraft (see below).

C.L. Air Surveys Ltd of The Airport, Doncaster, and at Manchester Ringway advertised 'Halifax and Dakota conversions a speciality'. Civilian Halifax aircraft that were handled at Doncaster, or registered to C.L. Air Surveys, included: G-AKJI (Air Freight Ltd), G-AIOH, and G-AIOI (C.L. Air Surveys). By September 1948, the company was in receivership.

Pegler Bros. & Co. (Doncaster) Ltd, 'Europe's largest' brass founders, built twenty Sopwith Cuckoo (N6930–N6949) from an order for fifty, the remainder being completed by Blackburn at Sherburn-in-Elmet. An order for fifty Sopwith Camel was cancelled. The first aircraft was completed in September 1918. The firm briefly continued their aircraft interests as the **Yorkshire Aeroplane Co.**, in 1919-1920. No products of this company are known, however.

G-PENY was a Sopwith Triplane replica built by **John Penny** of Eckington, and flown during the late summer of 1988. The aircraft was only loosely based on the Sopwith design, the fuselage being widened to accommodate two occupants, and power supplied by a Lycoming 0-320. Following a landing accident, David Silsbury rebuilt the aircraft in Devon. In its modified form, the fuselage was rebuilt to the original width and the engine replaced with a Warner Scarab radial for an altogether more original appearance.

Sopwith Triplane replica G-PENY is seen here in its original wide-fuselage form. (Author)

Tiger Cub RL5A-LW Sherwood Ranger G-GKFC *photographed at Henstridge in April 2004.* (Author)

Re-registered as G-BWRA and marked as N500, the aircraft was at Dunkeswell for testing during late 1996/early 1997. The first flight in its rebuilt configuration was made on 31 August 1996.

Phillips & Powis (Aircraft) Ltd received an order for 200 Miles Master to be built at Doncaster, with additional component manufacture at Sheffield. Only ten or so aircraft were actually built here, only one of which, DM200, is definitely known to have been flown at Doncaster. The remaining aircraft from this order were completed at the South Marston factory.

The **Sherwood** Ranger, a two-seat microlight biplane of very clean and pleasant lines, was first flown in October 1992. The type was being marketed by **Tiger Cub Developments Ltd** of Retford Road, Mattersey, Doncaster, in 1995. The first aircraft carried the registration G-MWND.

Westland (Doncaster) Ltd: Seventeen Lysander (W6939–6945, 6951–6960) are reported as having been built by Westland at Doncaster aerodrome, the works being used subsequently as a repair facility for Westland aircraft.

Netherthorpe Airfield (near Chesterfield)

The **Bonsall** Mustang G-BDWM is a large single-seat monoplane designed and built by David Bonsall, with styling that bears a passing resemblance to the North American Mustang. The type was selected as Best Homebuilt in the PFA Rally at Wroughton in 1991.

The **Szep** HFC125 is a single-seat, all-metal, low-wing monoplane. The sole example, G-BCPX, was flown in 1980 and was Best Original Design at the PFA Rally of that year at Leicester.

Sheffield

The **No.2 (Northern) Aircraft Repair Depot** and Aircraft Assembly Park, Coal Aston, Sheffield remanufactured various types during the First World War, including the Royal

The Bonsall Mustang G-BDWA *is one of the most powerful (if not the most attractive) of British homebuilt aircraft.* (Author)

G-BCPX *is an all-metal homebuilt aircraft constructed by Andy Szep as the Szep HFC125.* (Author)

Aircraft Factory RE8, Armstrong Whitworth FK.8, Sopwith 1½ Strutter and Sopwith Pup. The flying ground, workshops, erection sheds and hangars were located to the east of the Chesterfield Road and Dyche Lane, and to the south of the Greenhill to Jordanthorpe road.

Facilities included two flight sheds, three erecting shops and one dismantling shop together with sundry machine shops, test buildings and stores. Accommodation was provided in two camps to the north of the site, one of these being for German Prisoners of War.

The area has now been substantially altered with new roads and housing. Sheffield Tennis Centre occupies the portion of the site used for the erecting sheds and hangars. The flying field to the south of these sheds remains open space in use as playing fields.

Some 150 of the Daimler-built Royal Aircraft Factory BE12 were completed as BE12B, with 200hp Hispano Suiza engines being fitted at the Northern Aircraft Repair Depot at Coal Aston. Many of these engines were then subsequently removed for use in SE5A aircraft.

Craven Brothers of Sheffield were responsible, among many other dispersed contractors, for the manufacture of Horsa components, including 650 sets of outer wing and aileron components.

Phillips & Powis (Aircraft) Ltd built Miles Master aircraft components at Sheffield, supporting the factory at Doncaster.

Portass & Son of Buttermere Works, 70–72 Broadfield Road, Heeley, Sheffield, are reported to have built fifty Sopwith Snipe in 1918. The company was advertising in August 1918 'Aircraft, seaplane floats for all types'. The company was registered as **C. Portass & Son Ltd** in December 1918, with capital of £5,000, carrying out the business of 'Engineers, manufacturers, assemblers of aeroplanes, aeroplane parts and munitions, etc.'

Sheffield Simplex Motor Works Ltd, Tinsley, Sheffield. In July 1911 this company was advertising a Blériot cross-channel monoplane for sale – cheap. Other advertising during the First World War included, 'Central firm for the production of the ABC Dragonfly engine, acting on behalf of the Department of Aircraft Production, Ministry of Munitions' and 'Manufacturers of the Sheffield Simplex. *The most beautiful car in the world*'. This car was developed from the Brotherhood-Crocker design. The factory at Sheffield turned out up to twenty-five Sheffield Simplex chassis per month, but was not successful financially, closing in the mid-1920s.

West Yorkshire

The following unitary authorities are included within West Yorkshire: Bradford, Calderdale, Kirklees, Leeds and Wakefield.

Bradford

Bradford was the base for the Phoenix Dynamo Manufacturing Co. Ltd, which later became incorporated into the aviation interests of The English Electric Co. Ltd.

Phoenix Dynamo Manufacturing Co. Ltd, Trafalgar Works, Thornbury, Bradford. The Phoenix Dynamo company had a somewhat obscure and complex history, reflecting the rapid pace of development of the revolutionary electrical industry in the late nineteenth century. In 1895 'Phoenix' took over Wray Electrical Engineering Co., Soho Works, Thornton Road, Bradford. After a move to Hubert Street in 1896, more new works were opened at Joseph Street, Bradford in 1900. Finally, in 1903, the firm acquired the works of Rosling & Matthews (later Rosling & Flynn) at Trafalgar Works, Trafalgar Street, Manningham Lane, Bradford. This is where Phoenix Dynamo Manufacturing Co. Ltd was eventually to build aeroplanes. The Phoenix Dynamo Manufacturing Co. Ltd was itself incorporated on 11 June 1903 at Leeds Old Road, Thornbury, Bradford.

Some well-known individuals were involved in the first aircraft manufacturing efforts. These included Mr P.J. Pybus CBE (managing director), Capt. J.C. Crawshaw (managing director, Aircraft Department) and Mr W.O. Manning (technical manager) who had previously worked with Mr Howard Wright.

Aircraft known to have been built by Phoenix Dynamo include:

- Farman Longhorn (thirty ordered for use by the RNAS, and further aircraft supplied in component form for assembly by Brush Electrical at Loughborough);
- Short 184 (sixty-two);
- Short 225 Bomber (six);
- Felixstowe F.3 (thirty, plus twenty delivered to store, believed to have been produced under the supervision of **Dick, Kerr & Co.**);
- Felixstowe F.5 (fifty believed ordered from Phoenix via Dick, Kerr & Co., believed cancelled);
- Phoenix P.5 Cork (two). The Phoenix P.5 Cork N87 was first flown on 4 August 1918; the type being subsequently advertised by The English Electric Co. for civil use, although no aircraft were actually built for this role;
- Armstrong Whitworth FK.10 (two, tested at Boroughbridge).

The company advertised itself thus: 'Designers and constructors of all classes of aircraft, school machines, land bombers, chasers, patrol machines, torpedo carrying seaplanes. Speciality: LARGE FLYING BOATS.'

Phoenix Dynamo delivered its first Longhorn aircraft on 16 December 1916. Aircraft were sometimes delivered by rail (e.g. Longhorn), or by horse-drawn cart. A number were also flown out directly (usually to RNAS Killingholme) from the field next to the works. By April 1917, Short 184 seaplanes were being built, the first Phoenix-built Short 184 being flown at Great Yarmouth on 28 January 1916. Seaplane testing also took place using sheds on the Humber rented from Blackburn, and later taken over by the Admiralty as No.2 Marine Aircraft Acceptance Depot. Test flying was by pilots of the Clifford Prodger organisation. Flying boat hulls were sometimes sub-contracted to other suppliers. Thus the two Phoenix Cork hulls were constructed by **May, Harden & May**. See also **Christopher Pratt & Sons**, below.

Short 184, 8638, was the first of this type to be built by Phoenix Dynamo Manufacturing Co. Ltd at Bradford. (JMB/GSL collection)

The Felixstowe F.3 and F.5 were designed by Commander John Porte at Royal Naval Air Station Felixstowe, and drawings supplied to industrial contractors for production purposes. Aircraft of this type were ordered from Phoenix Dynamo in 1917, the precise numbers being somewhat uncertain due to the unclear contract/sub-contract arrangements with Dick, Kerr & Co. and Christopher Pratt & Sons. Flying boats were generally taken by horse and cart from Bradford to either Lytham, or Brough, for testing. Flying boat orders listed by Bruce Robertson in *British Military Aircraft Serials 1878-1987* include: (i) a mixed batch of seventy F.3 and F.5 starting at serial N4160 – at least thirty-nine of these aircraft were delivered, the first twenty-four of these being F.3 and the remainder F.5; (ii) thirty F.3 from N4400.

Phoenix were also involved in construction of the Fairey N.4 Atalanta N118. The responsibility for the hull construction and erection of the N.4 Atalanta and Titania machines is described inconsistently in various sources. The information presented here is drawn from a number of sources, including C.G. Grey's book *Sea Flyers* and Bruce Robertson's *British Military Aircraft Serials 1878-1987*, and is believed to correctly represent an undeniably complex saga. For convenience, the history of all three N.4 aircraft is summarised below.

Towards the end of the First World War, the Admiralty commissioned three large four-engine flying boats of nearly 140ft span: two Atalanta and one Titania, all known as the N.4 class. Construction and assembly of each aircraft was dispersed among a number of contractors, as follows:

- N.4 Mk I Atalanta N119: The hull for this aircraft was built by May Harden & May and was sent by road to Dick, Kerr & Co. at Lytham by a circuitous route to meet up with its superstructure. Robertson indicates that N119 was assembled by Dick,

Felixstowe F.3 fuselage production at the Phoenix Works. (JMB/GSL collection)

Phoenix P.5 Cork II N87 *at Brough*. (JMB/GSL collection)

Kerr & Co./English Electric Co. at Lytham, using a wing structure manufactured by Phoenix (other sources attribute the wing structure to Dick, Kerr & Co. themselves). This aircraft was taken by road to the Isle of Grain for test flying. Although completed in 1921, this aircraft was not flown until 4 July 1923.
- The other Atalanta (N118, which was completed but not flown) used a hull designed by Charles Nicholson and built by Gosport Aircraft Co. Ltd. (This does not correspond to Bruce Robertson's description, which states that the hull was built by Phoenix. It is, however, supported by contemporary photographs of an N.4 hull leaving the Gosport Aircraft works). This aircraft had its wing structure added by Phoenix, before being moved by road to the Isle of Grain. It was used for flotation tests but was never fully completed and remained unflown.
- The N.4 Mk II Titania, N129, had a hull of Linton Hope design. The Titania hull was constructed on the Clyde at the yard of the yacht-builders Fyffes, being delivered (again by road) to **The Fairey Aviation Co. Ltd** at Hamble for completion. The wing superstructure was manufactured in Hayes and sent 'piecemeal' to Hamble for erection. Eventually, another road journey took Titania to the Isle of Grain, where it was flown on 24 July 1925.

Throughout the First World War, work was sub-contracted by Phoenix Dynamo to **Christopher Pratt & Sons**, North Parade, Bradford (cabinet makers), and **Thornton Engineering Ltd**. Christopher Pratt received sub-contracts for the manufacture and sub-assembly of a range of components for at least six aircraft types (based on the evidence of blueprints discovered in the 1970s during building works at the company premises). These types were the Longhorn, Short 184, Short Bomber, Felixstowe F.3 and F.5, and Phoenix P.5 Cork. The Belle Vue Barracks Drill Hall, off Mannigham Lane, Bradford, was used for the assembly of some of the larger aircraft components.

One of the two Armstrong Whitworth FK.10 quadruplanes built by Phoenix Dynamo. (JMB/GSL collection)

Felixstowe F.5 flying boats being transported from Bradford to Brough. (JMB/GSL collection)

At the end of the First World War, parts were being manufactured for up to five aircraft per week. Peak employment during this period was 4,500 employees.

The English Electric Co. Ltd (Phoenix Works, Thornbury, Bradford, and Dick Lane Works, Bradford): 'The English Electric Co., which incorporates the Works of Messrs

The superlative Sopwith Triplane replica constructed by Northern Aeroplane Workshops, photographed at Old Warden in 2003. (Author)

Coventry Ordnance, Dick Kerr and Phoenix Dynamo Mfg Co., has consolidated the joint aircraft experience and plant of the three concerns in one large central factory, having exceptional manufacturing and testing facilities' (advertisement in 1919 *Jane's All the World's Aircraft*). The companies were amalgamated in December 1918 with the registered office in London, the centralisation at Bradford referred to above taking place in March 1919. The English Electric Co. stated at the time that every flying boat tested at the seaplane base at Brough had been of their manufacture.

The Phoenix Works at Thornbury (between Leeds Old Road and Gain Lane) are used today by GEC Alstholm, a successor to The English Electric Co. The dark brick works retain their Victorian character to this day. Close by lies Dick Lane, on the far side of which is Phoenix Park Sports Ground.

Heckmondwike, Dewsbury, West Yorkshire

Northern Aeroplane Workshops of Heckmondwike constructed a Sopwith Triplane G-BOCK 'N6290 Dixie II' to the original Sopwith drawings during 1990. The aircraft was (somewhat artificially) given the constructors number 153, as if it had actually formed part of the original production run. Although delivered by road to its owners (The Shuttleworth Trust) in June 1990, it did not make it first flight (at Old Warden) until 10 April 1992. The first flight was delayed by problems with the aircraft's Clerget engine, and was the culmination of a nineteen-year project.

In 1995, the Northern Aeroplane Workshops were constructing a Bristol M.1C monoplane to equally demanding standards, also for the Shuttleworth collection. This aircraft, G-BWJM/'C4918', was flown for the first time at Old Warden on 25 September 2000. The Northern Aeroplane Workshops have now moved their operations to Batley.

The pale green roof of the wartime factory of A.V. Roe & Co Ltd is seen here at the western end of the Yeadon runway. (Author)

Leeds (including Leeds-Bradford Airport, Yeadon)

Arrow Aircraft (Leeds) Ltd, Little Russel Street (off Whitehall Road), Leeds was registered on 9 April 1930. This company built two examples of the diminutive, fighter-like Arrow Active – G-ABIX and G-ABVE. The aircraft was powered by a 115hp Cirrus Hermes IIB and was intended for 'transitional training and advanced aerobatics'. When officially tested, the aircraft was found to have light, effective well-harmonised controls, and could be spun comfortably and smoothly with easy recovery at both forward and aft centre of gravity limits.

The two aircraft were built in 1931 and 1932 to the designs of A.C. Thornton, who was previously on the technical staff of the Blackburn Aeroplane & Motor Co. Ltd. (*Flight* attributes Mr Thornton with responsibility, under Major Bumpus, for the design of the original Blackburn Bluebird I).

A.V. Roe & Co. Ltd: The Avro factory at Yeadon, largest of all the A.V. Roe & Co. Ltd factories, is said to have been very carefully and cleverly camouflaged. The production facilities were partially below ground level, and the factory roof was camouflaged to tie in exactly with the surrounding countryside, complete with dummy cattle, farm walls, ponds, etc.

The main A.V. Roe & Co. Ltd production type at Yeadon was the Anson, some 3,400 of being built here. Yeadon was responsible for the later marks of Anson, the Anson XIX prototype G-AGNI making its first flight here on 30 December 1945. The last of nearly 11,000 Anson to be built, WJ561, was delivered to the RAF on 27 May 1952. Production is often quoted as 11,020, but is believed actually to have been 10,096 (reference: *Harry Holmes: Avro The History of an Aircraft Company*). At its peak of production, Yeadon was building up to 135 Anson per month. Other production by Avro at Yeadon included:

The delightful Arrow Active II G-ABVE shines like a fighter as it climbs away from the PFA Rally at Cranfield. (Author)

The last production Anson, WJ561, is seen here flying past the A.V. Roe & Co Ltd factory at Yeadon in May 1952. (BAE SYSTEMS plc)

The last of the Yeadon-built Lancasters climbs away at Yeadon in October 1945. (BAE SYSTEMS plc)

- A single Vulture-powered Hawker Tornado (R7936, built at Yeadon and flown from Woodford).
- York transports (the last seventy-seven aircraft, from October 1945).
- Lancaster (608).
- Lincoln (six examples only).

The A.V. Roe & Co. Ltd factory was closed in November 1946. This 1.5 million square foot site to the north of Yeadon airfield has now been covered with a modern pale green cladding, and remains relatively unobtrusive to this day.

The **Blackburn Aeroplane Co.** advertised in 1913 'Blackburn Aeroplanes Hydroplanes and Propellers'. The early specialisation of the company is reflected in its telegraphic address: 'Propellers, Leeds'. The company was registered as **The Blackburn Aeroplane & Motor Co. Ltd**, in June 1914 with £20,000 capital, and occupied various addresses in Leeds including (successively):

- Benson Street, off North Street, Leeds (1908 workshop, since demolished – a single room under a small clothing factory).
- 18 Spencer Place, Balm Road – disused stables rented from the Midland Railway (from early 1911).
- Olympia Works, a disused skating rink in Roundhay Road; test flying being conducted from the adjacent Roundhay Park.

Early flying was conducted at Filey, North Yorkshire, which see for further details of monoplanes flown prior to the outbreak of the First World War. During the First World War, Blackburn built the following types under contract: 111 BE2C, 186 Sopwith Baby, 162 Sopwith Cuckoo (at Sherburn-in-Elmet), and two AD Scout (other figures can also be found, for example in *The Blackburn Story 1909-1959*). A number of Blackburn designs were also produced including nine TB (Twin Blackburn); a single Blackburn Triplane N502

EVERY DESCRIPTION OF—

Metal Work for Aeroplanes, Forgings, Steel Stampings, Pressed Steel Brackets for "Gnome" and other Motors, Aluminium Seats, Iron Hangars, Steel Tape, Tanks, Wheels, Strainers, Eyebolts, Eyenuts, etc.

WHOLESALE & RETAIL MANUFACTURERS:

R. BLACKBURN & CO.,
BALM ROAD, LEEDS.

R Blackburn & Co. (Initial company name: Balm Road, Leeds, July 1911)

BLACKBURN
MONOPLANES.
TUITION.
Exhibition Flights Arranged.

The BLACKBURN AEROPLANE Co.,
BALM ROAD, LEEDS.

The Blackburn Aeroplane Co. (Balm Road, Leeds, August 1911)

The Blackburn Mercury III at Balm Road, Leeds. (JMB/GSL collection)

The Blackburn Aeroplane & Motor Co. Ltd, 'specialists in Torpedo Aircraft'. (BAE SYSTEMS plc)

flown in early 1917; two GP floatplane; and twenty Blackburn Kangaroo anti-submarine patrol bombers. The company later used a civilianised version of the Kangaroo to provide the fleet for its air transport company, The North Sea Aerial Navigation Co.

Seaplane work led to activity at Brough (which see), to which Blackburn eventually moved its headquarters. The Olympia Works were closed in around 1930 (*Flight* reported that the Blackburn Co. transferred its works and drawing offices from Leeds to the Brough seaplane

The Aircraft Manufacturers of Northern England, Scotland, Wales and Northern Ireland 181

A splendid photograph of BE2C 10000, the last example built by Blackburn under contract during the First World War. (Author)

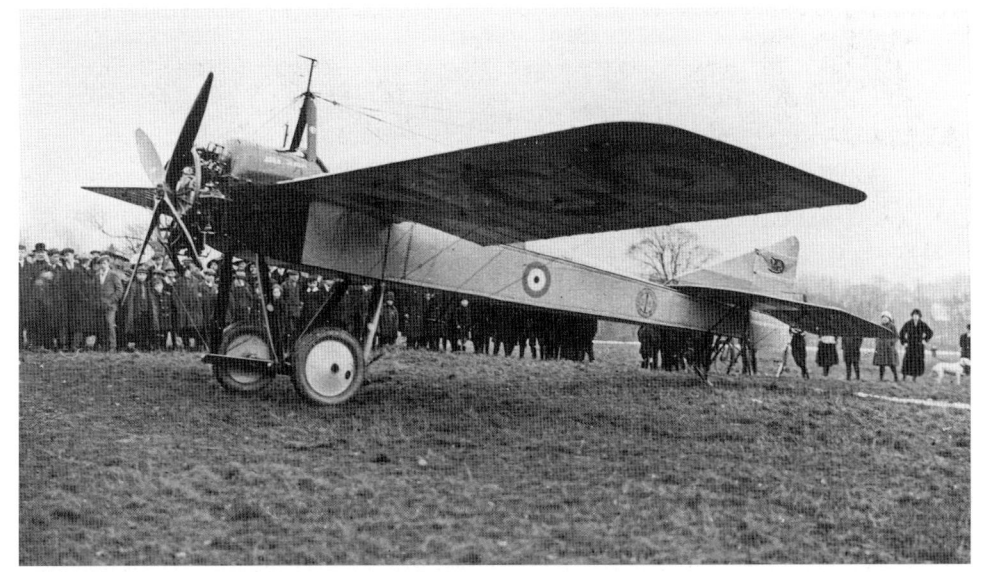

The Blackburn White Falcon monoplane photographed at Leeds Roundhay Park in 1915. (JMB/GSL collection)

Sopwith Baby production in full swing at the Olympia Works, Leeds. (JMB/GSL collection)

The unusually configured AD Scout 1536 *was one of two built by Blackburn; the type is also known as the* AD Sparrow. (JMB/GSL collection)

Production of the Armstrong Whitworth Siskin at Blackburn's Olympia Works in Leeds. (BAE SYSTEMS plc)

C8337 is a Sopwith Camel built by March, Jones & Cribb, seen here serving with the 17th Aero Squadron, U.S.A.S. (JMB/GSL collection)

station on the Humber in early 1929). The works at Leeds were, however, reopened in 1934 due to the demands of an increased workload. Slogans used included: 'Efficiency of design and construction. On Admiralty and War Office List', and, during the First World War 'Always at the Front'.

J. Curtiss & Son of Oxford Row, Leeds is listed in *The Aviation Pocket-Book of 1919-20* as an aeroplane manufacturer with propeller branch, nothing else known.

Haithwaite Aviation Co. Ltd of 10 Alfred Street, Leeds was registered in July 1918 with £1,000 capital as a dealer in aeroplanes and parts.

Thomas Horsman of 10–12 Mark Lane, Leeds is listed as an aeroplane manufacturer with propeller branch in *The Aviation Pocket-Book of 1919-20*, nothing else known.

March, Jones & Cribb built the at least thirty-eight AIRCO DH5 from an order for 100, together with 175 Sopwith Camel, and possibly up to 100 Sopwith Snipe. The initial Snipe order was for 100 aircraft from J301, but it is not known how many were delivered. Some sources indicate that ten aircraft were delivered from an order for fifty from J681, but Robertson in *British Military Aircraft Serials* indicates that this contract was cancelled. A total of 425 aircraft were ordered from this company of which, based on the above, at least 213 were built.

W.D. Oddy & Co. of Balm Road, Hunslet, Leeds and (from the end of September 1918) Globe Road, Holbeck, Leeds was a propeller manufacturer, using the slogans: 'Propellers only' and 'Contractors to HM Government'. The telegraphic address was 'Airscrews, Leeds'.

Scotland

Abbotsinch

Blackburn Aircraft Ltd carried out flight-testing of Shark and Botha aircraft at Abbotsinch Aerodrome. A purpose-built barge took landplanes from Dumbarton to Abbotsinch for flight-testing. The first Dumbarton-built Shark was air tested at Abbotsinch on 20 June 1938. Abbotsinch was used by Blackburn Aircraft for the modification of American-built naval aircraft to make them suitable for Fleet Air Arm service. The types handled included the Wildcat, Hellcat, Avenger and Corsair.

Scottish Aviation Ltd carried out assembly of American aircraft at Abbotsinch from July 1940, including a wide range of aircraft incapable of self-ferrying across the Atlantic. The types handled at Abbotsinch were mainly fighters, including the Tomahawk, Mohawk, Kittyhawk, Martlet and Kingfisher.

Aberdeen

The **Henderson Scottish Aviation Factory Ltd** at Aberdeen was one of many contractors to build the Avro 504. The total number of aircraft built is not clear. Research by Barry Abraham indicates that the factory was established at Forbesfield Road, with another assembly shop at Dafferish Place, Aberdeen. Bruce Robertson's *British Military Aircraft Serials* indicates that two batches of Avro 504 were built by Henderson Scottish Aviation Factory Ltd. These comprised 100 Avro 504J/K, the first example being D5851, and, from August 1918, 150 Avro 504K, with serials in sequence running from H201. The company is also referred to as Greig & Henderson, and as the Scottish Aircraft Factory.

Abbotsinch Aerodrome was used by Blackburn Aircraft for the test-flying of American-built naval aircraft including the Grumman Hellcat, following modifications for Royal Navy service. These aircraft were photographed on 18 November 1944. (BAE SYSTEMS plc)

Alloa

The British Caudron Co. Ltd, previously **W.H. Ewen Aviation Co. Ltd** of Hendon, set up an additional factory at Alloa, this being described in their advertisements as the company's 'Scottish factory and aerodrome'. W.H. Ewen had previously (1911) opened a flying school at Lanark Racecourse, the site of Scotland's first flying meeting in 1910. The W.H. Ewen Aviation Co. Ltd was renamed **The British Caudron Co. Ltd** in April 1914 and was soon building aircraft for both the RFC and the RNAS. The precise split in production between the British Caudron Scottish and English factories is not clear. Production included:

- One Caudron G.2.
- Sixty-one Caudron G.3.
- At least four of twelve Caudron G.4 ordered.
- Fifty AIRCO DH5 (believed to have been at Cricklewood).
- Fifty BE2C/E (believed to have been at Alloa).
- 100 Camel from orders for 350 aircraft.
- Fifty Handley Page O/400 (shared with Harris Lebus).
- Twenty Avro 504B (shared with The Regent Carriage Co.).

Of these, the fifty BE2C/E and 100 Camel were built at Alloa, and the shared O/400 and Avro 504B orders are most likely to have been built at Cricklewood, the collaborating companies being London firms.

The 1924 Ordnance Survey map shows an aerodrome at Alloa on the north bank of the Firth of Forth, immediately to the south-east of the town, and south-west of Clackmannan.

> CONTRACTORS TO H.M. ADMIRALTY, WAR OFFICE, AND FOREIGN GOVERNMENTS.
> # THE BRITISH CAUDRON CO. Ltd.
> SOLE BUILDING AND SELLING RIGHTS FOR
> ## Caudron Aeroplanes and Hydro-Aeroplanes
> — FOR —
> THE BRITISH EMPIRE AND DEPENDENCIES.
> HEAD OFFICE AND WORKS—BROADWAY, CRICKLEWOOD, N.W.
> CABLE AND TELEGRAPHIC ADDRESS—"CAUDROPLAN, CRICKLE, LONDON." PHONE—5551 HAMPSTEAD.
> SCOTTISH FACTORY AND AERODROME—ALLOA.
> CABLE AND TELEGRAPHIC ADDRESS—"CAUDROPLAN, ALLOA." PHONE.—52.

A 1917 advertisement for the British Caudron Co. Ltd operating at Cricklewood and Alloa.

The British Caudron Co. had factories at both Cricklewood and Alloa and built more than 300 aircraft of eight different types. This Airco DH5 was a product of the company's Cricklewood factory. (JMB/GSL collection)

Barrhead (south-west of Glasgow)

Barrhead was used as one of the earliest flying fields in Scotland, and is associated with the operations of the Barrhead Flying School, and the **Scottish Aviation Co.** of 185 Hope Street, Glasgow. In 1911, the School was advertising its facilities as the 'finest aerodrome in Scotland', this being a sixty-acre field, six miles from Glasgow. Tuition was offered on both Blériot and Farman types. In October 1911 there were six pupils and aircraft included Blériot, Farman, 'a new military passenger biplane', and two other machines under construction. In March 1912, the Barrhead Flying School was advertising: 'Tuition on monoplanes and biplanes till Brevet is obtained. £45 including Insurance against Breakages. Magnificent Aerodrome; Competent Instructors. £5 prize to pupils accomplishing 30 minute flight within a week of passing for Certificate.'

BE2E B6154 after a mishap at 31 Training Squadron, Wyton. This aircraft was built by The British Caudon Co. Ltd at Alloa. (JMB/GSL collection)

The Scottish Aviation Co. *Caledonia* monoplane was flying in November 1911 at Barrhead. The second Scottish Aviation type was the *Dart* monoplane, which was closely based on the Blériot monoplane, albeit with a modified undercarriage. In December 1911 the company negotiated the sole rights to build Avro designs in Scotland. In February 1912, the company was advertising the Caledonia-Avro biplane (under licence) for £500 including tuition. This Scottish Aviation Co. has no connection with the later Scottish Aviation Ltd of Prestwick. *British Aircraft Before the Great War* reports that a Farman-type biplane was also constructed and that all these aircraft were destroyed by fire at Barrhead on 13 April 1912.

Mr F. Norman, who flew the Scottish Aviation *Caledonia* monoplane in 1911, later set up the **National Aircraft Manufacturing Co. Ltd**, Printing House Yard, 15a Hackney Road, London, NE.

The Scottish Aviation Co. Dart was a modified Blériot monoplane. This photograph was taken in 1912 at the company's flying field at Barrhead. (JMB/GSL collection)

Two Opus 280 (a Rotax 912A-powered ARV Super 2) were built by Aviation Scotland Ltd in conjunction with ASL Sweden AB. (Author)

Blair Atholl (and Glen Tilt)

Lt J.W. Dunne, who worked at Farnborough as a designer of man-lifting kites, experimented with the design of inherently stable aircraft configurations from 1905 until 1913 at Farnborough, Blair Atholl and Eastchurch. Dunne's designs were tailless swept-wing biplanes with considerable wash-out of the wing tips. The Dunne D.3 and D.4 were tested at Glen Tilt and Blair Atholl, prior to official funding being withdrawn in 1909.

In July 1907 Dunne travelled to Glen Tilt (on the Blair Atholl estate, to the north of Blair Atholl) with a party of Royal Engineers to carry out trials in great secrecy. The initial trials were not successful and the party returned in September 1908, and achieved better success. The flying grounds used were, however, subject to high winds; later on the activity moved to a 'lower camp' in the Duke of Atholl's private grounds at Blair Castle.

After his funding was withdrawn, Dunne set up the Blair Atholl Aeroplane Syndicate to carry on with trials, which eventually led to the highly successful D.5 and D.8 designs. For further information, see the entry for the Isle of Sheppey in Volume Three of this series.

Burnbank, Hamilton

The works of **Aviation Scotland Ltd** were located at 9 Bertram Street, Burnbank, just to the east of Glasgow, the company producing the ARV Super 2. The first Aviation Scotland

An advertisement for William Beardmore & Co. Ltd of Dalmuir, reflecting their aircraft, engine and airship interests.

(ASL) aircraft flew in November 1992. In 1994, ASL announced that they had formed a joint venture in Sweden to market the aircraft with Rotax 912A power under the name Opus 280, the joint venture being named **ASL Sweden AB**. Two Opus 280 were constructed before this concern went out of business in 1995. In 1999, the design rights were transferred to Skycraft International of the USA.

Dalmuir

Wm. Beardmore & Co. Ltd (Aviation Dept), Dalmuir: This famous engineering company was founded in 1815. The company's first aircraft activity had German connections, through their initial licence in 1913 for the Porsche-designed Austro-Daimler engine, and the German DFW aircraft design in 1914. Two DFW biplanes were delivered to the Royal Navy (numbers 154 and 891).

With the coming of the First World War, the German connection was severed and Beardmore produced a wide variety of aircraft in its 98,000 sq. ft factory at Dalmuir, including:

- Fifty-six Royal Aircraft Factory BE2C from February 1915.
- Thirty-two Wight 840, twelve of which were delivered as spares.
- Fifty Nieuport 12.
- Fifty Sopwith Pup (an order for a further 150 was cancelled).
- Thirty Sopwith 'Ship's Pup' (Admiralty Type 9901A) with a skid undercarriage.
- Thirty Handley Page V/1500. Nine of the first twenty aircraft were delivered by air, the rest as spares. At least ten of a second order for thirty were also delivered.
- 140 Sopwith 2F1 Camel. These were ordered from Beardmore in two batches, the first (from N6750) of 100 aircraft; the second (from N7100) of fifty aircraft, of which the last ten (N7140–49) were sub-contracted to Arrol-Johnston for erection.

The company's own designs included:

- W.B. I, 'Adriatic' landplane bomber N525.
- W.B. II, one experimental aircraft F2995 flown on 30 August 1917.
- Two civilian W.B. IIB were built, G-EARX and G-EARY, these being large two-seat biplanes, powered by a 160hp Beardmore engine.
- W.B. III, a modified Sopwith Pup with folding wings, lengthened fuselage and undercarriage retracting into fuselage for shipboard use. Some 100 were ordered, and at least fifty-five built.
- W.B. IV, a tractor biplane with flotation gear in the fuselage, a dropping undercarriage, mid-fuselage engine installation and 'watertight' cockpit. One aircraft only, serial N38 first flown on 12 December 1917.
- W.B. V, a tractor biplane with folding wings, two aircraft only, serials N41 and N42.
- W.B. X, a large, nominally two-seat, two-bay biplane built for the 1920 Commercial Aeroplane Competition. The 185hp Beardmore-powered prototype was registered G-EAQS and proved entirely unsuccessful in competition, due to the combination of a failed cooling system and a centre of gravity location which prevented the passenger seat being used. A single flight was made, on 16 August 1920.
- W.B. 26, a single example of this angular biplane, designed by W.S. Shackleton, was built in 1925 against a potential Latvian contract.

Beardmore advertised that they had 'Aerodromes and Hangars at Dalmuir and Inchinnan', and that they were 'Builders of land machines and seaplanes. Contractors to The Admiralty and

1400, the first Wight 840 to be built by Wm. Beardmore & Co. Ltd under construction at Dalmuir. BE2C production is underway in the background. (JMB/GSL collection)

9209 was one of the fifty Nieuport 12 that were contracted to Beardmore.(JMB/GSL collection)

War Office'. Aircraft built by Beardmore were flown from 'nearby Robertson Park', to Renfrew and Inchinnan. Seaplanes were flown from the Clyde. It was reported in April 1919 that its 'war work included 650 aeroplanes from Baby Sopwith to large four-engined Handley Page bombers'. The company also manufactured the ABC Dragonfly and other engines.

George Richards, the designer of the Lee Richards annular monoplane, was the designer and assistant manager of the Aviation Department of Wm. Beardmore & Co. Ltd, becoming

This Beardmore Ship's Pup, believed to be 9922 shows clearly the skid undercarriage and hook fitted to assist in deck landings. (JMB/GSL collection)

Beardmore's first Handley Page V/1500 E8287 seen at the company's Inchinnan works. (JMB/GSL collection)

the general manager of Martinsyde Ltd from 1921 to 1923. Thereafter, he was a member of staff of the Science Museum.

The Beardmore aircraft department closed in 1921, but was then re-opened in 1924. W.S. Shackleton, from ANEC, was appointed chief designer and designed the Beardmore Wee Bee (similar to his ANEC monoplanes). The Wee Bee was flown in September 1924 and was entered in both the 1924 and 1926 Lympne trials. The Wee Bee won the 1924 two-seat light aircraft competition at Lympne, in doing so attaining some quite remarkable performance figures (a take-off run of 235 yards to 25ft; 79mph maximum speed;

The sole Beardmore W.B. II F2995 was a relatively clean two-bay biplane that was not selected for production. (JMB/GSL collection)

The sole example of the W.B. IV under test at the Isle of Grain on 27 September 1918. The mid-mounted engine can clearly be seen. (JMB/GSL collection)

distance flown during the week of competition 737.5 miles) under the limited power of its 1,096cc Bristol Cherub engine. Later registered as G-EBJJ, the Wee Bee was subsequently exported to Australia and it had a long flying life as VH-URJ, still being extant in 1949.

W.S. Shackleton was also responsible for the famous Beardmore Inflexible, based upon the structural concepts of Dr Adolph Rohrbach, from whom Beardmore took a manufacturing licence in 1924. Beardmore were then contracted to supply two Inverness flying boats, a version of the Rohrbach Ro IV. The first of these, N183, was built by Rohrbach and delivered to Felixstowe in September 1925. The second, N184, was built by Beardmore but did not fly until November 1928. In characteristic Rohrbach style, the Inverness featured resolutely rectangular flying surfaces, and monoplane wings of nearly 100ft span. The aircraft was regarded as unsatisfactory, whether in the air, or on the water.

Undeterred, Beardmore went on to build the much larger Inflexible J5557. The Inflexible was a three-engine landplane, with the staggering span of 157ft 6in. Its design was clearly based upon the ideas of Rohrbach, the indelible rectangular stamp of the Inverness being much in evidence. The Inflexible was taken by barge to Ipswich, from whence to Martlesham Heath for assembly and first flight on 5 March 1928. Its looks belied its behaviour, for the Inflexible proved to be very docile and easy to fly, taking off in a run of less than 350 yards. Perhaps it is now best remembered for the size of its wheels, one of which, at 7ft 6in diameter, was preserved in the Science Museum National Aeronautical Collection.

By 1930, Beardmore had withdrawn from aircraft production. W.S. Shackleton moved from Beardmore to become the Chief Engineer of the Larkin Aircraft Company at Melbourne from 1928 to 1932. On his return to England, he set up the famous aircraft sales agency W.S. Shackleton Ltd in 1932 and collaborated in the design of the Shackleton-Murray S.M.1 G-ACBP of 1933.

Dumbarton

The shipbuilder **Wm. Denny & Bros Ltd** was involved in early experimentation with a six-rotor helicopter, the rotors being based on ship propeller design. Despite its unlikely appearance, this machine (the **Mumford** Helicopter) succeeded in flying from the River Clyde in late 1914, travelling a distance of some 100 yards. This was the culmination of a series of experiments that had begun as early as 1906. During the First World War, the company, like many other shipbuilders on the Clyde, was engaged in aircraft production, building at least 150 Royal Aircraft Factory BE2C/E in two batches. These aircraft were tested at Cardross.

Blackburn Aircraft Ltd, Castle Road and Barge Park, Dumbarton: The Dumbarton operation of Blackburn Aircraft Ltd was formed as a joint venture with **Wm. Denny & Bros Ltd** in October 1936, with Sir Maurice Denny joining the Blackburn Aircraft board. The following types were handled at Dumbarton:

- Shark: Assembly, maintenance, repair and embodiment of in-service modifications to the Blackburn Shark III – initially carried out at a training school set up in a former tramway depot in Hartfield. The first Dumbarton-built Shark was air tested at Abbotsinch on 20 June 1938. The Shark activity was transferred to Barge Park in October 1939.
- 200 Botha, Dumbarton providing a second production line to that at Brough, where 380 of the type were built. Work on the Botha at Dumbarton started in mid-1939, with the first Dumbarton-built example L6347 flying in October of that year. Production continued at Dumbarton until June 1940.
- B-20 experimental flying boat: The Blackburn B-20 was a large machine powered by two Rolls-Royce Vulture engines, which featured a single retractable planing hull/float which could be raised to fair itself into the fuselage. The prototype, V8914, flew in March 1940, but was unfortunately destroyed in a fatal accident due to aileron flutter whilst test flying from Dumbarton on 7 April 1940.
- 250 Short Sunderland were manufactured at Dumbarton, made up of fifteen Mk I, five Mk II, 170 Mk III and sixty Mk V. The first Sunderland T9083 was flown from the river next to the factory, but subsequent aircraft were towed downriver and flown from the Marine Aircraft Experimental Establishment at Helensburgh. Alan Sherry reported that later aircraft were flown directly off from the factory, making use of the private

This BE2E presentation aircraft 'Hong Kong' is C6908, manufactured by Wm. Denny & Bros Ltd of Dumbarton. (JMB/GSL collection)

channel between the factory and the river. The last Dumbarton-built Sunderland, VB889, was completed on 25 October 1945 and flew on 8 November 1945.

Blackburn Roc L3057 and L3059 were fitted with floats at Dumbarton in October 1939, and tested at Helensburgh. Blackburn also converted the three Short S.26 'G-class' flying boats to military use in 1940, this adaptation including the fitting of ASV radar, gun turrets and bomb carriages. Dumbarton also controlled three sites (at Prestwick, Abbotsinch and the Ogston & Tennants soap works at Renfrew) that conducted preparation for service modifications to the Wildcat, Hellcat, Avenger and Corsair.

A purpose-built barge ferried landplanes from Dumbarton to Abbotsinch for flight-testing. The name of the barge – the *Dumbrough* – was indicative of the close collaborative enterprise between the Dumbarton and Brough factories of Blackburn Aircraft Ltd.

From April 1945, the Blackburn factory at Dumbarton, along with a number of other aircraft factories, was used for the production of aluminium housing, built at a rate of more than 200 units per week. In the mid-1950s, the factory was also engaged in the production of Beverley components (rear clam-shell doors, engine nacelles and undercarriage bogies), Buccaneer components and fuselage sections of the Britannia. Additional contract production included components for the Vampire, Venom, Canberra and Swift. At this time, the factory was referred to as **Blackburn (Dumbarton) Ltd**. The factory was finally closed in August 1960.

Dumfries

The **Arrol-Johnston Ltd** car company manufactured Beardmore aeroplane engines and the Sopwith 2F1 Camel during the First World War. A contract for ten 2F1 was sub-let from Beardmore, followed by a further direct contract for forty aircraft from N7350, of which at least twenty were delivered. A further order for twenty aircraft was cancelled. Arrol-Johnston was a Beardmore subsidiary, having been purchased by Beardmore in 1913, Sir William Beardmore acting as chairman. George Johnston had been a pioneer of the motor car, his

The first Dumbarton-built Sunderland T9083 *being moved from the factory on 17 October 1941.* (BAE SYSTEMS plc)

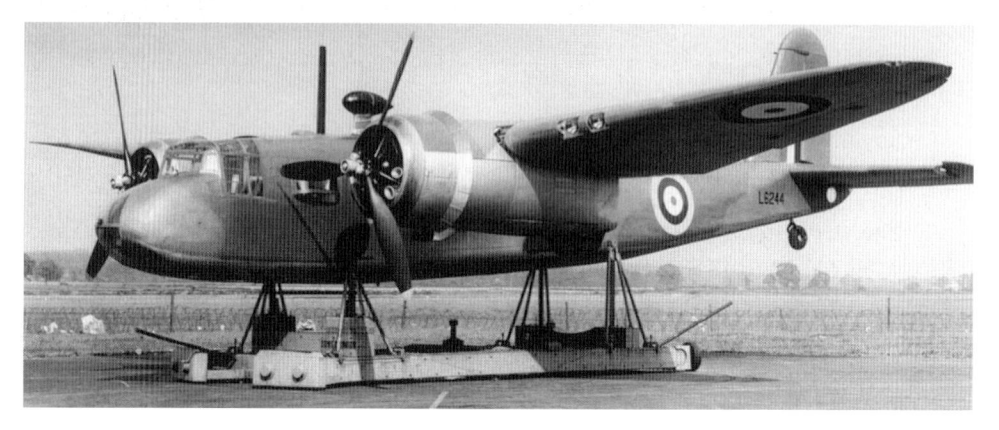

The Blackburn Botha was built at both Brough and Dumbarton. L6244 *is a Brough-built example, seen here undergoing compass swinging in the flight attitude, and with undercarriage retracted, on 16 August 1940.* (BAE SYSTEMS plc)

designs being manufactured by Arrol-Johnston from 1896. Sir William Arrol was the architect of the Forth Bridge. The factory at Dumfries was built in 1913, and was brand new when it was turned over to aircraft work. The car firm subsequently merged with the Aster company, with Arrol-Aster continuing in production until 1928.

The Galloway Engineering Co. Ltd of Shakespeare Street, Dumfries and Tongland, Kirkcudbright designed and manufactured the BHP (Beardmore–Halford–Pullinger) aero engine, which was also built by Siddeley-Deasy at Coventry. Galloway Engineering was, like Arrol-Johnston, a Beardmore subsidiary, and employed a largely female workforce, under female management. The company continued the manufacture of cars into the 1920s.

Edinburgh

Cooper biplane: This machine is described and illustrated in *British Aircraft Before the Great War*. The Cooper biplane of 1913 was designed and built by Mr G.T. Cooper, who had previously experimented with two glider designs. The biplane was a workman-like design of tractor configuration, with the pilot seated in a small faired nacelle. The machine was

The Watson No.2 biplane was unconventional in both configuration and means of control. (JMB/GSL collection)

powered by a Humber engine and was flown successfully at Crammond Sands in September 1913.

The **Ferranti Ltd** Flying Unit at Turnhouse flew a range of modified aircraft on radar and other equipment development for various aircraft. Types flown included the Dakota, Meteor, Varsity, Vampire, Sea Fury, Hunter, Gannet, Buccaneer, no less than eight Canberra aircraft, and, latterly, a BAC One-Eleven. Although not an aircraft manufacturer, the company's modifications were responsible for some considerable changes to the appearance of the aircraft in their test fleet.

Errol, Perthshire

Errol was used for the development of the **Watson** biplane series, designed and built by Mr Preston A. Watson from 1910 to 1914. This was an unusual design of inverted sesquiplane configuration, with an equally unusual control arrangement. The short upper wing was pivoted to allow it to be tilted laterally for control. The Watson No.2 biplane was flying at Errol in 1912 and featured a four-wheel undercarriage and twin tail booms, which carried the elevator and a very small fin. The small-span wing, which provided lateral control, was mounted on a cabâne above the pilot. The Watson No.3 competed in the 'Concours de la Sécurité en Aeroplane' competition in Buc, France in May 1914. *Flight* reported that 'several pilots have flown the machine and have found it easy to control'. (This quote possibly refers to the second machine). The third aircraft was being flown at Buc in June 1914, and crashed due to a broken rudder cable. This aircraft was said to have flown well 'once Mr Summerfield got used to the controls'.

Glasgow

A number of Clyde shipbuilders and engineering companies formed an aircraft-building combine during the First World War. Aircraft built by these companies are sometimes described as 'group-built' making it difficult to be certain of responsibilities between the companies. Those involved in aircraft construction included G. & J. Weir, Alexander Stephen, Wm. Denny & Bros Ltd, Clyde Shipbuilding & Engineering, Fairfield Shipbuilding & Engineering Ltd, North British Locomotive Co., Barclay Curle & Co., and Napier & Miller Ltd.

Alexander Stephen Ltd of Linthouse was a 'Scottish Group' manufacturer with responsibility for building Royal Aircraft Factory FE2B parts. 100 aircraft (from D9081) were built in conjunction with G. & J. Weir, with a further fifty aircraft to be delivered as parts for assembly by Barclay, Curle & Co. – it is not known whether these aircraft were actually delivered. The company received a further order for 100 FE2B, this being cancelled. An additional 150 FE2B (from A5650) are listed in *British Military Aircraft Serials* as 'group-built in Scotland', and it is very likely that Alexander Stephen had a part to play in the production of these aircraft. 300 Royal Aircraft Factory BE2C/D/E (from serial 4300) were group-built with G. & J. Weir, Alexander Stephen and the North British Locomotive Co. among the constructors. Alexander Stephen was later to become the Linthouse Division of Upper Clyde Shipbuilders.

Aviation Scotland Ltd of 205 Bath Street, Glasgow took over the ARV Super 2 from Island Aircraft in 1991. Further details can be found under the entry for Burnbank, Hamilton.

Barclay, Curle & Co. of Whiteinch, Glasgow was another of the Scottish Group of manufacturers. Precise numbers of aircraft manufactured by Barclay, Curle & Co. are not clear. The types involved included the BE2C/E, FE2B, Snipe (some sources – although the order for seventy-five aircraft from J3917–J3991 is believed to have been cancelled) and Fairey Campania. Royal Aircraft Factory BE2 production consisted of 150 BE2C/E; fifty FE2B to be built up from parts supplied by Alexander Stephen Ltd are believed not to have been delivered. Fifty Fairey Campania were ordered from the company with serials from N1840, but only twelve are known to have been delivered.

Beardmore Aero Engines Ltd, Parkhead Steelworks, Glasgow: see Dalmuir (Aviation Department).

Clyde Shipbuilding & Engineering Co. were part of the Scottish manufacturing group, although the company's precise contribution is not clear.

This FE2B D9104 is one of a batch of 100 aircraft that were built by Alexander Stephen Ltd in conjunction with G. & J. Weir Ltd. (JMB/GSL collection)

This BE2E of No.3 Training Squadron at Shoreham is one of 150 BE2C/E built by Barclay, Curle & Co. Ltd. (JMB/GSL collection)

Queen Bee LF858/G-BLUZ is one of sixty that were built by Scottish Aviation Ltd and local subcontractors at 39 West Campbell Street, Glasgow. (Alec Brew)

W.H. Ewen Aviation Co. Ltd, 28 Bath Street, Glasgow. This company was registered in January 1913, later evolving into the British Caudron Co. Ltd. For additional information, refer to the entries for Lanark, Hendon and Alloa.

Fyffes were a firm of yacht-builders who constructed the hull of the Fairey N.4 Titania N129. The hull was then moved by road to Hamble to be united with its superstructure. For further details, see Bradford, West Yorkshire.

Glasgow Corporation Tram Depot of Coplaw Hill undertook sub-contract construction for **Clyde Shipbuilding & Engineering Co**.

North British Locomotive Co. Ltd of Springburn undertook sub-contract construction for **Clyde Shipbuilding & Engineering Co**. 300 Royal Aircraft Factory BE2C/D/E (from serial 4300) were group-built with G. & J. Weir, Alexander Stephen and the North British Locomotive Co. among the constructors.

The **Scottish Aviation Co.** of 185 Hope Street, Glasgow set up a flying school at Barrhead, which see for further details.

Scottish Aviation Ltd: Sixty de Havilland Queen Bee were built by Scottish Aviation Ltd in a warehouse at 39 West Campbell Street, Glasgow, the principal sub-contractors including the **West of Scotland Furniture Co.** of Beith.

G. & J. Weir of Holm Foundry, Cathcart, Glasgow were an established engineering company, founded in 1871, which built aircraft during the First World War. The company then became involved in rotorcraft, initially carrying out experiments on their own account and subsequently becoming the backers of **The Cierva Autogiro Co. Ltd**.

The company was an important component of the Scottish Group of manufacturers, being engaged in substantial production of the BE2C/D/E, FE2B, and DH9. G. & J. Weir received contracts for 450 FE2B, 600 DH9 (200 of which were cancelled) and 100

G. & J. Weir was an important contract manufacturer during the First World War, building the BE2, FE2 and AIRCO DH9. This photograph shows DH9 production at Cathcart, c. 1918. (Weir Group plc)

A head-on view of the diminutive Weir W-2, taken at Cathcart on 10 July 1934. (Weir Group plc)

The Weir team (left to right: Messrs Hodgess, Bennett, Pullin, Boyer, Walker and Watson) inspect the Weir W-5; this was Britain's first successful helicopter, flown for the first time at Dalrymple on 6 June 1938. (Weir Group plc)

RE7 (cancelled). 300 BE2C/D/E (from serial 4300) were group-built with G. & J. Weir, Alexander Stephen and the North British Locomotive Co. among the constructors. 100 FE2B aircraft (from D9081) were built in conjunction with Alexander Stephen, with a further fifty aircraft delivered as parts for assembly by Barclay, Curle & Co. An additional 150 FE2B (from A5650) are listed in *British Military Aircraft Serials* as 'group-built in Scotland', and it is very likely that G. & J. Weir had a part to play in the production of these aircraft.

Tethered hovering of the Weir W-6 at Argus Foundry, Thornliebank in late 1939. (Weir Group plc)

The first Weir autogyro experiments were carried out on the Weir W-1 to W-4 from 1932 onwards. The W-1 was flown in May 1933; the W-2 was flown at Abbotsinch in March 1934; and the W-3 (a modification of the W-2), which was flown at Abbotsinch (by Alan Marsh) on 9 July 1936. The W-4 was tested at Abbotsinch in December 1937, but could not be persuaded to become airborne. The W-2 and W-3 were also flown at Hanworth. From 1937, these experiments were extended into the field of the helicopter, the company producing the first successful British helicopter to fly (if one discounts the experiments of Brennan at Farnborough, and the Mumford device described under William Denny & Bros Ltd at Dumbarton). This aircraft, the Weir W-5, was first flown on 8 June 1938, at Dalrymple, near Ayr. The Weir W-6 helicopter R5269 flew on 27 October 1939, flying for some eighty hours, before wartime priorities intruded. The W-6 was assembled at the Argus Foundry, Thornliebank, a few miles to the south of Cathcart.

Weir was also directly involved in the affairs of **The Cierva Autogiro Co. Ltd**, with C.G. Pullin of G. & J. Weir as managing director of Cierva, and J.G. Weir as chairman. Weir had a controlling financial interest in Cierva from 1939. The aircraft department moved to **Mollart Engineering**'s premises in Thames Ditton in 1943, before the final move of The Cierva Autogiro Co. Ltd to Eastleigh in 1946. The involvement of G. & J. Weir in the Cierva company is reflected in the latter company's products being designated W-9, W-11 Air Horse and W-14 Skeeter; the letter W standing for Weir, and the numerical sequence following on from Weir's own projects.

Wylie & Lochhead of 45 Buchanan Street, Glasgow, is listed as an aircraft manufacturer in *The Aviation Pocket-Book of 1919-20*. Nothing else is known.

Govan, Clydeside

The **Fairfield Shipbuilding & Engineering Co. Ltd** received a contract for 100 Sopwith Cuckoo in August 1917. The number completed and delivered is believed to be fifty aircraft built from N7000, the last fourteen being delivered directly to store. The first aircraft was completed on 6 August 1918 and delivered by road to No.6 Aircraft Acceptance Park at Renfrew. The father of Frank and Harold Barnwell (later of Bristol and Vickers, respectively) was managing director of Fairfield Engineering. See also Stirling for details of the Barnwell brothers pioneering experiments.

Greenock

The Osborne Aircraft Components Co. of Whin Hill, Greenock, were advertising in January 1917 as 'Aeronautical Engineers and Manufacturers' capable of the 'supply of all aeroplane fittings and components, mainplanes, tailplanes, ribs, fins and elevators'.

Scottish Aviation Ltd managed a Sunderland repair and overhaul facility and a Catalina reception centre at Caird's Yard, Greenock. (See Prestwick for further details). At the end of the war, these facilities were used to manufacture components for prefabricated housing, a relatively common occurrence within the industry at this time.

Helensburgh (near Glasgow)

After the outbreak of the Second World War, the **Marine Aircraft Experimental Establishment** (MAEE) was established at Helensburgh, replacing the vulnerably located activity at Felixstowe. Whilst the MAEE was not responsible for new designs, a number of experimental trials aircraft were flown here, these including two Blackburn Roc aircraft (L3057 and L3059) fitted with floats at Dumbarton in October 1939. The well-known Spitfire floatplanes were tested at the MAEE. The Saunders-Roe A.37 Shrimp G-AFZS/TK580 was also operated at the MAEE, and was used for the development of the Shetland hull shape, flying throughout the war, before moving to Felixstowe in 1945 and being scrapped in 1949.

Hillington (Glasgow)

The **Rolls-Royce Ltd** shadow factory at Hillington employed up to 26,000 people during the Second World War on Merlin and Griffon production. This factory was completed in October 1940, construction taking sixteen months; 50,000 engines were built at Hillington during the Second World War. The foundry facility at Hillington covered nearly 250,000 sq. ft. Post-war expansion of jet engine manufacture resulted in additional factories, including the present facilities at East Kilbride.

Inchinnan

Inchinnan was primarily used by **Wm. Beardmore & Co. Ltd** for airship construction; aircraft manufacture being centred on Dalmuir. Airships constructed by Beardmore included the R34 and R36. The site was, however, also used for test flying the Beardmore-built Handley Page V/1500 aircraft, for which a shed was constructed.

Irvine

In 1955, **Scottish Aviation Ltd** had insufficient production capacity available at Prestwick. The company therefore took over a disused laundry at Irvine, which was used for the manufacture of Twin Pioneer components, including rudders and wing slats.

Kirkpatrick

The shipbuilder **Napier & Miller** of Old Kirkpatrick, was one of the Scottish Group of manufacturers. The company assembled aircraft from components produced by sub-contractors. Orders were received for 150 Royal Aircraft Factory BE2E aircraft, one batch of fifty running from A1311, and a batch of 100 from C7101. Six aircraft from this second contract were subsequently issued with civil registrations.

This disused laundry at Irvine was used by Scottish Aviation Ltd from 1955 to provide additional capacity for the manufacture of Twin Pioneer components. (Scottish Aviation Ltd via Dougal McIntyre)

Lanark

Lanark was an early site of pioneer flying in Scotland; flying meetings were held here, and Drexel set a world height record of 6,750ft in a Blériot at Lanark on 12 August 1910. Lanark racecourse became the base for the early flying of **W.H. Ewen**, who set up his flying school here. Ewen's activities at Lanark were sporadically reported in contemporary issues of *Flight*, as follows: in July 1911 the Ewen school at Lanark was using a Blériot monoplane for training. W.H. Ewen became the sole Scottish agent for the **Deperdussin** concern, and at the end of August 1911 he used an aircraft of this type to make the first flight across the Firth of Forth. In November 1912, Ewen was reported to be seeking a new flying ground in Scotland, Lanark being too far from Glasgow, this presumably leading to his move to Alloa. In February 1913, he was reported to have commenced construction of six Caudron biplanes. W.H. Ewen later moved to Hendon, the company becoming **The British Caudron Co. Ltd** with works at Alloa and Hendon.

The **Barnwell** monoplane moved to Lanark in Autumn 1911 - for further details see Stirling.

Largs (on the Firth of Clyde)

During the Second World War, **Scottish Aviation Ltd** used a facility at Largs to provide dispersed repair and overhaul capacity for the Sunderland, see Prestwick for further details. The Largs facility was closed at the end of November 1944.

Leith (Edinburgh)

The **Gibson** biplane – a relatively crude Boxkite design – was reported to be flying at Leith in 1910, although in *British Aircraft Before the Great War*, these trials are reported to have been unsuccessful. The machine was built at the **Caledonian Motor & Cycle Works**.

ANOTHER HISTORIC FLIGHT

across

The Firth of Forth,

from Portobello to Kinghorn and back at an altitude of 1,000 feet,

by H. E. EWEN,

his first attempt

on a "Deperdussin" Monoplane

with a 28 H.P. 3-cyl. Anzani Engine.

12 MILES IN 10 MINUTES.

AVIATION SCHOOL AT BROOKLANDS.

Special Terms to Army and Navy Officers.

APPLY TO—

THE BRITISH DEPERDUSSIN AEROPLANE SYNDICATE, LTD.,
30, REGENT STREET, PICCADILLY CIRCUS, LONDON, S.W.

Telephone: 280 GERRARD.   Wire "SANTOCHIMO, LONDON."

CAUDRON Aeroplanes.

MONOPLANES

£380   fitted with 35 h.p. motors and upwards from   **£380**

BIPLANES

£400   racing type or two-seaters from   **£400**

HYDRO-AEROPLANES.

SOLE AGENT for Britain and Colonies: **W. H. EWEN** HENDON AND LANARK.

Above: The British Deperdussin Aeroplane Syndicate Ltd proudly records the flight across Firth of Forth, in 1911.

Left: W.H. Ewen (of Hendon and Lanark, 1912)

J. & G. Gibson, who were father and son, are then reported to have constructed a further ten aircraft. Their second machine was flown successfully in August 1910 and was a rebuild of the first machine, retaining the well-tried Boxkite configuration.

Maybole (south of Ayr)

Montgomerie Gyrocopters have developed an extensively modified Bensen design at the Montgomerie engineering business of Kirkmichael Road, Crosshill near Maybole, Ayrshire. G-BMUH first flew in mid-1988, and flew to the 1988 PFA Rally at Cranfield that year via a highly adventurous route including Scotland, Ireland, the Isle of Man, Wales, and England, the autogyro covering 395nm in seven hours forty-eight minutes. By 1994, the company had built forty-seven such aircraft. Other examples include G-BREU, G-BWJN and G-BXCL.

The Gibson biplane showing its conventional Boxkite configuration. (JMB/GSL collection)

G-BREU, seen making a 'hands-off flypast', is an example of the highly successful Montgomerie-Bensen B.8 Gyrocopter, built at Crosshill, near Maybole. (Author)

Montrose

Phillips & Powis (Aircraft) Ltd set up a repair depot at Montrose in May 1940. The main types to be repaired were the company's own designs, together with the Airspeed Oxford. RAF Montrose was used for flight-test purposes, although the repair organisation moved from a site on the airfield to a textile mill, the Chapel Works at Mill Lane, Montrose.

Perth

The first experimental **Kay** 32/1Gyroplane was built at Shields Garage, Perth and tested at RAF Leuchars from August 1932, before an improved machine (Type 33/1 G-ACVA) was built and flown at Eastleigh, Hampshire (see Volume Two of this series for further details).

Prestwick

Aircraft manufacture at Prestwick consists essentially of the history of Scottish Aviation Ltd and its BAe/BAE SYSTEMS successors, presented chronologically below.

Scottish Aviation Ltd was founded by Douglas Douglas-Hamilton, Marquis of Clydesdale and David McIntyre – the first men to fly over Mount Everest – on 9 August 1935 as the **Scottish College of Aviation Ltd**. Additional investment was provided by **The de Havilland Aircraft Co. Ltd**, the company being run as a civilian flying training school for the RAF. In February 1936 the company name was changed to Scottish Aviation Ltd, often abbreviated to SAL.

During the Second World War, aircraft modification, assembly and preparation-for-service work slowly increased. The first activity was Wellesley modifications transferred to SAL from W.A. Rollason Ltd. A range of minor contracts, including the manufacture of Hart and Hurricane rudders, followed this. Hurricane rudder work was to continue for much of the war. The No.3 factory building at Prestwick was acquired in 1940, and was originally built as the 'Palace of Engineering' building for the 1938 Empire Exhibition, being moved to Prestwick from its original site at Bellahouston Park, Glasgow. This huge building, which is still in use today, was disassembled, transported to its new site, re-erected, camouflaged and put into use in only four months.

One important wartime activity was Sunderland repair and overhaul, and Catalina reception, at Caird's Yard, Greenock, supplemented by dispersal capacity at Largs. Caird's Yard was requisitioned for this purpose on 1 June 1940. Largs provided supplementary flying boat capacity from September 1942. A batch of 195 Catalina 1B were delivered to Scottish Aviation from February 1941, passing from SAL to Saunders-Roe Ltd at Beaumaris for preparation for service.

Scottish Aviation managed a Spitfire and Hurricane Civilian Repair Organisation and acted as parent organisation for the **LMS Railway Wagon Works** at Barassie, whose Spitfires were flight-tested at Prestwick. In all, some 1,200 Spitfires were handled. Barry Abraham indicates (in correspondence with the author) that there was also an airstrip at Barassie that was used by these aircraft.

Prestwick was the principal terminal for the wartime transatlantic ferry operation. Scottish Aviation assembled many aircraft that arrived by ship (see Abbotsinch) – including Tomahawks, Mohawks, Kittyhawks, Kingfishers and Martlets – and modified the ferry arrivals for RAF use. The main aircraft handled were the Liberator, B-17 Flying Fortress, Dakota, Mitchell, Hudson and Canadian-built examples of the Lancaster and Mosquito. Six Grumman Martlet (from AX824) were among the American types assembled by the company. Liberator modifications included the installation of additional fuel capacity, weight saving modifications, equipment removal and the installation of UK-specific systems.

After the Second World War the company carried out many civil conversions of wartime transports, notably Dakotas, for airlines the world over. This is reflected in 1947 advertising:

Scottish Aviation Ltd – Construction, Conversions, Repairs, Overhauls. Founders of Prestwick Airport. Sole conversion, repair and overhaul centre in Great Britain for the Douglas Aircraft Co. Aircraft converted by Scottish Aviation Ltd are already flying for Aer Lingus, American Overseas Airlines, British Aircraft Services, DDL, DLM, Fred Olsen Transport (Norway), Portuguese Airlines, Sabena, Scottish Airlines, Swissair and TWA.

Additional orders were to be gained from, BEA, Ceylon Airways, Cyprus Airways, Abyssinian Airlines, Bharat Airways, CSA and many others. In 1950, SAL converted thirty-two BEA Dakota aircraft to an improved standard known as the Pionair Class.

During the immediate post-war years, SAL was forced to diversify to maintain factory throughput, producing a variety of products, which included lightweight tractor cabs, and bus and coach bodies for a wide range of manufacturers. The company also set up its own airline, Scottish Airlines, operating a diverse fleet, which included thirteen C-47; eight York; five B-24 Liberator transport conversions; two Proctor; two Walrus; and single examples of the Rapide, Oxford and Fokker F.XXII. The company made its last commercial flight on 9 November 1960.

Scottish Aviation Ltd created a niche market with their own designs – the Pioneer and Twin Pioneer STOL (short take off and landing) aircraft. The Pioneer was first flown as the A.4/45, G-31-1/G-AKBF/VL515, on 5 November 1947, being initially powered by a Gipsy

The first production Jetstream 31 G-TALL flies past the 1938 Palace of Engineering, at Prestwick, still in use by BAE SYSTEMS. (BAE SYSTEMS plc)

Scottish Aviation Ltd used facilities at Caird's Yard, Greenock, and at Largs for flying boat repair and overhaul work during the Second World War. (Scottish Aviation Ltd via Dougal McIntyre)

Queen 34 engine. The type proved its ability to operate out of extremely short strips in hostile terrain and high temperatures whilst serving with the RAF in Malaya. Strips as short as 160 yards were used operationally, and SAL claimed a 33mph landing speed and a minimum landing run of only 26 yards for the Gipsy Queen-powered prototype! A total of fifty-nine Pioneer aircraft were built (including one static test airframe), the first production aircraft flying on 25 June 1953. Contemporary advertising ran:

Scottish Aviation Ltd – Designers and manufacturers of the Prestwick Pioneer – a light aircraft specifically designed for use in undeveloped areas where airfield facilities are not available or are very restricted. [...] The remarkably slow flying characteristics of the Pioneer bring air transport to areas previously considered impossible for this form of communication.

The prototype Twin Pioneer G-ANTP flew at Prestwick (officially) on 25 June 1955 (there had been a brief unofficial hop the previous day), with the first production aircraft following on 28 April 1956. A total of eighty-seven Twin Pioneer aircraft were built, the type achieving civil and military sales, including forty operated by the RAF and five by the Royal Malaysian Air Force. The company advertising material (from March 1958) stressed the value of its ability to operate from short, unprepared strips:

Anywhere in the World is an Airfield. A hundred yards, or so, of reasonably level ground is all that the Twin Pioneer needs. It can land at bicycle speeds in 100 yards, and can take off in 85. With its unlimited utility and 'put down anyplace' performance, the Twin Pioneer can carry the countless benefits of air transport simply and cheaply, to anywhere in the world.

Another slogan was:

The Twin Pioneer makes air services to the 'Hundred Yard Airport' a practical proposition.

Spitfire repair work being carried out at in the 'Palace of Engineering' at Prestwick during the Second World War. (Scottish Aviation Ltd via Dougal McIntyre)

The success of the Twin Pioneer was hindered by the ready availability of cheap DC-3/C-47 aircraft, and further hampered by a fatal accident to demonstrator G-AOEO due to structural failure of a wing strut fitting, killing the crew, including David McKintyre, the co-founder of SAL and a driving force behind the company. By late 1958, the company was in financial difficulties.

The survival of the company was achieved mainly by its gaining significant overhaul and modification contracts for both civil and military operators, together with a wide range of non-aviation activities. The company carried out modification work on the Boeing Washington and conversion programmes on the Skyraider and Avenger. Additional military work handled included RCAF Sabre, CF-100, T-33 and CF-104 aircraft, and overhaul of the Rolls-Royce Griffon for the Shackleton. The RCAF CF-104 programme began with the arrival of the first aircraft on 15 January 1963 and involved as many as eighteen aircraft per month by 1965. By 1967, Scottish Aviation were conducting their 1,000th CF-104 test flight from Prestwick. In all, SAL provided nearly twenty-five years of continuous support to the RCAF.

A highly successful civilian repair and overhaul section (SALchek) worked on a large variety of types, handling 566 aircraft in 1968. Types handled included the Britannia, Viscount (notably conversion work for Aer Lingus), Friendship, Carvair, DC-7, Canadair CL-44, and numerous DC-8 and Boeing 707 aircraft. A wide range of piston engines were overhauled by SAL subsidiary Scottish Air Engine Services, including the Pratt & Whitney R-1830 and R-2000, as well as the Merlin and Griffon. The very last Merlin engine to be overhauled on a production basis was handled in April 1967, by which time SAL had complete responsibility for Rolls-Royce piston engine overhaul. A total of 1,910 Griffon overhauls were completed up to May 1981. In 1962, the company converted twelve Douglas

Scottish Aviation Ltd set up Scottish Airlines which operated a range of types, including transport conversions of the B-24 Liberator, the parent company also carrying out conversion work. (Scottish Aviation Ltd via Dougal McIntyre)

The Prestwick Pioneer prototype parachutes in to land with its extensive flap and slat system deployed, thus emphasising its similarities with the Fieseler Storch. (BAE SYSTEMS plc)

Skyraider aircraft as target tugs for use in Sweden; in 1954, the company had originally converted these same aircraft for Royal Navy use.

In April 1966 Cammel Laird brought the company, which then became involved in Jetstream wing production. Additional sub-contract work was obtained manufacturing 773 aircraft sets of C-130 Hercules fuselage panels and under-wing fuel tank pylons. SAL also acquired the spares responsibility for the Handley Page Dart Herald, taking over a factory at Cumnock that had previously operated as **Handley Page (Scotland) Ltd**. This latter company had been set up in 1970 as an associate company of C.F. Taylor (Holdings), part of the **Weir Group**.

In May 1970 SAL took over **Beagle Aircraft Ltd**'s Bulldog contracts, notably that for fifty-eight aircraft for the Swedish Air Force; 132 Bulldog aircraft were subsequently ordered for the RAF. In all, more than 330 Bulldog were built, the first Scottish Aviation-built example G-AXIG flying on 14 February 1971. The first RAF Bulldog T.Mk 1 XX513 flew on 30 January 1973.

From February 1972 onwards, production rights to the Jetstream were transferred to SAL, leading to production of the Jetstream T.Mk 1 for the Royal Air Force. The RAF had ordered twenty-six Jetstream in February 1972 for use as navigation trainers, the first of these, XX475, flying on 13 April 1974. The RAF ordered eight further Jetstream T.Mk 1 in October 1976. The Jetstream T.Mk 1 was withdrawn from RAF service at the end of March 2004.

BAe/BAE SYSTEMS: In 1977 the company was taken into **British Aerospace**, Scottish Aviation Limited ceasing to exist as a legal entity on 1 January 1978. Among the earliest work carried out at Prestwick for BAe was the completion for delivery of a small number of Hawker Siddeley HS.748 aircraft.

The Jetstream programme continued with fourteen Jetstream T.Mk 2 aircraft supplied to the Royal Navy for observer training and communications duties. BAe developed the Jetstream 31 with the US-built Garrett TPE331-10 engine, this programme being announced on 5 December 1978. The first Jetstream 31 development aircraft G-JSSD (a conversion of Jetstream 1 G-AXJZ) was flown on 28 March 1980, with the first production Jetstream 31 G-TALL flown on 18 March 1982. 381 Jetstream 31/32 were built, the last aircraft being delivered in 1993. The Jetstream 32 (originally known as Jetstream Super 31) introduced the more powerful TPE331-12 engine; 161 of this variant were built. Four Jetstream T.Mk 3 (equivalent to the Jetstream 31) were ordered by the Royal Navy, and two were exported for use by the Royal Saudi Air Force.

A separate organisation, **Jetstream Aircraft Ltd** (wholly owned by British Aerospace Regional Aircraft), produced the Jetstream 31, Jetstream 41 and Jetstream 61. The Jetstream 41 was a twenty-nine seat aircraft powered by two TPE331-14 1,650shp engines driving five-blade propellers. The prototype G-GCJL was rolled out on 27 March 1991 and first flew at Prestwick on 25 September 1991. BAe announced in May 1997 its decision to close the Jetstream 41 line and, with the Jetstream 41 and Jetstream 61 both out of production, it seems inevitable that the site will no longer be involved in the manufacture of complete aircraft. A total of 104 Jetstream 41 were built, the last aircraft G-4-104 leaving Prestwick for Hurn on 19 February 1998. This aircraft was eventually delivered to the Hong Kong Government in February 1999.

The Jetstream 61 was an ATP development, with increased power provided by PW127D engines replacing the PW126A of the ATP. The prototype Jetstream 61 G-JXLI first flew on 10 May 1994. ATP/Jetstream 61 production was phased out after the production of

Production Twin Pioneer VR-OAE *photographed in flight over Prestwick prior to delivery in 1958.* (Scottish Aviation Ltd via Dougal McIntyre)

Scottish Aviation Ltd received long-standing contracts for the maintenance of European-based RCAF aircraft. This busy scene of CF104 Starfighter maintenance was photographed in 1963. (Scottish Aviation Ltd via Dougal McIntyre)

sixty-seven aircraft, only four of which were Jetstream 61. The decision to withdraw the type from production coincided with the formation of the AI(R) consortium, which combined BAe and ATR regional aircraft interests. For further details of the ATP, see Woodford, Greater Manchester, where the type was originally developed and built.

Under **British Aerospace**, the Military Aircraft and Aerostructures group at Prestwick was used for the following production activities: Jetstream 41 wing and fuselage and components; work on BAe 146 engine pylons and Avro RJ wings; and Nimrod MRA.4 and Raytheon Hawker airframe components (following the closure of the Jetstream 41 production line). Raytheon Hawker 800 component manufacture at Prestwick includes control services, doors, tailplane and rudder. Airbus A320 sub-assembly work and trailing edge assemblies were transferred to Prestwick in 1997. In late 1998, BAe announced that it was making an investment of £6 million to transfer A319, A320 and A321 wing sub-assemblies to Prestwick from Samlesbury, with the first Prestwick deliveries to Airbus at Broughton in October 1999.

In November 1998, British Aerospace signed a contract to manufacture fixed leading edges for the Boeing 777-300ER. The first production item was delivered on 22 May 2002; the 100th set being delivered on 28 February 2003 in a programme that runs until 2009. A similar contract was signed in August 2000 for Boeing 767 wing components, with the deliveries commencing in August 2002.

Under BAE SYSTEMS, the Prestwick operation includes aerostructures and component manufacturing activity, and Regional Aircraft providing engineering support and customer training facilities (including an ATP simulator) for in-service turboprop regional aircraft.

Scottish Aviation inherited the Bulldog programme following the demise of Beagle Aircraft Ltd. This RAF Bulldog shows off a non-standard colour scheme as it flies past the RAF College at Cranwell. (BAE SYSTEMS plc)

A total of 381 Jetstream 31 aircraft were built at Prestwick, the type being widely exported. (BAE SYSTEMS plc)

Right: *Jetstream 41 G-JMAC pays tribute to another Prestwick product, Twin Pioneer VH-AIS.* (BAE SYSTEMS plc)

Below: *The Jetstream 61 was a 're-badged' version of the ATP, built at Prestwick. The prototype G-JLXI first flew in May 1994 and is seen here flying past the BAE SYSTEMS (ex Scottish Aviation) factory at Prestwick.* (BAE SYSTEMS plc)

Renfrew

Lockheed Overseas Corporation set up facilities at Renfrew during the Second World War as an extension of their activities at Speke (see also Langford Lodge and Belfast (Sydenham)). The main types handled at Renfrew were the Boston, Wildcat, Mustang and Lightning.

Scottish Aviation Ltd operated a support facility at Renfrew for RCAF and USAF aircraft in Europe from late 1954, dealing mainly with the Sabre (both nations) and the RCAF Avro Canada CF-100 and T-33. The RCAF support activity was ultimately transferred to Prestwick.

Stirling

Scotland's first really successful aeroplane was the **Barnwell** 1911 monoplane. The **Grampian Engineering & Motor Co.**, of Causewayhead, Stirling built this aircraft, which was owned by the Barnwell brothers, Frank and Harold. The Barnwell brothers started early, but unsuccessful, experiments on a large canard biplane in the summer of 1909, which is reported to have flown a distance of 80 yards in July 1909, with further short flights on 8–12 September 1909. The 1911 monoplane was noted for its clean lines, and was powered by a Grampian two-cylinder horizontally opposed engine. This aircraft later completed a one-mile flight, and gained the Barnwell brothers the J.R.K. Law Prize for the first flight over half a mile in an all-Scottish aeroplane for flights conducted on 14 January and 30 January 1911. In August 1911 the Barnwell (Stirling) monoplane was flying from Blair Drummond, moving to Lanark in October of the same year.

Frank Barnwell later became the famous chief designer for the Bristol Aeroplane Co. Ltd, Harold Barnwell carrying out flight-testing and design work at Vickers Ltd. Both brothers were to die in aircraft accidents; Harold whilst testing the prototype Vickers F.B.26 at Joyce Green on 25 August 1917; and Frank in his own Barnwell BSW.1 at Whitchurch on 2 August 1938.

Wig Bay

Wig Bay was used by **Short Bros. & Harland** as a Sunderland repair, modification and storage facility into the 1950s.

Wales

Abergele/Foryd (near Rhyl)

Vivien Hewitt was a notable pioneer of flying in Wales. He was based at Foryd aerodrome, Abergele, on the coast about two miles west of Rhyl. In 1911-1912, Hewitt was regularly flying a Blériot monoplane, and flew it across the Irish Sea in spring 1912, this being only the third successful crossing. The aircraft was progressively modified such that, by April 1913, the only original parts were the landing gear, engine and fuselage longerons.

In October 1915, *Flight* carried an advertisement for a 'Blériot monoplane, less engine and in need of slight repairs. Offered for sale at The Aerodrome, Foryd, Rhyl.' By November, the additional information was provided that the machine 'wants slight repair to warping gear', and that £35 would be accepted. Clearly no sale was forthcoming, and, by December, the asking price was £30, including two pairs of wings.

This location does not appear on modern maps, having been renamed Kimnel Bay.

Barry

The **Norman Aeroplane Co. Ltd** (previously **NDN Aircraft Ltd**) was established on 22 July 1985 and operated at Barry. Six Fieldmaster aircraft were built before NDN failed in August 1988. Croplease Ltd acquired the design and production rights in October 1988, contracting **Brooklands Aircraft Co. Ltd/Brooklands Aerospace Ltd** at Old Sarum to continue development. Croplease Ltd was based in Shannon, and transferred the rights in the Fieldmaster to **Croplease plc**, London. For related entries, see Bembridge, Goodwood, Old Sarum and Sandown in Volumes Two and Three of this series.

Beaumaris, Anglesey

In May 1912, *Flight* reported that 'Hydro-aeroplane experiments are being carried out by the **Marquis of Anglesey** and **Viscount Ingestre** in the Menai Straits.'

Auster Aircraft Ltd tested Auster Mk V VP-FAC on floats at Beaumaris from 6 September 1949, for use in the Falkland Islands. Auster J/5A G-AJYL was also tested on floats at Beaumaris in January 1951.

Saunders-Roe Ltd operated at Fryars from spring 1941, as sister design authority for the Catalina, carrying out modifications to meet Coastal Command requirements, including the installation of bomb racks, armament, and ASV radar. The company prepared for service 309 Catalina (including 195 PBY-5B in the serial range FP100–FP325); five Kingfisher; one Seamew; six Coronado (from April 1943); and twelve Martin Mariner flying boats, for a grand total of 333 aircraft. Beaumaris was the preparation centre for RAF Catalina aircraft, the transatlantic reception centre being at Caird's Yard, Greenock, this facility being run by Scottish Aviation Ltd.

Expansion of the activity at Fryars resulted in the requisition of a number of other buildings in the area, including stables at Red Hill and Baron Hill. Additional hangars were erected at Fryars in the autumn of 1942 (one), and in late 1943 (two more).

Experimental flying was also carried out here, well away from the risk of bombing. The Saunders-Roe A.37 Shrimp sub-scale experimental flying boat was based here from 1940. The Shrimp was operated at MAEE Helensburgh from August 1940, and was used by the MAEE for the development of the Short Shetland hull shape. In this guise, the type was modified to a single fin configuration, and allocated the serial number TK580. The Shrimp flew throughout the war, moving to Felixstowe in mid-1945, before being scrapped in 1949. Initial design of the Saunders-Roe SR.A/1 jet flying boat took place at Beaumaris from 1944.

In 1951, the Beaumaris works were transferred to the company's boat-building division; becoming **Saunders-Roe (Anglesey) Ltd**. Output then comprised small craft for naval use, aluminium airborne lifeboats, bus bodies and other products.

This Auster V was tested on floats at Beaumaris in 1949, prior to service in the Falkland Islands. (John Collier collection)

The Saunders-Roe hangars at Fryars are still a prominent feature of the landscape. (Author)

Vickers-Armstrongs Ltd tested the Supermarine Spitfire IX floatplane MJ892 at Beaumaris, it first flying on 6 June 1944.

A large number of hangars remain at Fryars, being used in 1997 by Faun Municipal Vehicles. From the shore road at Beaumaris, it only takes a little imagination to imagine the roadstead filled with flying boats, instead of yachts at their moorings.

Cardiff and Penarth

The Aircraft Manufacturing Co. Ltd: AIRCO formed a number of subsidiary companies to increase their production capacity, one example being Wycombe Aircraft Constructors at High Wycombe. Harald Penrose reported, in the *Great War and Armistice* volume of the *History of British Aviation* series, that AIRCO also set up a subsidiary at Penarth as part of this effort. Precise details of company name and address have not come to hand.

The **Watkins** 'Red Robin' monoplane of 1909 was designed and constructed by C.H. Watkins at Mynachdy Farm, Maendy, Cardiff at a cost of £300, which included the engine, which was also designed and constructed by Mr Watkins. Testing took place mainly in the early morning or late evening due to the problem of large crowds gathering to watch events in daytime. The aircraft was successfully flown on a number of cross-country flights, and the type is reported to have still been in occasional use as late as 1918 (*British Aircraft Before the Great War*). The machine was displayed in the RAF St Athan collection, having been stored for many years in the designer's Cardiff garage.

Crickhowell (Powis)

Noble Hardman Aviation Ltd developed an enclosed cabin, high-wing, two-seat microlight with conventional three-axis controls called the Snowbird. The prototype Snowbird G-MNHA was flown for the first time on 2 September 1984.

Dale (near Milford Haven)

Dale was used as an early experimental test base for **British and Colonial Aeroplane Co. Ltd** waterborne aircraft during 1912 and 1913. The Bristol TB8 was flown successfully here in 1913, after trials of the novel, but unsuccessful, Bristol Burney Hydroplanes.

Hawarden/Chester (Broughton)

The aircraft factory at Hawarden came into use as a shadow factory during the Second World War; it has been used by Vickers-Armstrongs Ltd; The de Havilland Aircraft Co. Ltd; and BAe/BAE SYSYEMS. This activity is presented chronologically below.

Vickers-Armstrongs Ltd: This major shadow factory, like that at Blackpool, was a product of the pre-war expansion schemes and was managed by Vickers-Armstrongs Ltd, using a large number of local sub-contractors for component supply. Wellington production comprised a total of 5,540 aircraft, made up of three Mk I, seventeen Mk IA, 1,583 Mk IC, 737 Mk III, 220 Mk IV, 2,434 Mk X, eight Mk XII, and 538 Mk XIV. In addition, 235 Lancaster Mk 1 were built at Chester between June 1944 and September 1945. This factory was also used for the assembly of a small number of Metropolitan-Vickers-built Lancaster aircraft.

After the Second World War, Vickers produced 28,000 aluminium bungalows at Chester to maintain production employment. The factory remained in use by Vickers until March 1948.

The de Havilland Aircraft Co. Ltd: In its 1948 annual report, the de Havilland company announced: 'For various national considerations, we are not able to expand our factories in Hertfordshire and the London area much beyond their present size, and to cope

Above: *The Noble Hardman Snowbird is a microlight with three-axis controls and a conventional configuration.* (Author)

Right: *This post-war view of Hawarden shows large numbers of aircraft in open storage on the airfield.* (BAE SYSTEMS plc)

with the export business obtained it has been necessary for us to secure the lease of a further factory near Chester. This is a modern factory, about as large as our main factory at Hatfield, and we expect to be able to develop an efficient aircraft assembly organisation there.' The company occupied the site from 1 July 1948.

The first aircraft to be built and flown by de Havilland at Hawarden was a Mosquito NF.38 flown on 30 September 1948. Aircraft types produced at Hawarden comprised the following:

- Mosquito – a total of eighty-one aircraft, including TR.37 Sea Mosquito (fourteen aircraft) and NF.38.
- Hornet and Sea Hornet – a total of 149 aircraft, including the NF.21 and PR.22, from March 1949.
- Vampire – a total of 792 single-seat fighter, sixty-two night fighter and 427 T.11.
- Venom – a total of 775 aircraft of all marks, including single-seat FB.1 and FB.4, and night fighter NF.2 and NF.3, built from 1952 onward.
- Dove – 209 aircraft from 1951 up to the end of 1959.
- Comet – One Comet 1, twelve Comet 4. Two Comet 4C airframes were also modified under Hawker Siddeley Aviation Ltd to become Nimrod development aircraft (XV147, XV148) in 1965-1967. XV148 flew for the first time on 23 May 1967.

This photographic period piece shows the frontage of the Vickers-Armstrongs Ltd shadow factory at Chester. (BAE SYSTEMS plc)

The well-known Lancaster PA474 operated by the RAF Battle of Britain Memorial Flight was built by Vickers-Armstrongs Ltd at Chester. (BAE SYSTEMS plc)

- Chipmunk – 889 aircraft from 1950 onward.
- Beaver – two production batches in 1961-1962, and in 1968.
- Sea Vixen FAW.2 – from 1962 until 1966.
- Heron – Chester production comprised forty-four Heron Srs.1 and ninety-seven Srs.2, and included those for the Queen's Flight.

Hawker Siddeley Aviation Ltd: The de Havilland factory at Broughton was amalgamated into HSAL in 1960, and from 1962, the HS125 was built at Broughton, the first Broughton-built aircraft flying on 12 February 1963. The aircraft was a long-lived commercial success, remaining in production for more than forty years.

British Aerospace (BAe) and **BAE SYSTEMS**: **BAe Corporate Jets** continued to produce the BAe 125 at Broughton until the business was sold to Raytheon Corporation in June 1993.

British Aerospace Airbus Ltd: The Broughton factory carries out wing manufacture for all types of aircraft in the Airbus range, and continued fuselage and wing manufacture of the Hawker 800 executive jet – the latest incarnation of the de Havilland DH125 – for Raytheon, after the sale of BAe Corporate Jets to that company.

The first A300 wing set was delivered from Broughton on 23 November 1971, and by February 2002, 3,000 Airbus wing sets had been delivered. Other significant Airbus wing production milestones are summarised below:

Date	Event
24 August 1990	First A340 wing box flown from Broughton by Super Guppy.
13 May 1992	1,000th Airbus wing set delivered.
August 1996	1,500th Airbus wing set delivered.
8 February 1999	2,000th Airbus wing set delivered.
18 February 2002	3,000th Airbus wing set delivered.
5 April 2004	Roll-out for delivery of first A380 wing.

Simultaneous production of the Dove, Hornet and Sea Hornet under way at Hawarden. (BAE SYSTEMS plc)

This immaculate Jordanian Dove banks gracefully during formation flying practice over the Hampshire countryside. (Author)

Above: *The Canadian-designed Chipmunk was built in quantity at Hatfield and Hawarden and remains a pilot's favourite due to its excellent control harmony.* (Author)

Left: *Like the Dove, a number of Herons were subsequently fitted with American engines, replacing the original Gipsy Queens. This example is preserved in Australia.* (Author)

Left: *The 500th aircraft of the HS125 family is seen here on the busy production line at Hawarden.* (Ken Ellis collection)

Opposite: *The first A340 wing leaves its jig at Broughton prior to being flown to Toulouse in August 1990.* (Airbus Industrie via Ken Ellis)

Wings for the later Airbus types were introduced on the Broughton production line as follows: A310 in 1978, A320 in 1986, A340 in 1990, A330 and A321 in 1992, and A319 in 1995. By the time of the thirtieth anniversary (23 November 2001) of the first Airbus wing delivery, a grand total of 2,934 Airbus wing sets had been delivered.

The company became **BAE SYSTEMS, Airbus** following the merger between British Aerospace and Marconi Electronic Systems. With the announcement of the **Airbus Integrated Company (AIC)** on 23 June 2000, it was indicated that the Broughton factory would be transferred to the re-constituted Airbus organisation.

Raytheon Corporation: Following the sale of BAe Corporate Jets Ltd to Raytheon, it was announced that existing contracts with BAe Airbus Ltd at Broughton for the supply of fuselages, wings and completion sets for the Hawker 800 and 1000 were to continue for up to three years from 1996, although aircraft final assembly was to transfer to Wichita by mid-1997. The decision was taken to end Hawker 1000 production in 1997, with about fifty aircraft sold.

The success of the DH/HS/BAe 125/Hawker 800XP continues almost undiminished, and some fifty aircraft sets were produced in 1998, with the 1,000th delivery of the type taking place in April 1998. As many as sixty aircraft sets were constructed in 1999, and the type continues in production in 2004, with a production run exceeding forty years. Airbus at Broughton continue to manufacture major assemblies, and in 2004 were responsible for fuselage, wing and tailplane manufacture and assembly. Some Raytheon manufacturing activity was transferred to Prestwick following the cessation of Jetstream J41 production.

On 7 March 2003, Raytheon Systems opened their new facility at Broughton for the preparation of Bombardier Global Express aircraft to fulfil their role as ASTOR (airborne stand off radar) aircraft for the Royal Air Force. Activities include systems integration for both the platform and its ground station. Five aircraft are to be procured, with the first being prepared in the United States, the remaining four making use of the new facilities at Broughton.

Llanbedr

Short Bros. & Harland were advertising in January 1955 for aircraft fitters and riggers for maintenance work on service aircraft (preference to be given to ex-service personnel with recent experience on jet aircraft) to be carried out at Llanbedr, Merioneth.

Llanddona (Anglesey)

William Ellis Williams was the first Professor of Electrical Engineering in the University of Wales, and designed and built his own aeroplane at Bangor. Ellis Williams flew this machine at Llanddona, Anglesey (a few yards away from Red Wharf Bay beach), his address whilst conducting these trials being 'The Aeroplane Shed, Llanddona'. After much modification and struggling, the aircraft flew in autumn 1911 with a JAP engine hired from A.V. Roe. A further engine, a 40hp Clément, was hired in 1912, and subsequently purchased for £25 and used for a further flying season in 1913. A successful flight was recorded photographically on 3 September 1913. The whole objective of this activity was research, and these experiments included some of the earliest to measure the aerofoil pressure distribution in flight!

William Ellis Williams continued his researches, and *Flight* records a publication received in May 1915, entitled 'On the motion of a sphere through a viscous fluid', written by W. Ellis Williams, University College, Bangor.

Red Wharf Bay is a glorious beach, which provides a vast area of sand at low tide. A narrow and steep road from Llanddona leads down to the beach, where at the end of a short stretch of unmade road there is a small car park. At the rear of the car park, there is a monument to Professor Williams inscribed as follows:

> *CYNGOR BWRDEISREF YNYS MÔN*
> *WILLIAM ELLIS WILLIAMS*
> *1881-1962*
> *MATHEMATEGYDD A PHEIRIANYDD*
> *BUN ARBROFI AC YN HEDFAN MEWN AWYREN*
> *AR Y TRAETH HWN YM MEDI 1911*

(for non-speakers of the Welsh language, this translates as '*Anglesey County Council, William Ellis Williams, 1881-1962, Mathematician and Engineer, He experimented in, and flew an aeroplane from this beach in September 1911*'). Here, at least, a piece of national aviation heritage is preserved for future generations.

Llandudno

A Short-Wright biplane and a Farman biplane were reported to be flying at the Llandudno and North Wales Aerodrome in August 1911. It is not known if any construction work was undertaken here.

Monmouth

Northern Aluminium Ltd: The Rogerstone Works at Monmouth was set up in 1939 to manufacture aluminium sheet. The Rogerstone Works went on to produce a huge quantity of aircraft extrusions including 40,000 Spitfire spar booms.

Northern Aluminium Ltd took control in June 1946 and the company became a mainstay of the post-war industry. Example products included the main spar of the Comet 3 and spar sections for the Beverley, Britannia, Canberra, and Vulcan; propeller blade forgings for the Hastings, Princess, Shackleton and Viscount; and forgings for the Heron, Vampire, Venom and DH110.

Parkes 1910 monoplane: This machine is described and illustrated in *British Aircraft Before the Great War*. The design (by the Parkes brothers) featured a monoplane wing, with front and rear stabilising surfaces, all heavily cambered. The engine was mounted ahead of the wing leading edge and drove a tractor propeller that rotated between the longitudinal members that

The Phillips Speedtwin is an original design with considerable potential, but the type has not yet entered production. (Author)

supported the foreplane. A small rudder surface was provided at the very rear of the machine. Despite its somewhat unusual configuration, it is reported (loc. cit.) to have flown on 7 July 1910, although no furher activity was subsequently reported.

Speedtwin Developments Ltd of Upper Cae Garw Farm, Trellech, Monmouth developed the Phillips ST1 Speedtwin. The Speedtwin was designed and built by Peter Phillips, the well-known Britten-Norman demonstration pilot. The type is an aerobatic twin-engine two-seat aircraft of fixed undercarriage tail wheel configuration. The prototype G-GPST was powered by two Continental O-200 engines, and was first displayed publicly in 1992.

Narbeth (between Carmarthen and Haverfordwest)

In September 1913, the **James** brothers flew a single-seat Caudron-like biplane from a small field near Narbeth. The machine was damaged during its first flight, and again, when it was flown in November 1913. By April 1914, the machine had been rebuilt in two-seat configuration, in which form it was known as the James No.2 biplane. In July of that year, the brothers were reported in *Flight* as planning to set up an aircraft factory at their hometown

The Parkes 1910 monoplane is reported to have been flown at Monmouth in July 1910. (JMB/GSL collection)

> **DUTTON AIRCRAFTS.**
> (T. M. DUTTON, A.M.I.E.E., Engineer.)
> **School of Flying at Chester Aerodrome,**
> Sealand, Chester.
> IDEAL FLYING GROUND EXTENDING OVER 150 ACRES.
> *IMMEDIATE VACANCIES.*
> All Particulars of Terms, etc., from Sub-Office,
> 52, Bridge Street, Chester.

Dutton Aircrafts (Sealand/Chester 1917)

of Narbeth. This would have been the first aircraft factory in Wales, but for the outbreak of the First World War. In 1915, the brothers took the No.2 biplane to the **Ruffy-Baumann School** at Hendon, where it was used as a trainer.

In June 1915, the brothers moved to the **Hall Aviation Co.** James Herbert 'Jimmie' James learned to fly at the **W.H. Ewen School** in 1912 and went on to test fly for **Nieuport & General Aircraft**, before becoming the first chief test pilot of the **Gloucestershire Aircraft Company**, holding this post until April 1923. He then moved on to Smiths Instruments in the old Nieuport works at Cricklewood.

St Davids (Pembrokeshire)

Airwork Ltd: In November 1954, Airwork Ltd were advertising for fitters and riggers for maintenance work on Meteor, Hornet and Mosquito aircraft, to be carried out at RNAS St Davids, Pembrokeshire.

Sealand

Dutton Aircrafts (sub-office 52 Bridge Street, Chester) were advertising during the First World War their 'School of Flying, at Chester Aerodrome, Sealand, Chester. Ideal flying ground extending over 150 acres'.

F. Hills & Sons Ltd: The Hillson-developed slip-wing Hurricane was flight-tested at RAF Sealand under the designation F.H.40 Mk1; for further details, see Barton, Greater Manchester.

Northern Ireland

Banbridge (Co. Down)

Miles Aircraft (Northern Ireland) Ltd: The first Miles factory in Northern Ireland was in a disused linen mill at Castlewellan Road, Banbridge, County Down, which was used for production of the Messenger. After construction, the aircraft were taken to Long Kesh to be assembled and test flown. The first Irish-built aircraft was G-ALAC, which flew at Long Kesh in August 1945. Production was moved in 1946 to a new factory at Ards Airport, Newtownards (Belfast), run by Miles Aircraft (Northern Ireland) Ltd.

Belfast

The most significant of the Belfast-based manufacturers is **Short Brothers plc** (now owned by Bombardier Aerospace Inc.), and its predecessor companies. This entry provides a chronological record of these companies; followed by an alphabetical listing of other Belfast-based firms.

The shipbuilders **Harland & Wolff Ltd** carried out aircraft construction during the First World War. Aircraft manufactured comprised:

- 300 AIRCO DH6 built in 1916.
- At least 505 Avro 504J/K from contracts totalling 600.
- A single Handley Page O/400, which was erected by Handley Page Ltd at Cricklewood from parts made by Harland & Wolff Ltd.
- Twenty Handley Page V/1500 with serials from E4304. For the first three of these, the parts were made by Harland & Wolff, but erected by Handley Page Ltd at Cricklewood. The next five were delivered by air from Aldergrove, with the remaining twelve aircraft delivered as spares.

Short & Harland Ltd was formed in June 1936 and was jointly owned by Short Brothers (Rochester & Bedford) Ltd and by Harland & Wolff Ltd. The works were at Queen's Island, Belfast, with Sydenham Airport being used for landplane assembly, test and delivery. Flying boats were flown from Belfast Lough. A further airfield at Nutts Corner, Long Kesh, Aldergrove was also used for assembly, test and delivery.

Short & Harland built fifty Bristol Bombay, starting with L5808, which was first flown at Sydenham in March 1939. This contract was followed by 150 Handley Page Hereford, the last eleven being delivered as Hampden. The first Short-built Hereford was L7271 (a conversion of the HP53 Hampden prototype), which flew on 6 October 1936.

The main wartime production was of 1,218 Short Stirling, including 266 Mk I, 342 Mk II, 450 out of 460 Mk IV, and all 160 of the Mk V transport variant. Stirling IV/V production was undertaken at Aldergrove (138 aircraft) and Maghaberry (ninety-eight aircraft), these factories being set up as satellites to the main works at Queen's Island. The first Belfast-built Stirling N6000 flew on 28 October 1940. Overall, Stirling production consisted of 2,383 aircraft at the following locations: Rochester/South Marston (two prototypes, and 543 production aircraft − 267 Mk I, 266 Mk II, ten Mk IV), Longbridge (Austin Motors production of 191 Mk I, 429 Mk II), Belfast (1,218 aircraft, details as above). (Other production details can also be found).

During the Second World War, Short & Harland built 133 Short Sunderland (fifteen Mk II, 71 Mk III, forty-seven Mk V) at Belfast. The last Belfast-built Sunderland SZ599 was flown on 14 June 1946. Short & Harland also converted five Sunderland aircraft for use in

Handley Page O/400 B9464 was erected by Handley Page Ltd using components manufactured by Harland & Wolff Ltd. (JMB/GSL collection)

The Short Brothers & Harland works at Queen's Island, with the adjoining Sydenham Airport, were used for assembly and landplane flight-test. (Bombardier Aerospace Belfast via Ken Ellis)

ML814 *is a Sunderland III, built by Short & Harland at Belfast.* (Author)

This evocative photograph shows Solent production in full flow. The aircraft in the foreground is G-AHIO Somerset, *a Solent 2 for BOAC.* (Bombardier Aerospace Belfast via Ken Ellis)

Sealand demonstrator G-AKLO, photographed in 1950, reportedly en route to the SBAC Show. (Bombardier Aerospace Belfast)

Argentina and Paraguay, this activity being followed by twenty-six of the twenty-seven Sandringham conversions (the prototype, later G-AGKX, having been converted from Sunderland III ML788 at Rochester). Production comprised one Sandringham 1 (at Rochester), three Sandringham 2, two Sandringham 3, four Sandringham 4, nine Sandringham 5 (one additional aircraft G-AHYZ was burned out during conversion at Belfast), five Sandringham 6 and three Sandringham 7.

The company carried out civil conversions of ten Junkers 52/3m for BEA, and modification of twelve Handley Page Halifax to Handley Page Haltons for passenger use by BOAC. Ninety-four Avro Lancaster and fifty Avro Lincoln aircraft came to Short & Harland for major overhaul, and twelve Lincoln bombers were reconditioned and converted for use by Argentina.

The Government, through the Minister of Aircraft Production, took control of **Short Brothers (Rochester & Bedford) Ltd** in March 1943, Oswald Short having resigned from the chairmanship of the company in January 1943. **Short & Harland Ltd** took over **Short Brothers (Rochester & Bedford) Ltd** in 1947, changing its name to **Short Bros. & Harland Ltd** in November 1947. The operations at Rochester, for both landplane and flying boat manufacture, were then transferred to Belfast. At the time of its formation, Short Bros. & Harland Ltd was owned 64 per cent by the Government, and 36 per cent by Harland & Wolff Ltd. By 1948, all design and manufacturing had been concentrated at Belfast, Short Bros. & Harland Ltd adopting a Short Brothers slogan, advertising themselves as 'The first manufacturers of aircraft in the world'.

Short Bros. & Harland Ltd continued the flying boat traditions of its predecessors with the Short Sealand amphibian. The prototype Sealand G-AIVX was first flown on 22 January 1948 from Belfast Lough. The Sealand was advertised as follows: 'Designed for areas where freight and passenger carriage is impracticable for normal aircraft – The Short Sealand' and 'The Sealand Amphibian – in service in Norway, Yugoslavia, Pakistan and now India. The

Indian Navy is to operate a fleet of ten Sealand based at Cochin. Each aircraft is fitted with dual controls, long-range tanks and has seating accommodation for six.' Production comprised the prototype, four pre-production aircraft, and twenty production machines, for a total of twenty-five aircraft.

The second Short Sturgeon RK791 was built at Rochester, but first flown from Sydenham, alongside the Queen's Island factory. The prototypes were followed by two Sturgeon 2 and twenty-four production Sturgeon TT.2, many of which were delivered to store. The last Sturgeon, WF632, was converted to Mamba turboprop power as the Short SB3, an unsuccessful competitor to the Gannet. The SB3 was first flown on 12 August 1950; a second prototype WF636 was not flown.

Sperrin VX158 is seen here in Short PD6 form, testing the de Havilland Gyron engine. (BAE SYSTEMS plc)

The SB5 experimental aircraft was built to investigate the low-speed characteristics of the highly swept thin wings proposed for the English Electric P.1. (Bombardier Aerospace Belfast)

Because of the expected high volume production, Comet 2 fuselage production and assembly was undertaken in Belfast. The original window shape is clearly shown. (BAE SYSTEMS plc)

The Short SB1 Sherpa research aircraft, used to investigate the properties of the aero-isoclinic wing, flew as a glider (G-14-5) at Aldergrove on 14 July 1951, being winch-launched for its first flight. On 30 July 1951, the Sherpa was able to make a longer flight, impressively towed by Sturgeon VR363. The Sherpa was rebuilt as a powered aircraft after an accident, flying in this form as Short SB4 G-14-1 on 4 October 1953, propelled by two Turbomeca Palas.

The Short SA4 Sperrin VX158 first flew at Aldergrove on 10 August 1951. The Sperrin was designed against specification B.14/46 as an insurance against the failure of the technically more adventurous V-Bomber prototypes. The Sperrin was powered by four Rolls-Royce Avon engines, wing mounted in stacked pairs. Two were built, VX158 and VX161; VX158 later being adapted as a test bed for the de Havilland Gyron. In this form the aircraft carried the designation Short PD6, being first flown on 7 July 1955 at Aldergrove.

The Short SB5 experimental aircraft was built to investigate the low-speed characteristics of highly swept wings in support of the English Electric P.1 programme. The SB5 WG768 was first flown at Boscombe Down on 2 December 1952, subsequently being based at RAE Bedford.

The Short SB6 Seamew was built and flown in less than eighteen months, the prototype XA209 flying on 23 August 1953. The type was intended to be based on escort carriers and to provide anti-submarine protection at a lower cost than the use of helicopters or the twin-turbine powered Fairey Gannet. Unfortunately, the Seamew proved to have complex handling and performance problems, which led to a lengthy and unsuccessful development programme. Three prototypes were built of which only two were flown. The prototypes were followed by a number of production aircraft, but when the programme was cancelled in 1957, only seven of the nineteen aircraft then built had been accepted into service at Lossiemouth. Following cancellation, the accepted aircraft were put into store and the remaining airframes were scrapped.

By July 1954, the ownership of Short Brothers & Harland was 69½ per cent by the Government and 15¼ per cent each by Harland & Wolff Ltd and The Bristol Aeroplane Co. Ltd. The interest in Short Brothers & Harland taken by The Bristol Aeroplane Co. Ltd was reflected in the decision to set up a second Bristol Britannia production line at Belfast in 1954, with specific responsibility for the production of the military transport version of the Britannia for the RAF. Short Brothers & Harland production of the Britannia comprised three Srs 252 and twenty Srs 253 for the RAF, and a total of twelve additional aircraft (two Srs 300, five Srs 305 and five Srs 314) under contract to The Bristol Aeroplane Co. Ltd. The first Short-built Britannia C.1 XL635 flew on 29 December 1958. Fuselage production and assembly for the de Havilland Comet 2 was undertaken in Belfast, supplementing the production capacity available at Hatfield in anticipation of an expected high volume of sales.

Two experimental Short SC1 vertical take off and landing (VTOL) aircraft were built, XG900 and XG905. These aircraft had a long testing career at RAE Bedford, and, on 6 April 1960, XG905 became the first United Kingdom jet VTOL aircraft to make a full transition between conventional and hovering flight. XG900 carried out initial conventional flying from Boscombe Down, flying for the first time on 2 April 1957. XG905 undertook tethered hover flight at Sydenham on 23 May 1958, followed by free hovering on 25 October 1958.

The resolutely utilitarian Skyvan is reputed to have had its origins in a re-evaluation of the Miles HDM.105, to which Shorts had acquired the design rights. The first prototype Skyvan G-ASCN flew at Sydenham on 17 January 1963. The aircraft was initially powered by two GTSIO-520 piston engines of 390hp, it was subsequently re-engined with 520shp Astazou II turboprops. The Astazou-powered Skyvan, which first flew on 2 October 1963, was known as the Skyvan 1A, becoming the Skyvan 2 in its fully developed production form. The first of three Skyvan 2 development aircraft, G-ASCO, was flown on 29 October 1965. The type was again re-engined with Garrett TPE331s to create the definitive production version, the Skyvan 3. The Skyvan 3 was first flown (G-ASZI) on 15 December 1967. Production comprised the prototype, nineteen Skyvan 2 and some 130 Skyvan 3 for a total of 150 aircraft.

In June 1964, the type was being advertised in the following terms:

SKYVAN – Versatility with Wings. There's a worldwide need for an all-purpose, robust, light freighter with good short field performance and the ability to carry a wide range of two-ton loads. So Shorts built the Skyvan.

The imposing Short Belfast transport aircraft for the RAF had its origins in a project to fit a specialist cargo fuselage to a wing adapted from that of the Britannia. This approach is directly analogous to the design concept of the Armstrong Whitworth Argosy, which exploited the wing design of the Avro Shackleton. These origins led to the Short Belfast being known initially as the Britannic. Wing design was by the Bristol Aeroplane Co. Ltd, with rear fuselage and loading ramp constructed by Saunders-Roe Ltd. The prototype Belfast G-ASKE/XR342 first flew at Sydenham on 5 January 1964. Production was limited to only ten aircraft for the RAF, the type serving from 1966 to 1976.

A stretched 'derivative' of the Skyvan, the SD330 G-BSBH first flew on 22 August 1974. A military variant of the SD330, the C-23 Sherpa, was first flown on 23 December 1982. The type was adopted by the US Air Force as the C-23A, and the US Army National Guard as the C-23B. A variant known by Shorts as the C-23B+ was a conversion from the later

Above: *The Belfast strategic transport flew in 1964. Only ten were to be built and by the end of 1976 the type had been withdrawn from RAF service.* (Author)

Left: *The Short SD330 was a stretched Skyvan derivative produced in both military and civil versions; G-BITX is seen here operating between Gatwick and the Channel Islands.* (Author)

SD360, itself an SD330 development. A further military derivative, the SH330-UTT was sold to the Thai Army, Navy and Police Force, and to the UAE and Venezuela. Production quantities, as supplied by Bombardier, were as follows: SD330 (and UTT variant) 104 aircraft; C-23A eighteen aircraft, C-23B sixteen aircraft; and C-23B+ twenty-eight aircraft.

In addition to the Bristol Britannia, Shorts were contracted to carry out repair, modification and overhaul work on the Hawker Sea Hawk, Vickers-Armstrongs Scimitar and de Havilland Sea Venom. Shorts held significant sub-contracts for the Swift and the cancellation of contracts for the Swift Mk 4 resulted in Shorts announcing job losses on 13 April 1955. The company was also contracted to supply Comet fuselages to the de Havilland Aircraft Co. Ltd and produced thirteen VC-10 fuselages for aircraft delivered to the RAF. The final significant production type was the English Electric Canberra, Shorts building sixty Canberra B.2, forty-nine B.6, twelve B(I).Mk 8 and twenty-three PR. Mk 9, for a total of 144 aircraft. The first Short Bros. & Harland Canberra PR. Mk 9 was flown on 26 July 1958. The company was also responsible for the development of the unmanned Canberra U.10, producing two prototypes and twenty-four production aircraft, followed by six Canberra U.14.

The name **Short Brothers Ltd** was re-adopted on 1 June 1977, at which time, 98 per cent of the share holding was Government owned. The company produced a stretched passenger derivative of the SD330, the Shorts SD360, which was distinguished by its single swept fin, compared with the twin fins of the Skyvan and SD330. The prototype G-ROOM first flew on 1 June 1981. 164 SD360 were built, the last being delivered on 28 June 1991.

The name **Short Brothers plc** was adopted in 1984. An extensively modified version of the Embraer Tucano was selected for RAF trainer use in March 1985, the aircraft being manufactured in Belfast. The initial RAF order for 130 aircraft was followed by sixteen supplied to Kuwait, and twelve to Kenya. One RAF airframe was destroyed by a bomb, and one of the export aircraft crashed during trials. These aircraft were replaced, making total airframe production of 131 for the RAF, and twenty-nine export examples. The first Shorts-built aircraft, ZF135, flew on 30 December 1986.

Like many other firms in the industry, the company has undertaken extensive sub-contract production for the worldwide aerospace industry, with particular emphasis on structural components and engine nacelle systems (see below). In its various guises, the company has also had a long-standing relationship with the Dutch company Fokker, being a risk sharing partner on the F28, Fokker 70 and Fokker 100.

Bombardier Inc. of Canada purchased Shorts from the British Government, the purchase being formally completed on 4 October 1989. Shorts is now the European Group of Bombardier Aerospace Inc., with major activities in component manufacture and jet engine nacelles.

Bombardier projects in which the company is involved include the design and manufacture of the centre fuselage, control surfaces and nacelles for the Canadair Regional Jet; design, development and production of the complete Learjet 45 fuselage; and work in support of the Canadair Global Express long-range business jet. Global Express responsibilities include forward fuselage and passenger doors, nacelles, under-fuselage fairing and tailplane. The company also manufactures engine nacelles and control surfaces for the Bombardier Dash 8-400.

Outside the Bombardier Group, Shorts were heavily involved in the Fokker 100 and Fokker 70 (having previously supplied wings for the Fokker F28), and have been concerned to make good business lost in this area following the collapse of Fokker in March 1996. The company is the sole source to Boeing for many airliner components, and is the prime supplier to Boeing of metal-bonded components for civil products, including 737 rudders, 747 landing gear doors, 757 flap components and 777 nose gear doors. Shorts is also under contract for structural work as part of both the UK Apache and the C-130J programmes.

Last of the Canberra variants to remain in front-line operations, the high altitude Canberra PR.9 was built in Belfast by Short Brothers & Harland Ltd. (Author)

The Short SD360 is a basic commercial aircraft that is distinguished from the closely related SD330 by its single swept fin. (J.S. Smith)

More than 2,000 Rolls-Royce RB211 nose cowls have been supplied, and the company, in partnership with IAE/Rohr, also supplies nacelles for the V2500 engine on the Airbus A319, A320 and A321, and the McDonnell Douglas MD-90. Other applications include CF34 on Challenger and Regional Jet, LF507 nacelles for the Avro RJ series, and, in partnership with Hurel-Dubois, nacelles for the Gulfstream V, the Bombardier Global Express and the Embraer 145. Shorts is also responsible for the nose cowling of the Rolls-Royce Trent 700.

J.B. Ferguson & Co. Ltd of Little Donegal Street, Belfast built the aircraft that made the first flight in Ulster on 31 December 1909, this being the Ferguson monoplane, a conventional tractor monoplane configured on broadly Blériot lines. The machine was designed and flown by Harry G. Ferguson of Ferguson tractor fame. Various iterations and developments with different engines and propellers flew very successfully between 1910 and 1913, first at Old Park, Hillsborough, County Down, then at Massareene Park, County Antrim and, from May 1910, at Magilligan Strand, Strangford Lough. From 15 July 1910, the aircraft was moved to Newcastle, County Down, Ferguson winning a £100 prize for being the first in Ireland to fly a distance of three miles, this flight being made on 8 August. The aircraft then returned to Magilligan Strand.

A second machine was built in June 1910 and was flown at Newtownards and at Magilligan Strand. *Flight* reported that splendid trial flights had been carried out from the shore of Strangford Lough on 17 October 1911, including the carriage of passengers. This machine continued in use until 1913.

Lear Fan Ltd: The Lear Fan Corporation of Reno, Nevada set up facilities for the manufacture of the Lear Fan 2100 at Aldergrove and at Newtownabbey. The Lear Fan was an all-composite corporate aircraft, featuring a PT6 twin-pack driving a single pusher propeller. The first prototype, N626BL, flew on 1 January 1981. Technical difficulties were encountered with certification of both the composite structure and the combining gearbox of the propulsion system. Lear Fan Ltd was formed in March 1980, as a result of an agreement between LearAvia Corporation and the British Government. Ownership and control was transferred to Fan Holdings Inc. of Delaware in September 1982. The project was transferred to Reno in 1983, with the company closing down not long after (90 per cent of the workforce had been laid off by August 1984).

The Aircraft Manufacturers of Northern England, Scotland, Wales and Northern Ireland 237

ZF417 is a Tucano T.1 (a highly developed version of the Brazilian Embraer Tucano) built by Short Brothers plc for the RAF training role. (Author)

Bombardier Aerospace is a major force in the manufacture of aerospace structures, supplying, for example, the complete fuselage of the Learjet 45. (Bombardier Aerospace Belfast via Ken Ellis)

The Ferguson monoplane made its first flight in Ulster on the last day of 1909. The aircraft went through a number of design changes; this is the third version of the No.1 monoplane, photographed in 1910. (JMB/GSL collection)

R. & W.A.C. McCandless Aviation Ltd produced the McCandless gyroplane. This type was initially derived from the Bensen design, the prototype M-4 G-ARTZ flying in 1965. The design was subsequently developed into the W.H. Ekin Airbuggy (see Crumlin).

Lockheed Overseas Corporation set up facilities at Sydenham during the Second World War as an extension of their activities at Speke (see also Langford Lodge and Renfrew). The main types handled at Sydenham were the Avenger and Corsair.

Miles Aircraft (Northern Ireland) Ltd was formed in May 1946 with an authorised share capital of £50,000. In 1946, a 250,000 sq. ft factory was built at Newtownards for Messenger production. Unfortunately, the company was forced into liquidation in November 1947 due to the financial difficulties of Miles Aircraft Ltd. Of eleven unfinished aircraft at Newtownards, nine were completed as Messenger 2A by Handley Page (Reading) Ltd.

Carnamoney (near Belfast)

Lilian E. Bland built the Bland 'Mayfly', which was initially tested as a glider. Miss Bland taught herself to fly the machine in late 1910, and she (and the aircraft) flew quite successfully. So successfully, in fact, that a new husband whisked her off to Canada at the end of 1911, bringing her aeronautical experiments to an end.

Crumlin (Co. Antrim)

W.H. Ekin (Engineering) Ltd was formed in March 1969 to build a productionised version of the McCandless autogyro. The company was contracted to build six McCandless Mk IV, following which the type was evolved into the W.H.E. Airbuggy. A total of twelve McCandless/Ekin machines were registered by 1974, the prototype flying on 1 February 1972.

G-AKIN *was, like most Messengers, built by Miles Aircraft (NI) Ltd at Newtownards.* (Author)

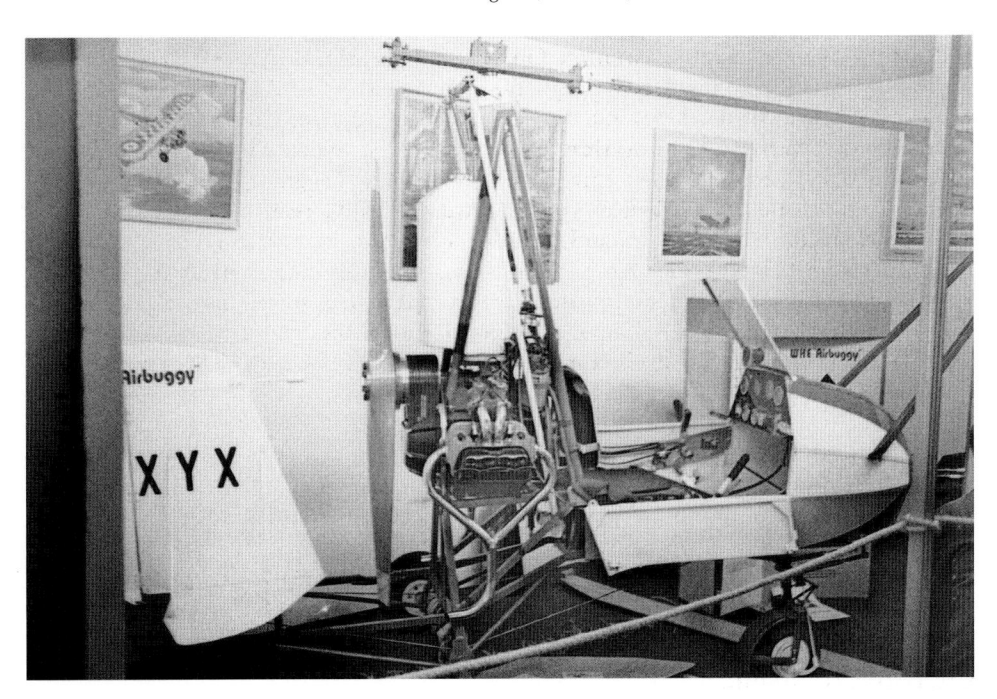

The W.H. Ekin Airbuggy was a developed version of the McCandless M-4 autogyro. (Author)

Langford Lodge, County Antrim

Lockheed Overseas Corporation ran a facility at Langford Lodge from August 1942 for repair and servicing of USAAF aircraft. This site also carried out the assembly of some Lend Lease aircraft, particularly the P-38 Lightning and the Brewster Bermuda.

Newtownabbey

Lear Fan Ltd had a production factory at 62 Church Road, Newtownabbey, Co. Antrim. See also Aldergrove.

Bombardier Aerospace Inc.: After Short Brothers plc were acquired by Bombardier in October 1989, the empty Lear Fan factory at Newtownabbey was purchased for use as a composite manufacturing facility.

Bibliography

50 Golden Years of Achievement, Hamble 1936-1986, (British Aerospace, 1986)
75 Years of Aviation in Kingston, 1913-1988, (British Aerospace, 1988)
Adventure with Fate, Harald Penrose, Airlife (1984)
The Aeroplane Directory of British Aviation, Staff of *The Aeroplane*, (Temple Press Ltd, 1953 edition)
The Aerospace Chronology, Michael J.H. Taylor (Tri-Service Press, 1989)
Aircraft made in Lincoln, John Walls, Charles Parker (Society of Lincolnshire History & Archaeology, 2000)
Aircraft of the Fighting Powers, Volume 1-5, Edited: D.A. Russell, Compiled: H.J. Cooper, Owen Thetford (Harborough Publishing, 1940-1944)
Aircraft of the Fighting Powers, Volume 6, Edited: D.A. Russell, Compiled: Owen Thetford, C.B. Maycock (Harborough Publishing, 1945)
Aircraft of the Fighting Powers, Volume 7, Edited: D.A. Russell, Compiled: Owen Thetford, E.J. Riding (Harborough Publishing, 1946)
Aircraft of the RAF, a pictorial record 1918-1978, Paul Ellis (Macdonald & Jane's, 1978)
The Aircraft of the World, William Green, Gerard Pollinger (Macdonald, 1953)
The Aircraft of the World, William Green, Gerard Pollinger (Macdonald, 1955)
The Aircraft of the World, William Green (Macdonald, 1965)
Airlife's General Aviation, R.W. Simpson (Airlife, 1991)
Armstrong Whitworth Aircraft since 1913, Oliver Tapper (Putnam, 1973)
Auster Aircraft –Auster Production List, N.H. Ellison, R.O. Macdemitria (AIR-BRITAIN, Second Edition, February 1966)
Aviation Archaeology, Bruce Robertson (Patrick Stephens Ltd, second edition 1983)
Aviation in Birmingham, Geoffrey Negus, Tommy Staddon (Midland Counties Publications 1984)
Aviation in Leicestershire and Rutland, Roy Bonser (Midland Publishing, 2001)
Aviation in Manchester, B.R. Robinson (Royal Aeronautical Society, Manchester Branch, 1977)
Aviation Landmarks, Jean Gardner (Battle of Britain Prints International 1990)
The Aviation Pocket-Book 1919-1920, R. Borlase-Matthews (Crosby, Lockwood & Son, seventh edition, 1919)
Avro (Archive Photographs series), Harry Holmes (Chalford Publishing, 1996)
Avro Aircraft since 1908, A.J. Jackson (Putnam, 1965)
AVRO The History of an Aircraft Company, Harry Holmes (Airlife, 1994)
Balloons to Buccaneers - Yorkshire's role in aviation since 1785, Brian Catchpole (Maxiprint, 1994)
Blackburn Aircraft since 1909, A.J. Jackson (Putnam 1989)
The BLACKBURN: Dumbarton's Aircraft Factory, Alan M. Sherry (Richard Stenlake Publishing, 1996)
The Blackburn Story 1909-1959, Blackburn Aircraft Ltd, 1960
Boulton Paul Aircraft (Archive Photographs series), Boulton Paul Association (Chalford Publishing, 1996)
Brassey's World Aircraft & Systems Directory, Michael Taylor (Brassey's (UK) Ltd, 1996)

Bibliography

Bristol Aircraft since 1910, C.H. Barnes (Putnam, 1964)
Bristol An Aircraft Album, James D Oughton (Ian Allan 1973)
'Britain's Air Strength', *The Air Defence of Great Britain*, Lt Cdr R. Fletcher, MP (Penguin, October 1938)
Britain's Motor Industry – The first hundred years, Nick Georgano, Nick Baldwin, Anders Clausager, Jonathan Wood (G.T. Foulis & Co., 1995)
British Aeroplanes, 1914-1918, J.M. Bruce (Putnam, 1962)
British Aerospace – The Facts, BAe Corporate Communications (British Aerospace, 1992 & 1996)
British Aircraft at War 1939-45, Gordon Swanborough (HPC Publishing, 1997)
British Aircraft Before The Great War, Michael H. Goodall, Albert E. Tagg (Schiffer Publishing Ltd, 2001)
British Aircraft Manufacturers since 1908, Günter Endres (Ian Allan Publishing, 1995)
British Aircraft of World War II, David Mondey (Chancellor Press 1994 edition)
British Aircraft, 1809-1914, Peter Lewis (Putnam, 1962)
British Aviation – Ominous Skies, Harald Penrose (HMSO, 1980)
British Aviation – The Adventuring Years, Harald Penrose (Putnam, 1973)
British Aviation – The Pioneer Years, Harald Penrose (Cassell Ltd, revised edition 1980)
British Aviation – Widening Horizons, Harald Penrose (HMSO, 1979)
The British Bomber since 1914, F.K. Mason (Putnam, 1994)
British Civil Aircraft since 1919, A.J. Jackson (Putnam, 2nd edition, Vol. 1 1973, Vol. 2 1973, Vol. 3 1974)
British Commercial Aircraft – sixty years in pictures, Paul Ellis (Jane's Publishing, 1980)
The British Fighter since 1912, F.K. Mason (Putnam, 1992)
British Flight Testing: Martlesham Heath 1920-1939, Tim Mason (Putnam, 1993)
British Floatplanes, G.R. Duval (D Bradford Barton, 1976)
British Homebuilt Aircraft since 1920, Ken Ellis (Merseyside Aviation Society, 2nd edition, 1979)
British Light Aeroplanes – Their Evolution, Development and Perfection 1920 – 1940, Arthur W.J.G. Ord-Hume (GMS Enterprises, 2000)
British Military Aircraft Serials 1878-1987, Bruce Robertson (Midland Counties Publications, 1987)
British Prototype Aircraft, Ray Sturtivant (The Promotional Reprint Co Ltd, 1995)
British Racing and Record Breaking Aircraft, Peter Lewis (Putnam, 1970)
Brush Aircraft production at Loughborough, A.P. Jarram (Midland Counties Publications, 1978)
Canada's Wings Vol. 1a The Blackburn Shark, Carl Vincent (Canada's Wings, 1977)
Cobham – The Flying Years, Colin Cruddas (Archive Photograph series, Chalford Publishing 1997)
In Cobham's Company – Sixty Years of Flight Refuelling Ltd, Colin Cruddas (Cobham plc 1994)
The Cold War Years – Flight Testing at Boscombe Down 1945-1975, Tim Mason (Hikoki Publications Ltd, 2001)
Dangerous Skies The, A.E. Clouston (Pan Books, 1956)
Discover Aviation Trails, Paul Shaw (Midland Publishing, 1996)
Dizzy Heights – The Story of Lancashire's First Flying Men, Chris Aspin (Helmshore Local History Society, 1988)
English Electric Aircraft and their Predecessors, S. Ransom, R. Fairclough (Putnam, 1987)
Fairey Aircraft since 1915, H.A. Taylor (Putnam, 1974)
Fairey Aviation (Archive Photographs series), J.W.R. Taylor (Chalford Publishing, 1997)
Fighters of the Fifties, Bill Gunston (Patrick Stephens Ltd, 1981)
Filton and the Flying Machine (Archive Photographs series), Malcolm Hall (Chalford Publishing 1995)
The First Croydon Airport 1915-1928, Douglas Cluett, (editor), Bob Learmonth, Joanna Nash (Sutton Libraries and Arts Services, 1977)
First Through the Clouds, F. Warren Merriam (B.T. Batsford Ltd, 1954)

The Flight of the Mew Gull, Alex Henshaw (John Murray, 1980)
Flying Corps Headquarters 1914-1918, Maurice Baring (Buchan & Enright, Publishers, Ltd (reprint), 1985)
The Flying Scots – A century of aviation in Scotland, Jack Webster (The Glasgow Royal Concert Hall, 1994)
Forever Farnborough – Flying the Limits 1904-1996, P.J. Cooper (HIKOKI Publications, 1996)
The Forgotten Pilots, Lettice Curtis (Nelson Saunders, third edition, 1985)
Forty Years of the Spitfire – Proceedings of the Mitchell Memorial Symposium, R.A. East, I.C. Cheeseman (Royal Aeronautical Society, Southampton Branch, 1976)
From Spitfire to Eurofighter, Roy Boot (Airlife, 1990)
Gloucestershire Aviation – A History, Ken Wixey (Alan Sutton, 1995)
The Great Aircraft Factory – Rootes Securities Ltd, Aircraft Division, Barry Abraham & Phil Butler, Article in Air-Britain Aeromilitaria, Vol 30, Issue 118 (Air-Britain, 2004)
Handley Page, Alan Dowsett (Tempus Publishing, Images of Aviation Series, 1999)
Hawker – A biography of Harry Hawker, L.K. Blackmore (Airlife, 1993)
Hawker Aircraft since 1920, F.K. Mason (Putnam, 1961)
Helicopters and Autogyros of the World, Paul Lambermont, Anthony Pirie (Cassell, 1958)
Hendon Aerodrome – A History, David Oliver (Airlife, 1994)
The History of Black Country Aviation, Alec Brew (Alan Sutton, 1993)
History of British Aviation 1908-1914, R. Dallas Brett (Air Research Publications & Kristall Productions. Eightieth Anniversary Edition 1988)
A History of the Eastbourne Aviation Company 1911 – 1924, Lou McMahon & Michael Partridge (Eastbourne Local History Society, 2000)
I Kept No Diary, Air Cdre F.R. Banks (Airlife, 1978)
Industry and Air Power. The Expansion of British Aircraft Production, 1935-1941, Sebastian Ritchie (Frank Cass, 1997)
The Jet Aircraft of the World, William Green, Roy Cross (Macdonald, 1955)
Knights of the Air, Peter King (Constable & Co. Ltd, 1989)
Lend-Lease Aircraft of World War II, Arthur Pearcy (Motorbooks International, 1996)
Leysdown – the Cradle of Flight, Brian Slade (Santa-Maria Publications, 1990)
Lion Rampant and Winged, Alan Robertson (Alan Robertson, 1986)
Mach One, Mike Lithgow (Allan Wingate, 1954)
The Magic of a Name, Harold Nockholds (GT Foulis & Co. Ltd 1949)
The Marshall Story, Sir Arthur Marshall (Patrick Stephens Ltd, 1994)
Men with Wings, W/Cdr H.P. 'Sandy' Powell (Allan Wingate, 1957)
More Tails of the Fifties, Editor: Peter G. Campbell (Cirrus Associates (SW), 1998)
Not much of an Engineer, Sir Stanley Hooker (Airlife, 1984)
Parnall's Aircraft, Ken Wixey (Tempus Publishing, Images of England Series, 1998)
Peaceful Fields.... Volume 1, The South, J.F. Hamlin (GMS Enterprises, 1996)
Plane Speaking, Bill Gunston (Patrick Stephens Ltd, 1991)
Per Ardua – The Rise of British Air Power 1911-1939, Hilary St George Saunders (Oxford University Press, 1944)
Proud Heritage - A Pictorial History of British Aerospace Aircraft, Phil Coulson (Royal Air Force Benevolent Fund, 1995)
Pure Luck - The Authorized Biography of Sir Thomas Sopwith 1888-1989, Alan Bramson (Patrick Stephens Ltd, 1990)
The Quick and The Dead, W.A. Waterton (Frederick Muller Ltd, 1956)
The Redwing Story, John Lane (Mrs Phyllis Lane, 1992)
The Royal Flying Corps, Terry C. Treadwell & Alan C. Wood (Images of Aviation series, Tempus Publishing Ltd, 2000)
The Royal Naval Air Service, Terry C. Treadwell & Alan C. Wood (Images of Aviation series, Tempus Publishing Ltd, 1999)
Schneider Trophy The, David Mondey (Robert Hale, 1975)
Sent Flying, A.J. 'Bill' Pegg (Macdonald, 1959)

Bibliography

Shoreham Airport, Sussex, T.M.A. Webb, Dennis L.Bird (Cirrus Associates (SW), 1996)
Shorts Aircraft since 1900, C.H. Barnes (Putnam, 1989)
Sigh for a Merlin, Alex Henshaw, Crécy Publishing, 1999 reprint
Slide Rule, Nevil Shute (Readers Union, 1956)
Sopwith – The Man and His Aircraft, Bruce Robertson (Air Review Ltd, 1970)
The Speed Seekers, Thomas G. Foxworth (Macdonald and Jane's, 1975)
The Spider Web, Sqn Ldr T.D. Hallam (Arms & Armour Press (reprint), 1979)
Spirit of Hamble – Folland Aircraft, Derek N. James (Tempus Publishing, 2000)
Spitfire - A Test Pilot's Story, J.K. Quill (John Murray, 1983)
The Spitfire Story, Alfred Price (Arms & Armour Press, second edition, 1995)
Staffordshire and Black Country Airfields (Archive Photographs series), Alec Brew (Chalford Publishing 1997)
Stirling Wings - The Short Stirling goes to War, Jonathan Falconer (Budding Books, 1995)
The Story of Acton Aerodrome and the Alliance Factory (London Borough of Ealing Library Service, second edition, 1978 with Addenda and Corrigenda)
The Story of the British Light Aeroplane, Terence Boughton (John Murray, 1963)
Supermarine (Archive Photographs series), Norman Barfield (Chalford Publishing 1996)
Supermarine Spitfire - 40 Years On, G.N.M. Gingell (Royal Aeronautical Society, Southampton Branch, 1976)
Sywell – The Story of an English Aerodrome 1928-1978, Christopher Paul (Sywell Aerodrome Ltd, 1978)
Tails of the Fifties, Editor: Peter G. Campbell (Cirrus Associates (SW), 1997)
Test Pilot, Nevil Duke (Allan Wingate, 1953)
Test Pilots - The story of British Test Flying 1903-1984, Don Middleton (Willow Books, 1985)
Testing Time, Constance Babington Smith (Cassell & Co Ltd, 1961)
That Nothing Failed Them, Air Cdre A.H. Wheeler (G.T. Foulis & C. Ltd, 1963)
Three Centuries to Concorde, Charles Burnet (Mechanical Engineering Publications Ltd, 1979)
A Time to Fly, Sir Alan Cobham (Shepheard-Walwyn, 1978)
Ultralights - The Early British Classics, Richard Riding (Patrick Stephens Ltd, 1987)
Vapour Trails, Mike Lithgow (Allan Wingate, 1956)
Vickers Aircraft since 1908, C.F. Andrews, E.B. Morgan (Putnam, second edition, 1988)
War in the Air, Edward Smithies (Penguin, 1992)
Westland 50, J.W.R. Taylor, Maurice F. Allward (Ian Allan, 1965)
Westland Aircraft since 1919, D.N. James (Putnam, 1991)
Wings over Woodley - The Story of Miles Aircraft and the Adwest Group, Julian C. Temple, (Aston Publications, 1987)
World Encyclopaedia of Aircraft Manufacturers, Bill Gunston (Patrick Stephens Ltd, 1993)

Magazines and other publications:

Flight: Numerous editions of "The First Aero Weekly in the World - A Journal Devoted to the Interests, Practice and Progress of Aerial Locomotion and Transport. Official Organ of The Royal Aero Club of the United Kingdom".
The Aeroplane: Numerous editions, Temple Press Ltd, Editors – C.G. Grey, Thurstan James
Aeroplane Monthly: Numerous editions, IPC Magazines Ltd.
The Aeroplane Spotter July 1941 - December 1945, Temple Press Ltd
Jane's All the Worlds Aircraft: various editions from 1909 to date, published by Samson Low, Jane's Information Group, and (reprints) David & Charles Ltd, Collins & Jane's.
Popular Flying, The Magazine of the Popular Flying Association
Royal Air Force Flying Review: 1954-55, 1957-58, 1961-62. A Mercury House Publication.

Cross-Reference Index between Volumes

The *British Built Aircraft* series presents a regional survey of aircraft construction in Britain. Whilst, in many cases, this local view is effective in giving a sense of time and place, it does not always provide a complete picture from an individual company perspective. This is particularly the case for the larger enterprises that have (or had) factories dispersed across the various regions of Britain, or whose activities moved from one site to another as they developed.

The table below is presented to assist the reader in finding references throughout the five volumes of this series to those companies that operated at several locations. Within the table one can find the name of the concern (and, where appropriate, its immediate successor); a list of major locations for the company; and an indication of other relatively minor references to the concern, which should also be consulted to provide a complete picture. Each location is followed by a numerical reference (e.g. (3)) to indicate in which volume this location may be found.

Company	Major Locations	Minor References
The Aeronautical Corporation of Great Britain Ltd (Aeronca)	Hanworth (1), Peterborough (4)	Horsey Toll (4), London (Central) (1)
Airbus	Broughton/Chester/Hawarden (5), Filton (2)	
The Aircraft Co. Ltd; The Aircraft Manufacturing Co. Ltd; AIRCO (successor The de Havilland Aircraft Co. Ltd)	Hendon (1)	London (Central) (1), Merton (1), Cardiff/Penarth (5)
Air Navigation & Engineering Co. Ltd (ANEC) (also Louis Blériot Aeronautics, Blériot & SPAD Manufacturing Co. Ltd)	Addlestone (3), Brooklands (3)	Lympne (3)
Airspeed Ltd; Airspeed (1934) Ltd. (also The de Aircraft Co. Ltd, Christchurch Division)	Christchurch (2), Portsmouth (2), York (5)	Harmondsworth (1), Sherburn-in-Elmet (5)
Alliance Aircraft Co. Ltd	Acton (1)	London (Central) (1)
Sir W.G. Armstrong, Whitworth Ltd; Sir W.G. Armstrong Whitworth Aircraft Ltd. (successor Hawker Siddeley Aviation Ltd)	Baginton (4), Bitteswell (4), Coventry (4), Gosforth (5), Hamble (2), Whitley Abbey (4)	Boscombe Down (2), Cramlington (5), London (Central) (1), Selby (5), Sywell (4)
Auster Aircraft Ltd. (successor Beagle Aircraft Ltd)	Rearsby (4), Thurmaston (4)	Beaumaris (5), East Cowes (2), Ratcliffe (4), Syston (4)
Austin Motors Ltd	Birmingham (4)	London (Central) (1)
A.V. Roe; A.V. Roe & Co. Ltd (successor Hawker Siddeley Aviation Ltd)	Alexandra Park (5), Brooklands (3), Brownsfield Mills (5), Chadderton/Middleton (5), Hamble (2), Leeds (Yeadon) (5), Miles Platting (5), Newton Heath (5), Ringway (5), Shoreham (3), Woodford (5)	Ashton under Lyne (5), Barrow in Furness (5), Blackpool (5), Boscombe Down (2), Bracebridge Heath (4), Dunsfold (3), Failsworth (5), Farnborough (2), Hackney (1), Langar (4), Lympne (3), London (Central) (1), Putney (1), Royton (5), Trafford Park (5), Waddington (4) Wembley (1), Windermere (5), Worthy Down (2), Wythenshaw (5)
Aviation Traders Ltd; Aviation Traders Engineering Ltd	Southend (3)	Stansted (3), London (Central) (1)
BAC/British Aircraft Co.	Hanworth (1)	Maidstone (3)
BAE SYSTEMS plc	Brough (5), Chadderton/Middleton (5), Farnborough (2), Filton (2), Hawarden (5), Prestwick (5), Samlesbury (5), Warton (5), Woodford (5)	Hatfield (3), London (Central) (1), Weybridge (3)
Beagle Aircraft Ltd	Rearsby (4), Shoreham (3)	Farnborough (2), London (Central) (1)
Wm. Beardmore & Co. Ltd	Dalmuir (5)	Inchinnan (5), London (Central) (1), Lympne (3), Martlesham (4)
Robert Blackburn; Blackburn Aeroplane & Motor Co. Ltd; Blackburn Aircraft Ltd; Blackburn & General Aircraft Ltd (successor Hawker Siddeley Aviation Ltd)	Brough (5), Dumbarton (5), Filey Sands (5), Holme-on-Spalding Moor (5), Leeds (5), Sherburn-in-Elmet (5)	Abbotsinch (5), Barnes & Putney (1), Brooklands (3), Carnaby (5); Hamble (2), Hanworth (1), Hendon (1), Leconfield (5), London (Central) (1), Lympne (3), Scarborough (5), Windermere (5)
Boulton & Paul Ltd; Boulton Paul Aircraft Ltd	Norwich (4), Seighford (4), Wolverhampton (4)	Boscombe Down (2), City (1), Perton (4)
British & Colonial Aeroplane Co. Ltd; Bristol Aeroplane Co. Ltd; Bristol Aircraft Ltd (successor British Aircraft Corporation)	Filton (2), Larkhill (2), Weston-super-Mare/Old Mixon (2)	Accrington (5), Banwell (2), Bristol (2), Brooklands (3), Dale (5), Farnborough (2), London (Central) (1), Lympne (3), Shoreham (3), Whitchurch (2)
British Aerospace; BAE SYSTEMS plc	Brough (5), Chadderton/Middleton (5), Dunsfold (3), Farnborough (2), Filton (2), Hamble (2), Hatfield (3), Hawarden (5), Holme-on-Spalding Moor (5), Kingston (1), Preston (5), Prestwick (5), Samlesbury (5), Warton (5), Weybridge (3), Woodford (5)	Bitteswell (4), Failsworth (5), London (Central) (1)

Cross-reference Index

Company	Major Locations	Minor References
British Aircraft Corporation (successor British Aerospace)	Filton (2), Hurn (2), Preston (5), Samlesbury (5), Warton (5), Weybridge (3), Wisley (3)	Boscombe Down (2), Fairford (2), London (Central) (1), Luton (4)
The British Caudron Co. Ltd (also W.H. Ewen)	Alloa (5), Cricklewood (1), Hendon (1), Lanark (5)	Glasgow (5)
Britten-Norman Ltd; Britten-Norman (Bembridge) Ltd; Fairey Britten-Norman Ltd; Pilatus Britten-Norman Ltd; B-N Group Ltd	Bembridge (2)	Ryde (2), London (Central) (1)
Cattle R., Ltd; Central Aircraft Co.	Kilburn (1), Northolt (1)	London (Central) (1)
Chrislea Aircraft Co. Ltd	Exeter (2), Heston (1)	
The Cierva Autogiro Co. Ltd (successors Saunders-Roe Ltd)	Eastleigh (2), Hamble (2), Hanworth (1), Redhill (3)	City (1), Glasgow (5), Henley-on-Thames (4), London (Central) (1), South Hampstead (1)
Comper Aircraft Ltd (successors Heston Aircraft Ltd, also Comper Aeroplanes Ltd)	Hooton Park (5), Heston (1)	London (Central) (1)
Coventry Ordnance Works (successors The English Electric Co. Ltd)	Brooklands (3), Coventry (4)	London (Central) (1)
The de Havilland Aircraft Co. Ltd (successors Hawker Siddeley Aviation Ltd)	Christchurch (2), Hatfield (3), Hawarden (5), Leavesden (3), Portsmouth (2), Stag Lane (1)	Acton (1), Fulham (1), Newbury (3), Hendon (1), Hurn (2), Lympne (3), Salisbury Hall (3), Tarrant Rushton (2), Whitway (3), Witney (Oxford) (4), Woodbridge (4)
Dick, Kerr & Co. Ltd (successors The English Electric Co. Ltd)	Preston (5)	South Shields (5)
Dunne, J.W.; The Blair Atholl Aeroplane Syndicate Ltd	Blair Atholl (5), Isle of Sheppey (3)	Farnborough (2), Hendon (1), City (1)
Edgar Percival Aircraft Ltd; Lancashire Aircraft Co. Ltd	Stapleford Tawney (3), Blackpool (5), Samlesbury (5)	
The English Electric Co. Ltd; English Electric Aviation Ltd (successors British Aircraft Corporation)	Bradford (5), Preston (5), Samlesbury (5), Warton (5)	Accrington (5), Acton (1), Boscombe Down (2), City (1), London (Central) (1), Lympne (3)
The Fairey Aviation Co. Ltd; Fairey Aviation Ltd (successors Westland Helicopters Ltd)	Harmonsworth (1), Hamble (2), Hayes (1), Heston (1), Northolt (1), Ringway (5), Stockport (5), White Waltham (3)	Aldermaston (3), Barton (5), Boscombe Down (2), Brentford & Isleworth (1), Hendon (1), Isle of Grain (3), Kingsbury (1), London (Central) (1), Warrington area (5), Weybridge (3)
F.G. Miles Ltd	Shoreham (3)	Ford (3), Redhill (3), Tangmere (3)
Folland Aircraft Ltd (successors Hawker Siddeley Aviation Ltd)	Chilbolton (2), Hamble (2), Staverton (2)	Boscombe Down (2), Cheltenham (2), Chipping Norton (4), Clevedon (2), Dunsfold (3), Eastleigh (2), Exeter (2)
Foster Wikner Aircraft Co. Ltd	Eastleigh (2)	Stapleford Tawney (3)
General Aircraft Ltd (successors Blackburn & General Aircraft Ltd)	Croydon (1), Hanworth (1)	Farnborough (2), Lasham (2), Tarrant Rushton (2), Hucclecote (2)
Gloucestershire Aircraft Co. Ltd; Gloster Aircraft Ltd	Cheltenham (2), Hucclecote (2), Moreton Valence (2)	Barford St John (4), Bentham (4), Boscombe Down (2), Brockworth (2), Bruntingthorpe (4), Calshot (2), Cranwell (4), Edgehill (4), Farnborough (2), Felixstowe (4), Lympne (3), Newent (5), Newmarket Heath (4)
Gosport Aircraft Co.	Gosport (2)	London (Central) (1)
The Grahame-White Aviation Co. Ltd	Hendon (1)	London (Central) (1), Park Royal (1)
Handley Page Ltd	Barking (1), Cricklewood (1), Hendon (1), Radlett (3), Reading (3)	Bicester (4), Boscombe Down (2), Brooklands (3), Carnaby (5), Clifton/Rawcliffe (5), Cranfield (4), Cumnock (5), London (Central) (1), Lympne (3), Wittering (4)
H.G. Hawker Engineering Co. Ltd; Hawker Aircraft Ltd (successors Hawker Siddeley Aviation Ltd)	Blackpool (5), Brooklands (3), Dunsfold (3), Hucclecote (2), Kingston (1), Langley (3)	Boscombe Down (2), Esher (3), Farnborough (2), Felixstowe (4), Lympne (3)
Hawker Siddeley Aviation Ltd	Bitteswell (4), Brough (5), Chadderton/Middleton (5), Dunsfold (3), Hamble (2), Hatfield (3), Hawarden (5), Holme on Spalding Moor (5), Kingston (1), Woodford (5)	London (Central) (1), Scampton (4)
Hendy Aircraft Co.	Shoreham (3), Yate (2)	Yeovil (2)
Heston Aircraft Ltd	Heston (1)	
Hewlett & Blondeau Ltd	Battersea (1), Luton (4)	Brooklands (3), Hendon (1), London (Central) (1)
F. Hills & Sons Ltd	Barton (5)	Blackpool (5), RAF Sealand (5)
Humber Motor Co. Ltd	Brooklands (3), Coventry (3)	
London & Provincial Aviation Co.	Hendon (1), Stag Lane (1)	
Luton Aircraft Ltd	Barton le Clay (4), Denham (3)	Heston (1)
Mann, Egerton & Co. Ltd	Norwich (4)	London (Central) (1)

Company	Major Locations	Minor References
Martin & Handasyde; Martinsyde Ltd	Brooklands (3)	Camberwell (1), Croydon (1), Hendon (1), London (Central) (1), Woking (3)
Martin-Baker Aircraft Ltd	Denham (3), Chalgrove (4)	Harwell (4), Heston (1), Northolt (1), Wing (4), Thame (3)
Metropolitan-Vickers Electrical Co. Ltd	Trafford Park (5), Woodford (5)	Baginton (4), Broughton/Chester/Hawarden (5)
Miles Aircraft Ltd; Handley Page (Reading) Ltd successor F.G. Miles Ltd	Reading (3), South Marston (2)	Banbridge (5), Belfast (5), Montrose (5),
Napier, D., & Son Ltd	Acton (1), Luton (4), Northolt (1)	
Nieuport & General Aircraft Ltd	Cricklewood (1), Hendon (1)	Acton (1), City (1), London (Central) (1), South Kensington (1)
Parnall & Sons; George Parnall & Co. Ltd; Parnall Aircraft Ltd	Bristol (2), Yate (2)	Andover (2), Filton (2), Cricklewood (1), Isle of Grain (3), London (Central) (1), Lympne (3)
Percival Aircraft Ltd; Hunting Percival Aircraft Ltd; Hunting Aircraft Ltd (successor British Aircraft Corporation)	Gravesend (3), Luton (4)	London (Central) (1), Maidstone (3), Rochester (3), Yate (2)
Phillips & Powis Aircraft Ltd (successor Miles Aircraft Ltd)	Reading (3), South Marston (2)	Doncaster (5), Willesden (1), Yate (2)
Pobjoy Airmotors & Aircraft Ltd	Hooton Park (5), Rochester (3)	
Robey & Co. Ltd	Lincoln (4)	City (1)
Robinson Aircraft Ltd; Redwing Aircraft Co. Ltd	Colchester (4), Croydon (1), Thornton Heath (1)	Elstree (3), Gatwick (3), Heston (1), Wolverhampton (4)
Rootes Securities Ltd	Blythe Bridge (4), Liverpool (5)	Meir (4)
Royal Aircraft Factory	Farnborough (2)	
Ruffy, Arnall & Baumann Aviation Co. Ltd (successors Alliance Aeroplane Co. Ltd)	Acton (1), Hendon (1)	London (Central) (1)
Sage, Frederick & Co. Ltd	Peterborough (4)	London (Central) (1)
Saunders, S.E., Ltd; Saunders-Roe Ltd (successors Westland Helicopters Ltd)	Beaumaris (5), East Cowes (2), Eastleigh (2)	Boscombe Down (2), Calshot (2), Somerton (2), London (Central) (1), Weybridge (3)
Scottish Aviation Ltd (successors British Aerospace plc)	Prestwick (5)	Abbotsinch (5), Glasgow (5), Greenock (5), Irvine (5), Largs (5), London (Central), Renfrew (5)
Short Brothers Ltd; Short Brothers (Rochester & Bedford) Ltd; Short Brothers & Harland Ltd; Shorts Brothers plc (successors Bombardier Aerospace Inc)	Belfast (5), Isle of Sheppey (Shellbeach, Leysdown, Eastchurch) (3), Rochester (3), South Marston (2)	Bedford (4), Boscombe Down (2), Bourn (4), Cambridge (4), East Cowes (2), Felixstowe (4), Gravesend (3), Kidderminster (4), Llanbedr (5), London (Central) (1), Lympne (3), Martlesham (4), Wig Bay (5), Windermere (5)
Simmonds Aircraft Ltd, Spartan Aircraft Ltd	East Cowes (2), Hamble (2)	
Slingsby Sailplanes Ltd; Slingsby Aircraft Ltd; Vickers-Slingsby Division of Vickers Ltd; Slingsby Engineering Ltd; Slingsby Aviation Ltd.	Kirbymoorside (5)	Dishforth (5), Scarborough (5), White Waltham (3)
Sopwith Aviation & Engineering Co. Ltd	Brooklands (3), Kingston (1)	East Cowes (2), Hamble (2), London (Central) (1), Southampton Water (2), Woolston (2)
Standard Motors Ltd	Coventry (4)	Ansty (4)
Pemberton-Billing Ltd; The Supermarine Aviation Works Ltd; Vickers-Armstrongs Ltd (Supermarine Works)	Castle Bromwich (4), Chilbolton (2), Eastleigh (2), High Post (2), Hursley Park (2), South Marston (2), Woolston (2), Worthy Down (2)	Aldermaston (3), Beaumaris (5), Blackbushe (2), Boscombe Down (2), Calshot (2), Chattis Hill (2), Cosford (4), Desford (4), Farnborough (2), Hamble (2), Henley-on-Thames (4), Itchen (2), Keevil (2), London (Central) (1), Lympne (3), Reading (3), Salisbury (2), Southampton Water (2), Trowbridge (2), Wisley (3)
Taylorcraft Aeroplanes (England) Ltd (successor Auster Aircraft Ltd)	Rearsby (4), Thurmaston (4)	Ratcliffe (4), Syston (4)
Vickers Ltd; Vickers-Armstrongs Ltd (successor British Aircraft Corporation)	Blackpool (5), Brooklands/Weybridge (3), Broughton/Chester/Hawarden (5), Hurn (2), Joyce Green (3), Wisley (3)	Bexleyheath (1), Byley (Cranage) (5), Cobham (3), Crayford (1), Erith (1), Farnborough (2), Hamble (2), London (Central) (1), Lympne (3), South Kensington (1), Windsor (3)
Weir, G. & J., Ltd	Cathcart, Glasgow (5)	Thames Ditton (3)
Westland Aircraft Works (Branch of Petters Ltd); Westland Aircraft Ltd; Westland Helicopters Ltd; GKN Westland Helicopters Ltd; AgustaWestland	Hayes (1), Weston–super-Mare/Old Mixon (2), Yeovil (2)	Andover (3), Boscombe Down (2), Doncaster (5), East Cowes (2), Eastleigh (2), Hamble (2), Hanworth (1), London (Central) (1), Lympne (3), Martock (2), Merryfield (2), White Waltham (3), Yeovilton (2)
White/Wight	East Cowes (2), Somerton IOW (2)	London (Central) (1)
Whitehead	Hanworth (1), Richmond (1)	Fulham (1)

Index

Abbotsinch, 150, 184, 185, 194, 195, 202, 207
ABC Motors Ltd, 137
Aberdeen, 184
Abergele, 216
Abingdon, 94
Accrington, 107, 108, 116
Aintree, 132, 133, 137
Air Service Training Ltd, 77, 81
Air Travel Ltd, 75
Airbus Integrated Company (also Airbus Industrie, BAe Airbus Ltd, BAE SYSTEMS Airbus Ltd), 11, 43, 47, 49, 51, 59, 120, 213, 221, 223, 225
A300-A380, 49, 50, 213, 221-223, 236
A400M, 49
AIRCO (also The Aircraft Manufacturing Co. Ltd), 16, 24, 25, 54, 218
AIRCO
  DH2, 20
  DH4, 16, 20, 21, 136
  DH5, 20, 184, 185, 186
  DH6, 15, 20, 134, 165, 227
  DH9 & DH9A , 16, 20, 21, 60, 73, 100, 132, 134, 136, 137, 150, 200
  DH10 and DH10A, 100
Aircraft Disposal Co. Ltd, The (also AIRDISCO), 23, 25, 73, 74, 75
Aircraft Repair Depot, 20, 168, 170
Airspeed Ltd (also Airspeed (1934) Ltd), 23, 27, 32, 54, 163, 165, 166
  AS.4 Ferry, 162, 163, 166
  AS.5 Courier, 166
  AS.10/AS.40 Oxford, 31, 33, 34, 207, 208
  AS.51 Horsa, 107, 110, 116, 166, 170
  AS.57 Ambassador, 36
  AS.65 Consul, 109
Tern glider, 166
Airwork Ltd, 87, 226
Aldenham, 31
Aldergrove, 227, 232, 236, 239
Alexander Stephen Ltd, 10, 198, 200, 201
Alexandra Park, 70, 73, 74, 87
Alloa, 6, 14, 19, 185-187, 200, 204
Anderson, L.G., 75
ANEC I & II, 165

Anglesey, 14, 216, 224
Angus Sanderson, Sir Wm., & Co. Ltd, 19, 139-141
Ansty, 31
Armstrong Siddeley Development Co. Ltd, 76, 79, 81
Armstrong Siddeley Motors Ltd, 81, 141
Armstrong Whitworth Aircraft Ltd, Sir W.G., 24, 30, 32, 37, 38, 40, 54, 79, 81, 141
  A.W.38 Whitley, 29, 101, 157
  A.W. 55 Apollo, 35
  A.W.650 & A.W.660 Argosy, 38, 40, 233
Argosy, 108
Siskin, 150, 183
Armstrong Whitworth Development Co. Ltd, 141
Armstrong, Whitworth & Co. Ltd, Sir W.G., 11, 18, 19, 21, 24, 25, 138, 141, 163
  F.M. 4 Armadillo, 138
  FK.2, 139-141
  FK.3, 18, 20, 139, 141
  FK.5, 141
  FK.7, 139
  FK.8, 18, 20, 139-141, 169
  FK.9, 140, 141
  FK.10, 141, 171, 174
  FK.12, 141
Arrol-Johnston Ltd, 19, 190, 195, 196
Arrow Aircraft (Leeds) Ltd, 176
Active, 176, 178
ARV Aviation Ltd
ARV1 Super 2, 51, 188, 189, 198
Ashton-under-Lyne, 69, 70
Auster Aircraft Ltd, 42, 216
  AOP. Mk V, Auster 5 Alpha, 216, 217
  J/5A, J/5 Adventurer, 216
Austin Motor Co. Ltd (also Austin Motor Co. (1914) Ltd and Austin Motors Ltd), 29, 31, 32, 101, 227
Aviation Scotland Ltd (and ASL Sweden AB), 188, 189, 198
Opus 280, 188, 190
Aviation Traders Engineering Ltd
Carvair, 210
Avro (A.V. Roe)
Roe I-IV triplanes, 70
Avro-Burga Monoplane, 70

Avro (A.V. Roe & Co.)
  500 & 502, 70, 71
  501, 67
  503, 70
  Type D, 13, 62, 70
  Type E, 70
Avro (A.V. Roe & Co. Ltd) , 6, 11, 14, 18, 19, 24, 25, 30, 32, 33, 37-41, 46, 54, 65, 67-76, 78-81, 83, 84, 87, 90, 94, 100, 104, 106-108, 115, 176, 178, 179
  504 (all variants), 15, 20, 24, 61, 68, 70, 71, 73-75, 77, 104, 108, 184, 185, 227
  521, 104
  536, 74, 108
  538, 73
  548, 74
  552, 75
  566/567 Avenger, 26
  581/594/616 Avian (all models), 24, 27, 71, 73, 75, 76, 89
  618 Ten, 75-77
  619 Five, 76, 87
  621 Tutor, 24, 71, 75, 77, 89
  624 Six, 76, 87
  626 and Prefect, 24, 75, 77, 78
  631/638/639/640/643 Cadet (all models),   24, 27, 75, 77, 78, 87, 89
  641 Commodore, 69, 87
  642/2m & 642/4m, 76, 77
  652, 652A Anson and Avro XIX, 24, 30, 34, 39, 61, 69-71, 75, 78-80, 87-89, 91, 158, 176, 178
  674, 75
  679 Manchester, 30, 75, 79, 83, 84, 99, 107
  683 Lancaster, 30, 31, 34, 35, 69-71, 78-81, 83, 87, 90, 99, 100, 107, 132, 179, 207, 218, 220, 230
  685 York, 35, 69-71, 75, 78-80, 83, 84, 86, 100, 107, 179, 208
  688/689 Tudor, 36, 71, 84-88, 90
  691 Lancastrian, 35, 71, 81, 87, 90
  694 Lincoln, 71, 75, 79-81, 84, 105, 107, 117, 179, 230
  696 Shackleton, 38, 71, 79-81, 87, 88, 91, 210, 224, 233
  698 Vulcan, 38, 39, 71, 79, 87, 88, 91-94, 224
  701 Athena, 87, 91, 92
  706 Ashton, 87, 90
  Tudor 8, 85, 87
BAE SYSTEMS plc, 6, 8, 9, 11, 47, 49, 51, 53, 54, 59, 79, 81, 82, 87, 96-98, 116-118, 120, 125, 127-131, 152, 153, 207, 212, 213, 220
  F-35 Joint Strike Fighter (with Lockheed Martin), 47, 48, 53, 120, 129, 153
  Nimrod MRA.4, 47-49, 82, 89, 98, 99, 130, 131, 213
Baginton, 30, 141
Banbridge, 227
Barassie, 33, 207
Barclay, Curle & Co. Ltd, 198, 199, 201
Barnwell brothers, 14, 202, 204, 215, 216
  monoplane, 204, 215

Barnwell BSW.1, 216
Barnwell, F.S., 216
Barrhead, 14, 186-188, 200
Barrow in Furness, 62, 63
Barry, 216
Barton, 11, 28, 30, 86, 101, 103-107, 155, 227
Baynes Bat, 163
Beagle Aircraft Ltd, 54, 211, 214
  B.121 Pup, 43, 46
  Beagle 206 and Basset, 43, 46
  Bulldog, 43, 211, 214
Beaumaris, 207, 216-218
Beccles, 13
Bedford, 232, 233
Belfast, 6, 11, 14, 19, 30, 32, 37, 42, 46, 122, 215, 227-238
Bembridge, 43, 216
Berkshire Aviation Co. Ltd (and Berkshire Aviation Tours Ltd), 74
Birmingham, 13, 31
Bitteswell, 30, 37, 47, 91, 141
Blackburn (Dumbarton) Ltd, 195
Blackburn Aeroplane & Motor Co. Ltd, The (also Blackburn Aircraft Ltd and Blackburn & General Aircraft Ltd),   6, 11, 19, 24, 30, 32, 33, 39, 40, 102, 143, 148, 150, 151, 154, 156, 162-165, 176, 177, 179, 184, 185, 194, 195
  AD Scout, 182
  B-2, , 144
  B-20, 194
  Baffin, 24, 144
  Beagle, 147
  Beverley (and Universal), 38, 39, 150, 151, 154, 195, 224
  Blackburd, 146, 147
  Blackburn, 143
  Bluebird, 24, 28, 144, 146, 147, 176
  Botha, 144, 148, 184, 194, 196
  Civil Monoplane and Civil Biplane, 147
  Cubaroo, 144, 147
  Dart, 24, 143, 147
  F.7/30, 24, 26
  Firebrand, 144, 149, 150, 156
  Firecrest, 149, 150
  Iris, , 147
  Kangaroo, 27, 143, 144, 180
  Land Sea monoplane, 67, 158
  Lincock, 147, 148
  Mercury monoplanes, 157, 180
  NA.39, 40, 150, 154
  Nautilus, 147
  Perth, 147
  Ripon, 24, 143, 144
  Roc, 24, 144, 195, 203
  Segrave, 148
  Shark, 24, 144, 145, 146, 148, 184, 194
  Skua, 24, 144
  Swift, 143
  Sydney, 147

Index

TB, , 179
Triplane, 179
Turcock, 147
Type L, 162
White Falcoln monoplane, 181
YA.7, YA.8 & YB.1, 150
Blackburn, Mr Robert (also R. Blackburn & Co.), 12, 14, 150, 157, 158, 177
Blackpool, 6, 11, 30, 37, 74, 106, 108-110, 120, 121, 167, 218
Blair Atholl, 14, 188, 189
Blair Atholl Aeroplane Syndicate Ltd, 189
Blake, J. & Co., 134, 136
Bland, Lillian, 14, 238
Blériot & SPAD Manufacturing Co., 73
Blythe Bridge, 30, 31, 134, 135
B-N Group, 6
Boldon Flats, 137
Bolton, 69, 70
Bonsall Mustang, 168, 169
Boscombe Down, 44, 86, 102, 115, 123, 232, 233
Boulton & Paul Ltd (also Boulton Paul Aircraft Ltd), 24, 102, 144
    Balliol, 92, 150
    Defiant, 33, 144
Bournemouth Aviation Co. Ltd, 74
Bowness, 64, 65, 67, 68
Brabazon Committee, 35
Bradford, 19, 112, 141, 143, 170-175, 200
British & Colonial Aeroplane Co. Ltd, The, 14, 24, 218
    Bristol F.2B Fighter, 16, 18, 20, 21, 25, 132, 139, 141
    Scout (all models), 20
    TB8, 218
Bristol Aeroplane Co. Ltd,   14, 24, 32, 39, 40, 55, 69, 107, 110, 216, 233
    Type 123, 24
    Type 130 Bombay, 30, 32, 227
    Type 133, 24
    Type 142M Blenheim, 29-31, 33, 34, 69, 70, 75, 79, 87, 134, 135
    Type 152 Beaufort, 34, 109
    Type 156 Beaufighter, 31, 33, 34, 86, 101-103, 109, 134, 135
    Type 167 Brabazon, 35
    Type 170 Freighter, 36, 39
    Type 171 Sycamore, 38, 40
    Type 175 Britannia, 36, 39, 40, 195, 210, 224, 233, 234
    Type 192 Belvedere, 38, 40
Bristol Aircraft Ltd, 55, 123
Bristol engines (including Bristol Siddeley and Rolls-Royce Ltd (Bristol)), 90
British Aerospace plc , 6, 8, 43, 46-50, 53, 54, 56, 58, 59, 69, 79, 81, 87, 93, 95-97, 112, 115-117, 121, 127, 130, 152-154, 207, 212, 213, 218, 220, 221, 223
    ATP (and Jetstream 61), 49, 81, 82, 88, 95, 97, 212, 213, 215

    BAe 146, HS146, Avro RJ, RJX, 43, 49, 81, 88, 89, 96-98, 213, 236
    EAP, 128
    Jetstream 31 & 32, 49, 208, 212, 214
    Jetstream 41, 49, 212, 213, 215, 223
    Sea Harrier, 47, 153
    T-45 Goshawk (with Boeing), 47, 117, 152
British Aircraft Corporation, 6, 22, 41-43, 46, 47, 53, 54, 58, 112, 115-117, 121, 123, 125, 127, 132
    BAC 167 Strikemaster, 46, 125-127
    Concorde, 43
    One-Eleven, 43, 197
    TSR.2, 41, 44, 46, 107, 116, 117, 119, 124, 125
British Caudron Co. Ltd, The, 19, 73, 185-187, 200, 204
    Caudron G.2, 185
    Caudron G.3, 185
British Deperdussin Co. Ltd, 140, 205
British South American Airways Corporation, 84, 85
Britten-Norman Ltd (and its successors), 6, 225
    Islander, 43, 46, 51
Brockworth, 31
Brooklands, 10, 12, 13, 30, 65, 67, 70, 71, 74, 138, 158
Brooklands Aircraft Co. Ltd (also Brooklands Aerospace Ltd), 216
Brooklands Aviation Ltd, 33, 167
Brooklands Rotorcraft Ltd, 68
    Mosquito, 68
Brough, 9, 11, 12, 19, 47, 129, 130, 143-153, 154, 156, 172, 174, 175, 180, 194-196
Broughton (Chester/Hawarden), 11, 30, 37, 47, 59, 213, 218-223, 225
Brownsfield Mills, 14, 65, 70, 71
Brush Electrical Engineering Co. Ltd, The (also Brush Coachworks Ltd), 31, 73, 171
Burnbank, 189, 198
Burnley, 110
Burtonwood, 62, 102, 110, 121, 135
Burtonwood Repair Depot Ltd, 102, 103, 110
Byley (Cranage), 59
C.L. Air Surveys Ltd, 167
Caledonian Motor & Cycle Works, 204
Calgarth, 68
Cambridge, 33
Camsell Monoplane, 156
Cardiff, 14, 218
Carlisle, 63
Carnaby, 150, 153, 154
Carnamoney, 14, 238
Castle Bromwich, 31
Castle Donington, 159, 160
Central Aircraft Co. Ltd, The, 24, 74
Chadderton, 11, 47, 70, 73, 79-83, 91, 94, 100, 106, 117, 130
Chattis Hill, 20
Cheshire, 8, 59-62, 87, 103
Chichester Miles Consultants Ltd
    CMC Leopard, 161
Chorley, 111

Christchurch, 37, 47, 163
Christopher Pratt & Sons, 171-173
Cierva Autogiro Co. Ltd, The, 200, 202
    C.25 (Comper-built), 61
    C.30A (Avro 671), 27, 75
    W-9, 202
    W-11 Air Horse, 202
    W-14 Skeeter, 202
Civilian Aircraft Co. Ltd, 156
    Coupé, 156
Clarke Cheetah, 153
Clyde Shipbuilding & Engineering Ltd, 198, 200
Coal Aston, 20, 168, 170
Cobham, 158, 166
Cody, S.F., 12, 132
Comper Aircraft Co. Ltd, 59
    C.L.A.7 Swift, 28, 59-62
Compton Paterson, 133, 134
Cook Flying Machines (and associated companies), 51, 53
    Shadow and Streak Shadow, 51
Cooper biplane, 196
Coventry, 24, 31, 55, 80, 141, 196
Coventry Ordnance Works Ltd, 55, 113
Cowley, 31
Cramlington, 138
Cranfield, 62, 68, 206
Craven Brothers, 170
Crickhowell, 218
Croplease Ltd (also Croplease plc), 216
Crosby (Andreasson) BA-4B, 62, 165
Crosby Aviation Ltd, 62
Crossens, 132, 136, 137
Crossley Motors Ltd, 79, 100, 103
Croydon, 23, 27, 74, 75
Cumbria, 8, 59, 62-68
Cumnock, 211
Cunliffe-Owen Aircraft Ltd, 32
    Concordia, 35
Currie Wot, 142, 160
Curtis, J., & Son, 184
Curtiss, 65, 67, 133
Daimler Co. Ltd, The, 29, 170
Dale, 218
Dalmuir, 16, 19, 165, 189-194, 198, 203
Darwen, 111
Dawson, John, & Co. (Newcastle-on-Tyne) Ltd, 8, 19, 142
de Havilland Aircraft Co. Ltd, The (see also AIRCO), 11, 23, 24, 31, 32, 38, 39, 40, 54, 59, 207, 218
de Havilland Aircraft Co. Ltd, The
    DH53, 153
    DH60 Moth (all models), 26, 76, 146
    DH82 Queen Bee, 199, 200
    DH82 Tiger Moth, 31, 33, 34, 160
    DH84 Dragon, 25
    DH87 Hornet Moth, 7
    DH89 Dragon Rapide (and Dominie), 25, 31, 34, 109, 208

DH98 Mosquito (and Sea Mosquito), 31, 34, 61, 103, 121, 207, 219, 226
DH100 Vampire (all marks), 32, 37, 86, 102, 115, 117, 119, 195, 197, 219, 224
DH103 Hornet (and Sea Hornet), 38, 219, 221, 226
DH104 Dove (and Devon), 36, 37, 38, 39, 219, 221, 222
DH106 Comet, 36, 37, 40, 43, 44, 91, 96, 219, 224, 232, 233, 234
DH110 Sea Vixen, 38, 40, 220
DH112 Venom (all marks including Sea Venom), 38, 86, 102, 195, 219, 224, 234
DH114 Heron, 39, 220, 222, 224
de Havilland (Canada) DHC1 Chipmunk, 38, 220, 222
de Havilland, Geoffrey, 14
Denny, Wm. & Bros. Ltd, 54, 148, 194, 195, 198, 202
Derby, 33
Dick, Kerr & Co. Ltd, 19, 55, 103, 112-114, 143, 171-174
Dishforth, 157
Dobson & Barlow, 69
Doncaster, 33, 166-168, 170
Dumbarton, 6, 11, 30, 144, 148, 150, 184, 194-196, 202, 203
Dumfries, 19, 195, 196
Dunkeswell, 168
Dunne, J.W., 14, 188
    Dunne D.3 & D.4, 188
    Dunne D.5-D.10, 189
Dunsfold, 37, 47, 82, 129, 131, 152, 153
Durham & Cleveland, 8, 59, 68, 69
Dutton Aircrafts, 226
East Yorkshire, 143-156
Eastbourne Aviation Co. Ltd, 13, 73, 74
Eastchurch, 12, 13, 28, 67, 188
Eastleigh, 202, 207
Edgar Percival Aircraft Ltd, 109, 120
    E.P.9 Prospector, 109, 120
Edgley Aircraft Co. Ltd
    Optica, 51
Edinburgh, 196, 204
Ekin, W.H., (Engineering) Ltd, 238
    Airbuggy, 238, 239
Ellis Williams, W., 14, 224
English Electric Co. Ltd, The (and English Electric Aviation Ltd), 6, 11, 23, 30, 32, 37, 38, 41, 46, 54, 55, 94, 107, 108, 112-118, 121-123, 170, 171, 173-175
    Ayr, , 113
    Canberra (all marks), 37, 38, 46, 53, 94, 107, 115, 117, 120-123, 195, 197, 224, 234, 235
    Kingston, 113-115
    P.1, P.1A & Lightning, 38, 46, 107, 115-117, 119, 123-125, 127, 232
    Wren, 114
Errol, 197
Errwood Park, 7, 30, 31, 86, 100-103
Eurofighter Gmbh

Index

Eurofighter (and Typhoon), 47, 48, 53, 117, 118, 127-129
Europa Aircraft Co. Europa, 11, 51, 53, 161, 162
Ewen, W.H. (later W.H. Ewen Aviation Co. Ltd), 14, 185, 200, 204, 205, 225
F. Hills & Sons Ltd, 11, 30, 87, 104-106, 109, 227
    Hillson Bi-Mono, 106, 109
    Hillson F.H.40 Mk 1, 104, 106, 109, 227
    Hillson Helvellyn, 105
    Hillson Pennine, 105
    Hillson Praga, 28, 105, 106
Failsworth, 69, 70
Fairey Aviation Co. Ltd, The (also Fairey Aviation Ltd), 6, 24, 30-33, 37, 40, 42, 62, 85-87, 100-103, 105, 110, 173
    Albacore, 31
    Barracuda, 31, 33, 34, 62, 85, 86, 102, 150
    Battle, 24, 29, 31, 33, 85, 101, 102, 105
    Campania, 198
    Fairey Delta 1, 86, 102
    Firefly, 31, 34, 85-87, 102, 103
    Fulmar, 86, 101
    Gannet, 40, 102, 150, 197, 231, 232
    Gyrodyne and Jet Gyrodyne, 38, 40
    Hendon, 13, 24, 101, 104, 105
    N.4 Atalanta and Titania, 112, 113, 172, 173, 200
    Rotodyne, 38, 40
    Spearfish, 86, 102
    Swordfish, 30, 33, 85, 107, 150, 153, 164, 165
Fairey, C.R. Mr (later Sir Richard Fairey), 14
Fairfield Shipbuilding & Engineering Co. Ltd, 198, 202
Farnborough, 9, 12, 20, 21, 91, 130, 188, 202
Felixstowe (Seaplane Experimental Station), 115, 172
    F.3, , 16, 112, 113, 143, 171-173
    F.5, , 112, 171-174
Ferguson, J.B., 14, 236, 237
Ferranti Ltd, 197
Field, C.B., 75
Filey Sands, 12, 14, 157, 158, 179
Filton, 31, 47, 81, 98, 130, 135
FLS Aerospace (Lovaux Ltd)
    Sprint, 51
Flying Flea, 28, 105, 111
Folland Aircraft Ltd, 32, 38, 54
    Gnat (fighter and trainer), 38
Ford Motor Co. Ltd, 61, 103, 107
Ford Trimotor, 61
Fredk. Sage & Co. Ltd, 73
Freshfield, 14, 132-134, 137
Fryars, 217, 218
Fyffes, 173, 200
G. & J. Weir group (also G. & J. Weir Ltd and Weir Group plc), 19, 198, 200-202, 211
    W-1 to W-4 autogyro series, 201, 202
    W-5 and W-6 helicopters, 201, 202
Galloway Engineering Co. Ltd, The, 196
Gaunt Baby, 136
General Aircraft Ltd, 27, 54, 150, 154
    Hotspur, 158

George & Jobling biplane, 141
Gibson biplane, 204, 206
Glasgow, 11, 186, 189, 197-204, 207
Glasgow Corporation Tram Depot, 200
Gloster Aircraft Co. Ltd, 31, 32, 38, 54, 79, 81
    Gladiator, 24
    Javelin, 37, 38
    Meteor (all marks), 37, 38, 121, 197, 226
    SS.37, 24
Gloucestershire Aircraft Co. Ltd, The, 24
Gnosspelius, O.T., 65, 68
Goodwood, 216
Gosforth, 6, 138-141, 163
Gosport Aircraft Co. Ltd, 173
Govan, 202
Grahame-White Aviation Co. Ltd, The, 24, 73, 74
Grampian Engineering & Motor Co., 215
Gravesend, 27
Great Yarmouth, 171
Greater Manchester, 8, 11, 59, 69-107, 213, 227
Greenock, 203, 207, 209, 217
Grey, C.G., Mr, 147, 172
Gyroflight Hornet, 68, 69
Hafner Rotabuggy & Rotajeep, 165
Haithwaite Aviation Co. Ltd, 10, 184
Hall Aviation Co., 225
Halton Aero Club
    HAC.1 Mayfly, 153
Hamble, 26, 47, 70, 73-76, 78, 104, 173, 200
Handley Page (Reading) Ltd, 238
    HPR.3 Herald and HPR.7 Dart Herald, 40, 44, 211
    Marathon, 36
Handley Page (Scotland) Ltd, 211
Handley Page Ltd, 24, 31, 32, 37-40, 42, 44, 54, 65, 74, 94, 115, 132, 153, 156, 227, 228
    HP12 O/400, 16, 100, 185, 227, 228
    HP15 V/1500, 190, 192, 203, 227
    HP52 Hampden, 29, 30, 32, 33, 61, 101, 115, 116, 118, 227
    HP53 Hereford, 30, 32, 227
    HP57 Halifax (all variants), 30-34, 85, 86, 101-103, 109, 115, 116, 118, 119, 134, 135, 156, 167, 230
    HP67 Hastings, 38, 39, 224
    HP68 Hermes, 36, 37
    HP70 Halton, 35, 109
    HP88, 150, 153, 154
    HP80 Victor, 38, 94, 150, 153, 154
    HP137 Jetstream, 44, 49, 53, 107, 211, 212
Hanworth, 27, 61, 75, 202
Harland & Wolff Ltd, 19, 23, 73, 227, 228, 230, 233
Harris Lebus Ltd, 185
Hatfield, 27, 37, 43, 47, 49, 81, 95, 97, 115, 219, 222, 233
Hawarden, 36, 37, 59, 218-223
Hawker Aircraft Ltd (also H.G. Hawker Engineering Co. Ltd), 11, 24, 32, 38, 40, 54, 79, 81, 109
    Audax, 75, 94
    Hart and Hart Trainer, 207
    Henley, 31

Hunter, 37-39, 46, 108, 109, 197
Hurricane, 30, 31, 33, 34, 102, 106, 107, 109, 207, 227
Osprey, 147
P.1127 and Kestrel, 38, 53
Sea Fury, 38, 153, 197
Sea Hawk, 37, 38, 40, 234
Tempest (all marks), 34
Tornado, 94, 95, 179
Typhoon, 31, 34
Hawker Siddeley Aviation Ltd, 6, 41, 43, 46, 49, 50, 53, 54, 59, 78, 79, 81, 87, 94, 151, 152, 154, 220
 Andover C. Mk 1, 88, 94, 95
 Buccaneer, 40, 45, 46, 150-152, 154, 155, 195, 197
 DH121 Trident, 43, 46
 Harrier (all marks), 38, 46, 47, 53, 82, 117, 130, 131, 153
 HS1182 Hawk, 46, 47, 53, 107, 127, 129, 130, 152, 153
 HS125 (and DH125, BAe125), 43, 46, 49, 50, 53, 107, 127, 220-222
 HS748, 40, 45, 46, 49, 81, 82, 88, 89, 93-95, 97, 212
 Nimrod, 46, 47, 53, 88, 94, 96, 98, 220
 Nimrod AEW.3, 91, 92
Hayes, 173
Heaton, 28, 142
Heaton Chapel, 7, 30, 31, 86, 100-103
Heckmondwike, 175
Hedon (Hull), 155, 156
Helensburgh, 194, 195, 203, 217
Henderson School of Flying Ltd, 74
Henderson Scottish Aviation Factory, 73, 184
Hendon, 12, 13, 65, 67, 118, 158, 185, 200, 204, 205, 225
Henlow, 20, 33
Heston, 60, 61, 78, 147
Heston Aircraft Ltd, 32
Hewitt, Vivien, 216
Hewlett & Blondeau Ltd, 73, 139
Heysham, 111
High Wycombe (also Booker), 165, 218
Hillington, 203
Holme-on-Spalding Moor, 47, 152, 154, 155
Hooton Park, 28, 59-62, 160
Horsman, Thomas, 184
Hucknall, 81
Humber Motor Co. Ltd, 73, 135
Hunday, 142, 143
Hunting Percival (and BAC) P.84 Jet Provost, 46, 125
Hurn, 47, 212
Inchinnan, 190, 192, 203
Ipswich, 194
Irvine, 203, 204
Isaacs, John, 28
Isle of Grain, 113, 173, 193
Isle of Sheppey, 12, 189
Isle of Wight, The, 43, 165

J. Samuel White & Co. Ltd
 Wight Type 840, 190, 191
James brothers, 14, 225
Jetstream Aircraft Ltd, 212
Jezzi brothers, 28
Joyce Green, 20, 216
Kay Gyroplanes Ltd, 207
 Type 32/1, 207
 Type 33/1, 207
Kendal Mayfly, 143
Kent, 75
Kingsbury Aviation Co. Ltd, 74
Kingston upon Thames, 30, 47, 109
Kingswood Knoll, 75
Kirkbymoorside, 11, 150, 158-163
Kirkpatrick, 203
Kitchen, Mr J.G.A., 111, 112
Knutsford, 62
Lakes Flying Co., The (also Northern Aircraft Co., The), 13, 14, 63-68, 70, 142
 monoplane, 65
 PB.1 & PB.2, 67
 Sea Bird, 64, 65, 70
 Water Bird, 64, 65, 70, 71
 Water Hen, 64, 65
Lanark, 14, 185, 200, 204, 205, 216
Lancashire, 8, 59, 107-132
Lancashire Aircraft Corporation Ltd, 84, 109, 121
Langford Lodge, 121, 135, 215, 238, 239
Langley, 30
Largs, 204, 207, 209
Larkhill, 13
Lea Marshes, 12, 70
Lear Fan Ltd, 236, 239
Lear Fan, 236
Leavesden, 31, 32
Lee Richards Annular Monoplane, 191
Leeds, 7, 11, 12, 14, 19, 143, 150, 158, 162, 163, 170, 175-184
Leeming Prince Wood glider, 73
Leiston, 51
Leith, 204
Leysdown, 12
Linthouse, 198
Liverpool Area, 134-136
Liverpool Aviation Co. Ltd, The, 10, 134, 137
Liverpool Motor House Ltd, 133
Llanbedr, 223
Llanddona, 224
Llandudno, 224
LMS Railway Wagon Works, 207
LNER, 166
Lockheed Overseas Corporation, 135, 215, 238, 239
London & Provincial Aviation Co. Ltd, 74
London Aircraft Co. Ltd, 73
London Aircraft Production Group, 31, 32
Long Kesh, 227
Longbridge, 101, 227
Loughborough, 31, 171

Index

Lowe HL(M)9 Marlburlian, 28, 142
Luton, 27, 81, 123, 125
Lympne, 26, 105, 114, 146, 192
Lynden Aurora, 63
Lytham St Annes, 112-115, 172, 173
Magilligan Strand, 236
Maidstone, 135
Manchester Area, 70-100
Manchester Aviation Co. Ltd, 73
Manning, W.O., 115, 170
March, Jones & Cribb, 19, 183, 184
Marine Aircraft Experimental Establishment (MAEE), 203, 217
Marshall of Cambridge Aerospace Ltd (and related companies), , 33, 82
Martin Hearn Ltd, 61, 160
Martin-Baker Aircraft Ltd
  MB5, 33
Martinsyde Ltd (also Martinsyde Aircraft Co.), 24, 54, 192
  F.3, , 21
Martlesham Heath, 105, 148, 194
Martyn, H.H., & Co., 54
Mather & Platt Ltd, 71, 73
Maurice Farman
  S.7 Longhorn, 171, 173
  S.11 Shorthorn, 20
May, Harden & May, 54, 113, 171
Maybole, 206
McCandless, R. & W.A.C., Aviation Ltd
  gyroplane, 238
McDonnell Douglas F-4 Phantom, 46, 152, 154
Meir, 135
Merseyside, 8, 59, 132-137
Metropolitan-Vickers Electrical Co. Ltd, 30, 80, 81, 87, 90, 99, 100, 105-107, 218
Miles Aircraft (Northern Ireland) Ltd, 227, 238
Miles Platting, 14, 19, 70, 71
Miles, F.G., Mr, 43
ML Engineering Co. Ltd (also ML Aviation Co. Ltd)
  Rotachute, 87
Monmouth, 224, 225
Montgomerie Gyrocopters, 206
Montrose, 20, 207
Moore-Brabazon, J.T.C. (later Lord Brabazon of Tara), 12
Morgan & Co. Ltd, 73
Morris Motors Ltd, 31, 32
Morrisons Engineering Ltd / Morrisons Aircraft Services, 33
Moss Brothers Aircraft Ltd (also Mosscraft Ltd), 111
  M.A.1, 111
  M.A.2, 111
Mumford, W., 194, 202
  Helicopter, 194
Napier & Miller Ltd, 198, 203
Narbeth, 14, 225
National Aircraft Factory, 100, 132, 133, 137
National Aircraft Mfg. Co. Ltd, 187

Navarro Aircraft Syndicate (also Navarro Aircraft Co. Ltd, Navarro Safety Aircraft Ltd and Navarro Aviation Co. Ltd), 74
NDN Aircraft (UK) Ltd (also NDN Aircraft Ltd), 216
  Fieldmaster, 216
Netherthorpe, 168, 169
Newcastle, 11, 19, 137, 138, 141, 142
Newton Heath, 19, 70, 71, 73-79
Nieuport & General Aircraft Ltd, 24, 226
Nipper Aircraft Ltd, 159, 160
  Nipper Mk III, 159, 160
Noble Hardman Aviation Ltd, 8, 218
  Snowbird, 218, 219
Norman Aeroplane Co. Ltd, 216
North British Locomotive Co., 198, 200, 201
North Yorkshire, 156-166
Northern Aeroplane Workshops, 10, 175
  Bristol M.1C replica, 175
  Sopwith Triplane replica, 175
Northern Aircraft & Engineering Ltd, 69
Northern Aluminium Ltd, 224
Northern England, 59-184
Northern Ireland, 227-239
Northolt, 20
Northumberland & Tyneside, 8, 59, 137-143
Norwich, 20
Oddy, W.D., & Co., 184
Old Sarum, 216
Ord-Hume, A.W.J., Mr, 9, 156
Osborne Aircraft Components Co., The, 203
Panavia, 46, 126, 127
  Tornado, 45-47, 53, 82, 107, 117, 126-128
Parker, John Lankester, 65, 67
Parkes monoplane, 224, 225
Parkside, 141
Parnall & Sons Ltd (also George Parnall & Co. Ltd), 24, 73
Pashley, C.L., 74
Pegler Bros. & Co. (Doncaster) Ltd, 19, 163, 167
Pemberton Billing, Mr, 21
Pemberton-Billing Ltd, 55
Penarth, 218
Penny, John
  Sopwith Triplane replica, 167
Penrose, Harald, 60, 147, 218
Percival Aircraft Ltd (and Hunting Percival Aircraft Ltd), 23, 27, 33, 39, 41, 55, 123
  Merganser, 35
  P.40 Prentice, 38, 150
  P.56 Provost, 38
  Pembroke, 38, 39
  Prince & Sea Prince, 36
  Proctor, 11, 30, 34, 87, 104, 106, 109, 208
Perry, Beadle & Co., 68
Perth, 207
Petter, W.E.W., 115
Phillips & Powis Aircraft Ltd (also Miles Aircraft Ltd), 23, 27, 32, 54, 167, 168, 170, 207, 238
  Hawk Speed Six, 27

M.14 Hawk Trainer III & Magister, 34
M.38 Messenger, 227, 238
Master, 31, 34, 167, 168, 170
Phoenix Dynamo Mfg. Co. Ltd, 19, 55, 112, 113, 141, 143, 170-174
  P.5 Cork, 171, 173
Pilatus PC9, 127, 152
Planes Ltd/Mersey Aeroplane Co., 14, 132-134
  monoplane, 134
Pobjoy Airmotors & Aircraft Ltd, 62
Popular Flying Association, 68, 142, 143, 168, 206
Portass, C., & Son Ltd, 10, 170
Portsmouth, 27, 162, 163, 166
Portsmouth Aviation Ltd
  Aerocar, 35
Practavia Ltd, 165
  Sprite, 131, 132, 165
Preston, 7, 11, 19, 30, 32, 37, 46, 47, 103, 112-116, 123, 132, 143
Prestwick, 7, 9, 11, 33, 42, 47, 49, 130, 150, 187, 195, 203, 204, 207-215, 223
Procter (later Nash) Petrel, 132
Radlett, 37, 42, 88
Radley-England
  Waterplane, 65
RAF Clifton/Rawcliffe, 33, 156
RAF Kemble, 33
RAF Leconfield, 149, 156
RAF Scampton, 154
RAF Shawbury, 135
Raytheon Corporation, 49, 59, 213, 220, 221, 223
  Hawker 800, 49, 213, 221, 223
  Hawker 1000, 49, 223
Rearsby, 42, 43
Regent Carriage Co. Ltd, The, 73, 137, 185
Renfrew, 135, 190, 195, 202, 215, 238
Rhyl, 216
Ringway, 62, 70, 80, 83-87, 90, 101-103, 105, 167
Rochester, 31, 227, 230, 231
Rolls-Royce Ltd, 59, 203
Rootes Securities Ltd, 11, 29, 30-32, 69, 134, 135
Rosefield, David, Ltd, 107
Rover Company Ltd, The, 29, 111
Royal Aircraft Factory, The, 15
  BE2 (all models), 15, 16, 20, 21, 136, 138-141, 179, 181, 185, 187, 190, 191, 194, 195, 198-200, 203
  BE12, 15, 170
  FE2 (all models), 15, 20, 21, 198, 200, 201
  RE8, 15, 20, 141, 169
  SE5, SE5A, 15, 20, 21, 170
Royton, 70, 100
Ruffy-Baumann School, 225
Samlesbury, 11, 30, 32, 37, 46, 47, 82, 115-121, 123, 153, 213
Samlesbury Engineering Ltd, 109, 120, 121
  Lancashire Prospector, 109, 120, 121
Sanders Aeroplane Co.
  Type 2, 13
Sandown, 216

Saunders, S.E., Ltd, 24, 73, 79
Saunders-Roe (Anglesey) Ltd, 217
Saunders-Roe Ltd, 40, 42, 79, 148, 207, 217, 233
  A.37 Shrimp, 203, 217
  P.531, 38, 43
  Princess, 35, 224
  Skeeter, 38, 40
  SR.A/1, 217
Savages Ltd, 73
Scarborough, 157, 158, 162, 163
Scotland, 6, 8, 11, 14, 15, 30, 38, 59, 184-216
Scottish Aviation Co., The, 14, 186-188, 200
  Caledonia monoplane, 14, 187
Scottish Aviation Ltd, 6, 11, 33, 40, 42, 54, 84, 184, 187, 199, 200, 203, 204, 207-209, 211, 213, 214, 217
  Pioneer, 38, 40, 208, 209, 211
  Twin Pioneer, 38, 40, 203, 204, 208-210, 212, 215
Sealand, 106, 109, 226, 227
Selby, 139, 140, 163
SEPECAT, 117, 125
  Jaguar, 46, 47, 117, 125
Shackleton, W.S., Mr, 165, 190, 192, 193, 194
Shackleton-Murray S.M.1, 165, 194
Shaw, 28, 100
Sheffield, 166, 168-170
Sheffield Simplex Motor Works Ltd, 170
Sherburn-in-Elmet, 7, 30, 62, 150, 162-167, 179
Shoreham, 13, 43, 67, 70, 112
Short Brothers Ltd
  Short-Wright biplane, 12, 224
Short Brothers (Rochester & Bedford) Ltd, 24, 32, 68, 227, 230
  Short 184, 15, 143, 171, 173
  Short 225 Bomber, 171, 173
  S.23 C-Class (and S.30, S.33), 26
  S.25 Hythe, 35
  S.25 Sandringham, 35, 230
  S.25 Sunderland, 30, 32, 33, 35, 68, 148, 194, 195, 196, 203, 204, 207, 209, 216, 229, 230
  S.29 Stirling, 30, 31, 32, 34, 35, 227
  S.35 Shetland, 203, 217
  S.45 Solent, 35, 229
  SA1 Sturgeon, 231, 232
Short & Harland Ltd, 30, 32, 227, 229, 230
Short Bros. & Harland Ltd (and Shorts plc, Bombardier Aerospace), 6, 11, 22, 37-39, 42, 49, 54, 115, 223, 227, 228, 230, 233-239
  SA4 Sperrin, 231, 232
  SA6 Sealand, 230, 231
  SB1, SB4 Sherpa, 232
  SB3, 231
  SB5, 231, 232
  SB6 Seamew, 232
  SC1, 233
  SC5 Belfast, 45, 46, 233, 234
  SC7 Skyvan, 43, 49, 233, 235
  SD330, 49, 52, 233, 234, 235, 236
  SD360, 49, 107, 234, 235, 236

Tucano, 49, 53, 235, 237
Short Brothers Repair Organisation (SEBRO), 33
Siddeley-Deasy Motor Car Co. Ltd, The, 24, 141, 196
Silsbury, David, 167
   Sopwith Triplane replica, 168
Simmonds Aircraft Ltd, 115
Slingsby Aviation Ltd (also Slingsby Sailplanes Ltd, Slingsby Aircraft Ltd, Slingsby Engineering Ltd), 6, 11, 51, 61, 157-163
   T3 Grasshopper, 160
   T6 Kite, 61, 158
   T7, T8 Kirby Kadet, Cadet & Tutor, 61, 158, 160
   T18 Hengist, 157, 158
   T21B Sedbergh, 61, 158
   T22 Petrel, 158
   T29 Motor Tutor, 160
   T31 Tandem Tutor, 61
   T37, T41, T43, T50 Skylark, 158
   T45 Swallow, 158
   T49 Capstan, 158, 160
   T51 Dart, 158
   T56 SE5A replica, 160
   T57 Camel replica, 160
   T58 Rumpler C.IV replica, 160
   T61E Venture, 160
   T67 & Firefly, 51, 52, 160, 161
Smith, Barry, 68, 69
   Acro Advanced, 68
Snellings Light Aircraft Service, 8, 111
Society of British Aircraft Constructors, 6, 22, 23, 91
Sopwith Aviation Co. Ltd, The, 24
   1½ Strutter, 16, 20, 169
   Baby (and Fairey Hamble Baby), 143, 179, 182
   Camel, 16, 20, 167, 183-185, 190, 195
   Cuckoo, 163, 167, 179, 202
   Dolphin, 21
   Pup, 16, 20, 169, 190, 192
   Ship's Pup, 190
   Snipe, 10, 16, 132, 170, 184, 198
Sopwith, T.O.M. (later Sir Thomas Sopwith), 14
South Marston, 31, 168, 227
South Shields, 112, 143
South Yorkshire, 166-170
Southport, 19, 74, 133, 136, 137
Speedtwin Developments Ltd, 225
   Phillips ST1 Speedtwin, 225, 226
Speke, 7, 11, 30, 134, 135, 215, 238
Spennymore, 68
Squires Gate, 108-110, 121
Staffordshire, 30, 134, 135
Stag Lane, 27
Standard Motor Co. Ltd, The, 29, 31, 32
Stanley Park, 108, 109
Stansted, 109, 121, 154
Stirling, 14, 202, 204, 215, 216
Stockport, 7, 33, 37, 69, 86, 87, 100-103, 105
Stockport Aviation Co. Ltd, 101
Stretton, 62, 102
Sunbeam Motor Car Co. Ltd, The, 73, 135

Supermarine Aviation Works Ltd, The (also The Supermarine Aviation Works (Vickers) Ltd), 24, 55
   Stranraer, 150
   Walrus, 34, 208
Surrey Flying Services, 74
Sydenham, 135, 215, 227, 231, 233, 238
Szep HFC125, 168, 169
Taylor, John, 28
Taylorcraft Aeroplanes (England) Ltd, 23, 33, 54
The Varioplane Co. Ltd, 165
   Alula-winged DH6, 164, 165, 166
Thetford, 20
Thornton Engineering Ltd, 173
Tiger Cub Developments Ltd, 168
   Sherwood Ranger, 168
Tipsy Aircraft Co. Ltd
   Belfair, 165
Trafford Park, 30, 73, 100, 103-107
Turner Super Wot, 142, 143
Turweston, 28
Usworth, 142, 143
Vickers Ltd, 14, 24, 74, 158, 216
   Vimy (and Vimy Commercial), 16
Vickers-Armstrongs Ltd (also Vickers Ltd (Aviation Dept), Vickers (Aviation) Ltd, Vickers-Armstrongs (Aircraft) Ltd), 11, 30-32, 38, 39, 40, 55, 59, 110, 123, 218, 220
   Seafire, 34, 102
   Supermarine Attacker, 38, 153
   Supermarine experimental jet prototypes, 153
   Supermarine F.7/30, 24
   Supermarine Scimitar, 38, 234
   Supermarine Spitfire (all marks), 25, 26, 30, 31, 33, 34, 203, 207, 210, 218, 224
   Supermarine Swift, 38, 195, 234
   Type 246 Wellesley, 29, 207
   Type 271 Wellington (all models), 30, 34, 59, 101, 108, 110, 218
   Type 300 (later named Spitfire), 25
   Type 491 VC1 Viking (all models), 36
   Type 630/700/800 Viscount, 36, 37, 40, 43, 121, 210, 224
   Type 637 Valetta (all models), 38, 39
   Type 648 Varsity, 38, 39, 197
   Type 680 Valiant, 38
   Type 950 Vanguard, 40, 43
   Type 1100 VC10 and Type 1151 Super VC10, 43, 53, 55
Vulcan Motor & Engineering Co. (1906) Ltd, 8, 19, 132, 136, 137
Wales, 216-227
Waring & Gillow Ltd, 107, 110, 116, 132, 136, 137
Warrington area, 62, 102, 103
Warton, 9, 11, 44, 46, 47, 99, 115-117, 119, 121-132, 152, 153
Waterloo Sands, 74, 134, 137
Watkins monoplane, 14, 218
Watson biplane series, 197

Welford monoplane, 137
West of Scotland Furniture Co., 200
West Yorkshire, 170-184, 200
Westland (Doncaster) Ltd, 168
Westland Aircraft Works (Branch of Petters Ltd) (also Westland Aircraft Ltd), 24, 32, 40, 102
   Lysander, 34, 150, 168
   Westland F.7/30, 24
   Wyvern, 38, 40, 149
Westland Helicopters Ltd (also GKN Westland Helicopters Ltd, AgustaWestland), 6, 22, 43, 50, 51, 54
   Dragonfly, 38
   EH101 and Merlin, 50, 52, 53
   Lynx, 43, 50, 52, 53
   Sea King, 43
   WAH-64 Apache, 50
   Wasp, 43
   Wessex, 43
   WG30, 50
   Whirlwind, 38, 43
Weybridge, 30, 47
Whitchurch, 31, 216
White Waltham, 160
Whitley Abbey, 141
Wig Bay, 216
Willys Overland Crossley Ltd, 24, 100
Winchester, 28
Windermere, Lake, 7, 14, 30, 63-68, 70, 71, 142, 158
Witney, 74

Wm. Beardmore & Co. Ltd, 16, 19, 23, 100, 189-195, 203
   Inflexible, 165, 193, 194
   Inverness, 193, 194
   W.B. 26, 190
   W.B. I, 190
   W.B. II & W.B.IIB, 190, 193
   W.B. III, 190
   W.B. IV, 190, 193
   W.B. V, 190
   W.B. X, 190
   Wee Bee, 165, 192, 193
Wolverhampton, 144
Woodford, 8, 11, 37, 47, 49, 70, 71, 73, 78- 84, 87-100, 107, 130, 179, 213
Woodley, 27
Woolston, 31
Wren Aircraft Co., 63
   Goldcrest, 63
Wright, Howard, 170
Wycombe Aircraft Constructors Ltd, 54, 218
Wylie & Lochhead, 202
Wythenshawe, 70, 107, 155
Yate, 20
Yeadon, 11, 30, 70, 78, 80, 84, 89, 94, 176-179
Yeadon Engineering Ltd, 109
Yearby, 68
Yeovil, 50
York, 27, 156, 163, 166
Yorkshire Aeroplane Co., 167

If you are interested in purchasing
other books published by Tempus, or in case you have
difficulty finding any Tempus books in your local bookshop, you can also place
orders directly through our website

www.tempus-publishing.com